# Creative Writing
# Anthology 2008

egg box

# UEA Creative Writing Anthology 2008

First published by Egg Box Publishing, 2008.

International © retained by individual authors.

A CIP record for this book is available from the British Library.

UEA Creative Writing Anthology 2008 is typeset in Oranda 9pt on 12pt Leading.

**Printed and bound by:**
Biddles, King's Lynn
www.biddles.co.uk

**Designed and typeset by:**
Kettle of Fish Design, Norwich
www.kettleoffishdesign.com

**Proofed by:**
Sarah Gooderson

**Distributed by:**
Central Books, 99 Wallis Road
London, E9 5LN

**ISBN:** 9780954392079

# Acknowledgements

UEA Creative Writing Anthology 2008

Thanks to the following for making this anthology possible: The Random House Group, the Malcolm Bradbury Memorial Fund, the Centre for Creative and Performing Arts at the University of East Anglia and The School of Literature & Creative Writing at UEA in partnership with Egg Box Publishing.

We'd also like to thank the following people:

Trezza Azzopardi, Jon Cook, Andrew Cowan, Mark Currie, Geoff Dyer, Siân Evans, Giles Foden, Janet Garton, Sarah Gooderson, Rachel Hore, Kathryn Hughes, Michael Lengsfield, Jean McNeil, Denise Riley, Rob Ritchie, Michèle Roberts, Helen Smith, Val Striker, George Szirtes, Val Taylor, Ardashir Vakil and Jeremy Webb at UEA.

Nathan Hamilton at Egg Box Publishing, and Catrin & Dylan Lloyd-Edwards at Kettle of Fish Design.

**Editorial team:**
M. Colleen Burns
Anna Giokas
Lauren Higbee
Tadzio Koelb
Jesse Kuiken
Nicole Lawrence
Ben Parker
Gena Schiffenhaus

# Contents

# Foreword

*by* **Anne Enright**

For a long time, when asked about creative writing courses, I said that no one taught me anything in UEA. This, strictly speaking, was true. I could neither spell nor punctuate when I left, had vague ideas about how a paragraph might be constructed, and I used words like 'denouement' with the greatest contempt. At least I had heard them, I suppose. But though I had not been taught anything I did learn a lot: this is a nice distinction but a crucial one. Writing is learned from the inside out; it is not like mathematics, it is more like a spiritual or physical discipline; the doing is everything – and no one else can do it for you. The job of the teacher is to feed the students and to keep them safe. Angela Carter did the first, with a scattering of photocopies, musings and anecdotes (she never mentioned my work, I think), and Malcolm Bradbury did the second, by smiling a lot, and liking books, and keeping quiet (I don't think he ever mentioned my work either. I might be wrong). The other students did mention my work, they had various opinions about it, but that was fine, because Malcolm was there to like us all and keep us safe.

Both my teachers died when I was a baby writer. I didn't miss Angela much when she went, despite the fact it was her work that had called me to UEA in the first place. I miss her now, though – quite keenly. It came to me quite recently, how the world would be so much better if she were still here.

I was with a good bunch of people in East Anglia, but they couldn't make the place less flat. Being an artist, I had no money and, being an exile, I had severed all my connections to home. I suffered slightly from an idea of the Irish that was prevalent in Middle England in the 1980s: not that I was dirty-lazy-drunk-and-stupid (chance would be a fine thing), but that I could write, of course I could, because that's what Irish people did. I myself was of the contrary opinion. I did not write like any other

Irish person I had read. Also, in actual fact, I didn't think I could write at all.

Of course, in the grand scheme of things, I was a wonderful writer. I was destined and marvellous. These things were very clear, they just were not clear on the page. In fact, to be honest, there wasn't very much on the page – if by 'page' you mean that white sheet of paper with words on it, or not. I had scraps and fragments, little rushes of stuff that might actually be ok; there were phrases and headlines in different coloured marker stuck to the walls. Index cards – I had them too. I had intimations of the most fabulous book, with very few intimations of what it might contain. The only idea I had was this large idea of myself as a writer. I was like a balloon – the bigger my ambition, the less there was inside. And balloons (to overstretch the metaphor) are liable to burst.

This is how the day went in UEA. I would get up sometime after midday and meet the other students in the refectory. Louise Doughty was in my year and Mark Illis, Fadia Faquir and others who have published since. It was a friendly group. We were chatty and supportive of each other, we met for lunch. This was always, for me, a ham and coleslaw roll. The others would have been up since eight, and some of them took a proper meal. They had all, without exception, written five hundred words before noon. Some had written more. After lunch they might suggest a walk (I think I went, once) or plan an event at the weekend.

Sometimes these events would be exciting: too much red wine at Malcolm and Elizabeth's, a couple of agents down from London, Anthony Thwaite in a green velvet smoking jacket, some literary women who looked terribly, terribly middle-aged. Sometimes they would be dull: two halves of lager and a game of pool in the Student Union, then home to bed because there were five hundred words to be done early the next day.

All years are different: some are wild and wrongheaded and disastrous and wonderful, and some are not. For me, all the drama of that year happened in my head.

I never worked in the morning. I started at four in the afternoon and went through to four am. Or I might go from after dinner until dawn. I didn't see a lot of daylight. Every time I counted my words the number had shrunk (this remains true of my work, to this day). I sat at the desk all night and lost words. I got up the next day and met people who ate properly and went home for weekends and made it, one painful chapter at a time, through the book they had somehow decided to write.

By springtime I was working on a novel that took place simultaneously in three different centuries. It was also written in three different styles – you might even say three different languages, all of them versions of English. I have never been psychotic (I know, how can I tell?), but I have had a glimpse of it: sitting in a breeze block student room reading Lacan and ignoring the walls, with their messages all written in different coloured pen.

When I fell apart, over the Easter break, I was set back to rights with great kindness by some of my fellows, who could mend me a little, but not mend my book – because writing is learned from the inside, and there's no one who can do it for you, much as they might want to help.

The book went in the bin (a few box files sitting on my bottom shelf) and I went home and started to write for real. I learned all the hard things at UEA – difficulty, incapacity, failure, humility, the importance of working more on the page than in your head. Now when I hear of people taking a year off to write, I worry that a year might not be enough. You must fail as a writer for much longer than that, I think, before you know what failure is and what use you might make of it. I didn't realise, when that first book fell apart, that every book falls apart. That this is the gig. You sit there and watch your word count drop, and you hold your nerve. I have survived this process now many times. But the first time was the worst, and I was lucky to be among friends.

AE

# Prose

*Introduction by* **Giles Foden**

*Claire Anderson-Wheeler*

*J.W. Arble*

*Gabrielle Barnes*

*Natalie Butlin*

*Tamsin Evans*

*Elisabeth Fairchild*

*Anna Giokas*

*Alastair Hadden*

*Ben Harvey*

*Eli Herman*

*Anjali Joseph*

*Tadzio Koelb*

*Jesse Kuiken*

*Georgina MacArthur*

*Tammer Mahdy*

*Justine Mann*

*Tracy Maylath*

*Lauren Owen*

*Salman Shaheen*

*Kelly Smith*

*Alistair South*

*Christie Watson*

*Naomi Wood*

Books might be taken as sins of commission and I've committed a few, but in the teaching of creative writing I'm a relative innocent. One thing I was sure of from the start, however, was that certain aspects of the novel could be objectified and therefore taught. Other aspects I was sure were educationally intractable: these largely concerned the nexus of creativity and the individual psyche.

Then my mind went back to my only personal experience of creative writing teaching, which was by Paul Muldoon in an informal academic setting. A very lucky young man I was, in that respect. I remember something he said that made a powerful impression on me. This was unusual as it was often the things which Paul did not say that spoke loudest. The utterance was: 'find your territory'. That is something I have encouraged students of this MA to do, and it relates after all to those 'unteachable' elements.

I think all these writers have found their territory, psychic or geographical or stylistic. From Tadzio Koelb's Brussels to Jesse Kuiken's Astora, from Anna Giokas's Greece to Gabrielle Barnes's Digbeth, from Naomi Wood's baroque dystopia to J.W. Arble's dystopian baroque, and many other places beside, the fire of creativity – dread word – has been lit.

As it cheerfully burns, let us focus on something else happening in the corner of the workshop. The most satisfying element of the teaching process has been seeing students and tutor reach a common understanding of fictional technique. About character, for instance: check out *inter alia* Naomi Wood's crazy Granny, Tammer Mahdy's scary Sam Hatch, and Anjali Joseph's amorous taxi driver.

Achieving technical excellence (or even competence) involves stripping out personality, developing that splinter of ice in the heart of which Graham Greene once spoke. It is a lifelong struggle. Often writers lose their way – as they must, for what is involved is nothing less than the *mise en abîme* of the self.

But once it is understood that the legend of intention, that repository of practical artistic choices which constitutes a text, is also an existential document, the coldness is ready for transfiguration. It takes another party to make the fire and the ice one, and that is the reader. That self also must be lost. So step up, play your part, be off with you into these pages.

GF

# Claire Anderson-Wheeler

## *Vernissage*

Mothers clustered outside the school gates. They chattered; and those waylaid by the dull or domineering rattled keys at intervals, announcing a departure they could not quite achieve.

Alex's mother was waiting in the car. Her hand signalled to him out of the open window, brisk as a lollipop lady's. He hoisted his satchel up a notch. Opening the car door, he accidentally bumped one of the mothers with his satchel. She turned, looking over her shoulder and then down to locate him. Benevolence displaced annoyance, and she smiled. Her fingernails on the strap of her handbag were red. Alex got in the car.

There was a shopping bag in the back seat.

'How was school?'

'OK.'

'What did you do?'

'We got a project. For Nature class. I'm doing earthworms. Sam got beetles.'

'Earthworms?'

'I wanted beetles.'

'I'm sure earthworms are just as interesting.'

'Ms Swanson told me there are no such things as boy or girl earthworms. They're all just worms.'

'Is that so?'

There was paper in the bag, crêpe paper like from art class, but it was white instead of coloured. Alex could hear it rustling when the bag shifted.

'What's in the bag?'

'It's a dress,' his mother said.

'Is it new?'

'Of course it's new. I just bought it.'

'While I was at school?'

'Yes.'

'What did you buy a dress for?' he asked.

'It's for tonight.'

'For the vernissage?' He stretched the word out like chewing gum.

'Yes. For the vernissage.'

It sounded like a person, that was how Alex liked to think of it: Vernie Sadge. He would be tall, with a big thick neck, and glasses, and a moustache like a nailbrush. He would have big eyes behind the glasses, with eyelids at a sly half-mast. He would smoke cigars.

Alex imagined Vernie Sadge dancing with his mother at the party tonight. Her hand would be on his shoulder, only her nails wouldn't be long and red like that woman by the car. Hers were short as short, with twiggy bits at the sides. Still, she would dance. He looked into the bag but he didn't want to disturb it. The crêpe paper was folded carefully as bedsheets. The car went up and over the speed ramps. They were striped black and yellow, like a wrong zebra. From inside the bag came rustle, rustle.

'Is the new dress so as you look pretty for Vernie Sadge?' Alex asked.

His mother looked at him in the rear-view mirror. She had a funny face on, like the one Tracy Walsh made if you ever asked to borrow a pencil – like she didn't trust you to give it back. Then his mother laughed and the look went away, all except for a little bit in her eyes that stayed.

'I hope so, Alex,' she said.

At home she made him a banana sandwich. There was something about banana sandwiches, sweet and soft, that made him think of babyfood. Maybe he was getting too old for banana sandwiches. He thought about saying that he didn't want to eat them anymore. But he liked them: he liked to eat them after he had left them a little while, when the circles of banana had started to go black at the edges. He peeled back the top of his sandwich, examining the fuzz of white bread that remained stuck to the butter, stuck in turn to the pieces of banana. The banana was still firm and yellowy-white.

'Alex! Stop messing with your sandwich.' His mother was unstacking the dishwasher.

He patted the top back down on his sandwich and began to eat it, with both hands. He was glad that she had cut it in triangles.

'When are you going to Vernie Sadge?'

'It starts at eight, but your father has to be there earlier. He has to talk with the gallery owner.'

'What about you?'

'Me?'

'Who will you talk to?'

'Oh, I expect there will be lots of people I ought to talk to.'

'What will you talk about?'

'Different things.'

He felt the mulch of sandwich against the roof of his mouth. He imagined how it would look, all white and yellow-white like mashed potato. He watched his mother take out another dish, a big one, and put it away. She had to take three other dishes out of the cabinet, put the big one in, then put the other three back on top. They all clanked, and clanked again when she closed the cabinet.

'Your father will be home around six,' she said. Sometimes the way she said 'your father' sounded proud, like he was something special that she and Alex had made together. 'And Anne-Marie,' she continued, 'should be here around half past.'

Anne-Marie was the babysitter. Alex didn't like her, there was fat under her eyes and she called him 'Ally', which was a girl's name. If she was a food she would probably be a banana sandwich. Suddenly the taste in his mouth was sickly-sweet, and he gulped it down quickly.

He heard his mother's voice downstairs, calling him. She probably wanted him to do his homework, but it was better doing it when Anne-Marie was there: she just smiled and blinked instead of checking it properly. His mother's step on the stairs now: unusual persistence. Before she rounded the stairwell, he had pushed open the door of his parents' bedroom. If she found him upstairs now, undeniably within earshot, she would be annoyed. He hesitated, then crept under his parents' bed.

The footsteps didn't move towards his room as he had expected; instead Alex saw his mother's legs appear in the doorway. She prised off her shoes – toe to heel, toe to heel – and crossed the room. So she wasn't looking for him. She was wearing tights, and the band across her toes made a brown beak at the ends of her feet. Alex could smell her feet-smell, different from his own. It was sort of sweet as well as salty; sweet like old things. Maybe it was the tights that made them smell that way. He didn't like the smell, it was too private.

She was standing at the dressing table, her palms down flat, leaning in towards the mirror. Veins stood out under pressure on her wrists, and below that, the beginnings of her palms showed pink. Alex noticed the carrier bag from the car was on the dressing table now: she took out the dress and put it on a hanger, suspending it on the outside of the wardrobe door. Alex couldn't see her face but thought from her stillness she must be admiring the dress. It was purple, with a sheen on it, like a plum turned this way and that under the light.

Alex heard the front door and his father's step in the hall. It must be six o'clock already. He hoped his father would not come looking for him – but that would be unusual.

His mother moved back to the mirror. She reached down and picked up a lipstick. He heard the pop like lips smacking as she opened it. She put it on, put her head to one side, and sighed. She whisked a tissue from the tissue box, and Alex thought she was going to rub it all off, but she must have changed her mind: she put the tissue down, slowly.

Footsteps, and Alex's father came in the bedroom door: another set of legs.

'Frances.'

'Hello, darling.' The two pairs of legs kept their distance, about three feet between them. 'How are you feeling about tonight?'

'OK. It should all go OK, I think.'

'Of course it will. It will be great, John.'

'Mm.'

Alex watched his father's feet – brown leather shoes – move along the foot of the bed, and over to the window, toes pointing towards the garden.

'Don't worry.'

'Mmn. No.' He seemed to rouse himself. 'No, I'm not worried.' The legs turned back in towards the room. 'What's that?'

'I told you I was going to buy a new dress; for tonight. Remember?'

'Oh, right.'

'Do you like it?'

'The dress?'

'Yes.'

'It's very nice.'

'I'm glad you like it. You've said before how the colour suits me.'

'Did I? I'm sure it does.'

She took a step towards the dress and put out a hand to it, making the light move on the fabric. 'I'll put it on for you.'

'Yes,' he said, 'We'd better get moving, all right.'

Alex saw his mother open the bottom button of her blouse, and he closed his eyes. He heard the rattle of the hanger against the wardrobe door. His father had gone into the bathroom and was brushing his teeth. The sound it made was regular as steps in snow, wish-wish, wish-wish.

Then Alex heard a zip. He opened his eyes.

His father came out of the bathroom.

'What do you think?' his mother asked, and Alex wondered if the dress had done something to her voice as well, because now it, too, seemed full of plums: dark and round and soft.

But his father's voice was the same as usual. 'It's very nice, Frances. Lovely.' That voice Alex knew. It was the same voice that he heard when he showed his father something he'd made in school.

There was a silence. A restless kind of silence, like when you wake in the middle of the night and your room is full of no one. Alex watched his mother walk over to his father. She seemed stiff – was she holding her breath? Alex realised he was holding his breath, maybe that was it. His father didn't move. He coughed, though.

The woman stopped. Alex could see up to their shoulders, but no faces. He saw the woman reach out and take the man's hand. Her right hand, his right hand. She pulled it towards her and took a half-step closer. Alex felt a wave of dread, and tasted banana sandwich in the back of his mouth, sick-sweet. The woman took the hand and cupped it round her left breast. She held it there, as though it were a weak runt of a thing. She breathed out: she had been holding her breath. Then the man coughed again.

'Thanks, Fran,' he said. 'I know how much you've put into tonight.' He moved the hand up onto the woman's shoulder. 'Really,' he said. Then he moved over to the wardrobe, opened it and took out a pair of black shoes. He sat on the bed, and Alex felt it sag. A sound of fingers picking at knots.

When both shoes were on, his father stood up. 'I'd be lost without you, you know that?'

'I know.'

'Oh, Frances – that shirt –'

'I stopped by the cleaners. It's on the hall table.'

He left the room, and his voice drifted up from the stairs. 'What time is the babysitter?'

She made no answer, just stood in the silence. Then she sighed, and turned, and went into the bathroom. The room was empty. Alex pulled himself out from under the bed in a snake-wriggle. His neck was stiff from keeping his head to one side. He stood up. He saw himself in the mirror, one cheek flushed and carpet-mottled. The lipstick was still there, in the middle of the dressing table. She had put the lid back on, like you were supposed to. Two sets of shoes lay abandoned on different sides of the room.

Alex walked across the landing, not into his own bedroom but into the bathroom, and took down his toothbrush. It was green, a crocodile, yellow eyes. This too, he decided, was a child's thing. He would ask his mother for a new toothbrush, one that was a toothbrush and nothing more. Though it was very far from bedtime and he would be having dinner soon, he began to brush his teeth. He brushed them for a long time, steadily. Wish-wish; wish-wish.

---

**Claire Anderson-Wheeler** was born in Washington DC and has lived in Dublin, Geneva and Brussels. She was shortlisted for a Fish Publishing prize and appeared in their 2007 anthology, and was placed third in the 2007 Over The Edge 'New Writer of the Year' competition. She is currently working on a novel.

# J.W. Arble

## Will You Be My friend?

*Extract from a short story*

Dan, who has been travelling, and the narrator, a young actor referred to by Dan as 'Pixie', have met, by chance, in a London bar for the first time in several years. Throughout the evening Dan has been attempting to pitch his idea for a screenplay to Pixie, with little success. In between efforts he has sabotaged Pixie's attempt to pass a beer mat, with his phone number on it, to a pretty girl. Nevertheless the girl and a large gentleman (both of whom are dressed in entirely orange sales uniforms) are now approaching Dan and Pixie's table...

...I looked up. The girl in orange was crossing the room towards us. She was swinging her hips. The Honey Monster followed after her, dragging his feet and carrying the drinks. Seeing him I slid the beer mat with the message into my pocket, just in case.

'I'm not talking to her,' Dan said. 'I told you I'm not going to fucking talk to her, no way.'

She arrived at our table. She was definitely smiling at me now.

'Hi,' she said.

'Hi,' I said.

'So I dropped something?'

'Maybe,' I said. My eyebrows were working overtime.

'Nice dictator,' she said to Dan. He scowled, put the Mao keyring in his pocket and reached for one of the shandies.

'I think we've met before,' I lied. 'You're an actor too, aren't you?' Dan began to gargle his drink. 'You don't call them actresses, Dan, not anymore.' I was going to use him whether he spoke or not. 'I've told him before but it's like he's living in the dark ages. I told him, we're all actors in this game, nowadays.'

'You're an actor, interesting.' The girl fluttered her lashes. The Honey Monster lumbered up beside her. She tugged his sleeve. 'Tony, this guy says he's an actor.'

'OK,' said Tony, the Honey Monster. He said it quietly; a beaten man already.

'All right mate,' I greeted him. 'Now what are you guys drinking? I know, have either of you ever had a Cuba Sunrise?' I gestured towards the shot glasses.

'A Cuba Sunrise?'

'You never forget them.' I felt on top of my game. 'Isn't that right, Dan? Cuba Sunrise: once seen, never forgotten.'

'Cunt,' said Dan, looking up at the girl.

'What?' she hissed. Suddenly the colour in her cheeks clashed with her clothes.

'Fucking orange cunt,' he repeated.

'What did you just say?' Tony asked.

'Oh fuck,' said Dan. Certain cogs were shifting into gear.

Tony began putting his drinks on the table with a purposeful alacrity.

'Fuck,' said Dan again. Then he added, 'Cunt, wank, crap, I have fucking Tourette's shitting, fuck, balls, piss, todger, nose.' He began twitching.

'No!' said the girl. 'Tourette's? Like on TV? Has your friend really got Tourette's?' She looked at me and I just nodded. Tony finished putting the glasses on the table. Dan knocked one of them over.

'There's no way that freak has Tourette's. My mum works with kids with Tourette's.' Tony brushed his hands on his trousers. 'But don't worry, son. I'm not going to hit you. Come on Jenny, these two aren't worth it. Let's get you home.'

He turned and started to walk away. Jenny looked sick.

'Grow up,' she said. Then she turned on her orange heel and followed him out of the bar.

'Cunt deserved it,' said Dan, when they were out of earshot. 'Did you see that fucker, right? He was going to hit me! Ha! For slagging his tart! He was going to hit me! Nut-job! Hey, look! They've left their drinks.' He drank from the one closest to him. 'What! It's just lemonade, just fucking mixer. You all right, Pixie?' He pulled out his keyring and danced Mao across the tabletop. 'You know that's the worst thing about this country, Pix. You carry a knife, they fucking bust you. How are you meant to defend against that kind of guy? How are you?'

He started to shake my shoulder. I felt too exhausted to argue. I had the odd thought that somehow Dan had arranged the entire evening. His words seemed rehearsed; his expression was expectant. I needed an out.

'Stop Dan,' I sighed. 'Tell me about your screenplay.'

'You want to know?' he put the keyring back in his pocket and stretched his arms. 'You really want to know? All right then. Actually, it starts with one line, best line ever, voice-over: *That morning she woke up and he did not.* Isn't it a fucking good line?'

'It's good,' I said.

'It's the best fucking line. *That morning she woke up and he did not.* They're a young married couple, both training to be doctors. They fuck all the time, everywhere, all the time, and they think they love each other, right? They can't really love each other because they're too young; they're rich, they have careers, they read books – they like each other, they spend time with each other. And they're both swingers but that's not important. They love each other, but it's only English love; they don't need each other. If one goes the other can just say fuck it, and go back to being a doctor and fucking around. But, anyway, that's not the point. As far as the audience knows they love each other: proper true love and they're happy. One night, they fuck – a long fantastic fuck – that's the first scene. Then they go to bed, he goes to sleep, but she can't sleep and she lies there. She thinks, what's wrong with me? She stares at the ceiling, she looks out the window, she cries, she wanks herself off, then finally she gets right to the edge of sleep. She's there, if you see what I'm saying, but she's not quite there '

'She's hypnagogic,' I suggest.

'Hypna-what?'

'That's the word for when you're about to fall asleep, the liminal moment. The best acting is hypnagogic.'

'Whatever, it's just a word. Will you stop interrupting me? And that's when, just as she's there right on the edge of sleep, she thinks, "God, I love him." She says it aloud, "God, I love him," and she smiles, big happy smile so everyone in the audience knows this is true. Then she goes to sleep. She shuts her eyes, she snores, you know she's asleep. And then she gets up. You see what I'm saying? And she starts sleepwalking. This has never happened before. No history of this stuff. She's never so much as talked in her sleep. No one in her family has ever done any sleepwalking, none of that shit. Completely out of nowhere.

'Anyway. She gets out of bed and starts sleepwalking. She moves across the bed and she straddles her boyfriend, like she's kind of squatting above his head, right? She has her legs by his ears. Then she picks up a pillow and she puts it over his head. And she suffocates him! She holds the pillow down over his face and he suffocates, right? He thrashes around and stuff for a while, but he can't get it off. She's too strong – because she's done so much fucking she's got these iron hips and so on. And besides, sleepwalking people are stronger because they can't feel pain. Then she puts the pillow back, she gets back in bed and she goes back to sleep. He's dead, she sleeping. *That morning she woke up and he did not.* So it goes. And she remembers nothing. She doesn't know what has happened. She screams, she cries, she calls the police, the neighbours come round because of how much she's screaming. All she knows is they fucked and they went to sleep. And after that everything starts happening. She calls the police, the detectives, she tells his parents. No one can believe he's dead, they think maybe someone broke in and killed him. They start looking for a killer – any kiddie-fiddlers who have stopped taking their medication, that kind of thing. But one policeman, he's just had this divorce. He's bitter, he's mean. He decides she did it. No other explanation – she must have done it. And he proves it, he works it all out. And slowly he convinces everyone. One by one, they realise he must be right. No other explanation: she must have killed him. They examine the pillow and it's got the husband's phlegm on it; whatever evidence they need, it's all there. The copper's cracked it. The police arrest her. And everybody starts to hate her: the press, the police, the other doctors, her neighbours. No one wants to fuck her anymore, nobody even talks to her. Even her own parents hate her, because all the time she keeps denying it, she keeps saying, "I don't remember anything. I didn't do it. I don't remember anything." They put her in gaol. The jury find her guilty. The judge says maximum fucking life imprisonment.'

He picked one of the shandies and drained it.

'And?' I asked.

'And, what? That's it. The end.'

'I don't see the point.'

'That is the fucking point,' said Dan. 'That's the whole fucking point. There isn't one. You know that's why I left university: 'cos of cunts like you.' He picked up the last Pimp and downed it. 'Not that I hate you kind of people anymore. Now I've met you properly, Pixie, I even sort of like you. Ha! Right, stay there. I need a slash.'

He put his arm on my leg for leverage as he stood up. I moved aside to let him through. He made a beeline towards the bathroom.

While Dan was gone I finished my fifth lager. I worried a beer mat until it crumbled and remembered the one with my number on it, still in my pocket.

That was what I needed. I made a break for the stairs, but when I was halfway across the room, Dan came out of the swinging door and we saw each other. For a second we both stopped and I looked into his face under the blue spotlights, very pale with a beard just starting to sprout. Standing apart from the crowd, he pulled the Chairman Mao keyring out of his pocket and began swinging it like a prison guard.

I just nodded and left the bar.

---

J.W. Arble was educated at Eton College and St Andrews University where he was awarded the prize for Best Dissertation at Honours Level from the School of English. His play *FortyFive* premiered at the *Edinburgh Fringe* 2005. He has published poetry and is working on his first novel. He lives in London.

# Gabrielle Barnes

## *Digbeth, November*
*An extract from a novel*

Ayesha pressed the buzzer for Flat 3. She waited. The snow was falling faster now; huge, tattered flakes caught on her coat lapels and in the tassels of her scarf. Despite the cold, she was sweating. She'd trudged right across the city, not wanting to squander £2.40 on the bus, and now her feet ached like an old aunty's. She shifted on them uneasily.

The speaker fizzed. Someone gave a deep cough into it before speaking. 'All right?' The voice was male, groggy, and definitely not Rav.

'All right,' said Ayesha. There was an awkward pause, then they started together:

'– This is the bit where you say who you are, man.'

'– I need to talk to Rav.'

There was another pause, while each party deciphered what the other had said.

'Oh right yeah –' the voice slid into friendliness '– is that Nish? You didn't sound like you man, how's it going?'

*Nish?* Who was Nish? Ayesha took a deep breath and folded her lips together, trying to concentrate. 'Look, is he in?'

'Well, yeah, course, it's Saturday innit, I thought he'd arranged –'

'Please, just tell him it's Ayesha,' she said, quickly. 'He'll know who I am.'

There was a short silence. Then, quietly: 'Fu-cking hell.'

She pulled a face. 'Please,' she repeated. 'Just let him know I'm here.'

The speaker went dead. She chewed her thumbnail through her glove. The wool squeaked against her front teeth and a shudder ran through her. The unknown flatmate would be walking to Rav's room now, he would be saying her name. It had been four whole months since Rav had last heard from her. Shit. She had no idea what she was going to say. She'd rehearsed the conversation in her head – of course she had, all the way here, reciting into the wind – but now she found that all those careful words had dispersed like so much snow. Shit, shit, shit.

Someone was coming downstairs; she could hear them behind the front door. Rav and she had checked this place out together, in the spring term, when it had been under the tenancy of two final year students. Rav had said, back then, that he would get her a key cut. Someone was fiddling with the lock now, on the other side of the door. Ayesha looked at the scraped paint around the keyhole, where student after drunken student had struggled to fit their key in the slot.

The door pulled back.

He'd grown a short beard since Ayesha had last seen him. His jaw line was emphasised; his mouth framed. It was nearly midday but he was still in his boxer shorts and the awful Homer Simpson *Doh!* T-shirt his mum had given him for his last birthday. His eyes were unreadable in the white light reflecting from the snow; Ayesha found she couldn't hold his gaze for long.

'Hello,' she said, addressing his feet instead. They were bare and looked incredibly clean against the scrubby pile of the doormat. In the heels and balls of her own sore feet, she felt her blood pound.

'I wasn't sure when –' he said. 'You must be third trimester – I'd thought –' he gave up, cleared his throat, as if to start again, but said nothing more.

Ayesha looked down and saw how her size ten winter coat buttoned only to the bottom of her bust before it split across her belly like the skin of an overripe fruit. Beneath that, impossible for her to see without a mirror, was the shameful safety-pin, hooking together her jeans where the button and hole no longer met.

'Can I come in?' she asked.

He stepped aside in answer; she stepped in. As he secured the lock, she noticed the tense dent in the right corner of his mouth. They traipsed up the two flights of stairs in silence.

The flat door opened onto a boyish hovel. The air was slightly smoky, and there was a strong smell of cooked fat. Polystyrene take-away cartons cluttered the coffee table; newspapers and medical textbooks were splayed half-read all over the place; a decaying teabag sat forgotten on a bookshelf. Rav's flatmate lay on the sofa, swathed in a ratty dressing gown, his skinny legs cocked over the arm. He had a book open, but he was using this conspicuously as a screen around which to peer at Ayesha.

*Digbeth, November*

'This is Gurjit,' said Rav, closing the door behind them.

'All right,' said Gurjit, letting both the book and the pretence drop. His gaze settled on Ayesha's bump.

'All right,' said Ayesha. She peeled her handbag from her shoulder and held it primly in front of her midriff, cutting off Gurjit's line of vision. She turned to Rav. 'Can we please talk in private?'

'Yeah – sure.' Rav edged past her and indicated a doorway. 'In here.'

His bedroom at least was clean, if not tidy: the radiator was colourful with drying socks, and the single bed was unmade but the sheets on it looked fresh. Ayesha sat on the desk chair without waiting for it to be offered. While Rav pulled the duvet and pillows into hasty arrangement, she cast her eye over the anatomical posters, flow-charts and notes on the wall behind his desk. She wondered whether the Nish girl had lain on those bedsheets.

'So,' said Rav, sinking onto a corner of the bed. Ayesha swivelled on the chair to face him. The snow on her clothes had melted; she was damp and uncomfortable.

'You've got a beard,' she said.

'You've covered your hair.'

Her fingers lifted to the sweep of scarf, checked its edges around her face. 'Yeah,' she said.

'So, you a proper Muslim now or what?'

She shrugged. 'People stare less when I cover.'

A silence hardened between them.

'I'm sorry I haven't – been in touch,' she tried.

Nothing. His toes clenched and unclenched on the carpet, and she watched the fine bones rise and fall beneath his skin.

'I thought it was best,' she continued, 'that I just made the decision for both of us. I didn't want you to feel – you know – responsible.'

'But I wanted to see you,' he said, slowly, as if only just realising this himself. 'After I got your letter. I didn't – didn't know, you know, about turning up at your house, about your parents, what they'd do – so I borrowed a mate's car, parked down the road early one morning. Watched them leave for work. I went to your door. I wanted to see you, Yeesh –' she flinched at this, at his name for her ' – I really, really wanted to see you. I must have rung your doorbell fifty times in those first couple of weeks, man.'

'I left home,' she said. 'Four months ago. The same morning I posted your letter.'

'Oh.' Rav swallowed awkwardly. 'Did they –?'

'No, no no,' she said, her mind jumping to the same place as his. 'I wasn't kicked out, don't stress; I went of my own accord.' She looked away, to a hand-drawn diagram of a heart, its cavities neatly labelled in Rav's tight handwriting. 'I left them a note. On my bed.'

'Letters for everyone.' Rav shook his head. 'Fuck, Ayesha, you're a fucking coward.'

Instinctively, she curled her arms across her belly, spreading her fingers. 'Don't swear,' she said. 'It can hear.' Her face was sweating and she wiped it with her coat sleeve. The flat's heating seemed to be on full blast. She felt light-headed and far more flustered than she'd anticipated. 'And I'm not a coward,' she said, and began to struggle out of her gloves and coat.

'God, Ayesha. You don't return my texts, you don't pick up your phone, what else am I gonna think? I mean, you move house and don't even bother to let me know.'

'I lost my mobile,' she lied, miserably.

'So? Big deal, you could've come round. Clearly, you know where I live.'

'You don't understand.' She closed her eyes so she didn't have to look at him. 'I did the right thing,' she said.

Rav made an explosive, derisive little noise. 'And where did you run away to? Where do you live?'

'With a friend.'

'A boyfriend?'

She opened her eyes and looked at him, steadily. 'No, Rav, a girlfriend from school. Anyway, I know about Nish so don't hassle me.'

'Nish?'

'Yeah, Nish.' She tried to keep her tone light. 'Your flatmate mistook me for her. Obviously that was before he saw my great big melon-belly.'

Rav sighed. 'Nish is just a mate from my year, a med student, I study with her. I'm not going out with her.'

'Sikh?'

'Yeah. Sikh. Not that it's relevant because I'm not going out with her. Or sleeping with her, before you ask.'

'Right.'

'You look like shit, Ayesha.'

'Cheers a bunch,' she snapped. 'And don't swear.'

'Right, sorry. But you do, you look awful. You don't look like you any more.'

She knew how she looked – she'd stared at herself in the mirror before she'd left her house that morning and she'd seen the dark dips beneath her eyes, the paleness of her face, and the dried blood on her lips where they'd cracked from the cold. The sight of herself had almost stopped her from coming here.

'I'm six months pregnant, Rav,' she said. 'I'm *not* me any more. I'm us.'

He had been going to say something more, but now he closed his mouth. His eyes were wet, hurt.

'Look,' she said, her voice taut. 'I've been having some problems.'

'The baby?' Rav's hands went out, and halted a little way from her belly. He held them there, still and curved in the air like a prayer gesture.

'The baby's fine,' she told him.

'Thank God,' he said.

There was a knock. Gurjit popped his head round the door just as Rav took his hands away. Gurjit watched, and his eyebrows flexed up into a double arc. He blinked a bit as he looked from Rav to Ayesha and back again.

'Er,' he said. 'I was just wondering, would anyone like a cup of tea?'

'No,' said Rav, impatiently.

'No, thanks,' said Ayesha.

'Right,' said Gurjit. 'Sorry.' He backed out, closing the door with a tender click.

'Look,' said Ayesha, 'these problems, they're the reason that I needed –'

'Can I show you something?' interrupted Rav.

'Yeah,' she said, after a moment. 'Sure.'

He stood up and went over to the bookcase. His hand travelled halfway along the top shelf and yanked out a textbook. He brought it over and held it out to her with the spine facing the carpet.

'Take it,' he said.

She took it.

'Open it. But let it fall open.'

Obediently, she brought the book up so that the spine rested on the dome of her belly, and, dropping a palm either side to catch the halves, she let the pages slump apart. She looked.

'Oh,' she said.

Rav crouched down beside her, beside the book, and traced a finger from diagram to diagram, foetus to foetus. She could feel the gentle pressure of his touch, spread across her skin by the cover of the book.

'I've been following you,' he said. 'Every day.'

She looked at his fingertip, and at the baby printed beneath. She thought, I shouldn't have come here.

---

**Gabrielle Barnes** grew up in the West Midlands. She was this year's recipient of the David Higham Award. Previously, she has had short fiction published in *Southwords*, and won first prize at the Mere Literary Festival. *Digbeth, November* is an extract from her novel-in-progress.

# Natalie Butlin

## *Scarlet's Birthday*

**M**ary feels a bit funny in the evening. Geoff drives her to the hospital and her waters break on the way there. The doctor says 'push' and the baby slides out into his hands. It opens its eyes but doesn't cry. The nurse dabs at it with swabs as the umbilical cord is cut. The doctor's forehead wrinkles in concern and Mary's lips tighten. Still holding the baby, the doctor pushes through the swing doors. His steps can be heard fading down the hallway. Geoff tries to ignore the pain in his fingers as Mary squeezes tighter and tighter.

'Breathe,' Geoff says.

Mary breathes.

They wait for the return of the doctor. The nurse tidies away, pulling the blanket over Mary's legs and straightening the pillows behind her. Footsteps. The doors swing open. The doctor, with a now pristine baby, re-enters the room.

'It's as I thought,' he says, fetlock sticking to his glistening forehead. Even the nurse freezes. 'I'm afraid your baby –' he pauses and touches his hand to his lips. He starts again, lowering his voice. 'I'm afraid your baby has been born without a personality."

Mary and Geoff stare at each other. Her eyes dart about his face.

'I don't understand, won't it grow? I mean won't she develop one?' says Mary; she is frantic. 'I thought they developed as you got older, isn't that right?'

The doctor remains silent.

'She doesn't need one now, she's only a baby, it's natural isn't it? That's how it's meant to be, your personality develops!' Her hands scratch frenziedly at her neck.

The doctor shakes his head. "There has to be a seed, something to start from, predispositions, basic tendencies…' he tails off, shrugging his shoulders.

'It's there! She's got a seed, she's just a baby, you can't tell!' She sits up towards the doctor.

The doctor shakes his head. 'There's nothing,' he says, opening his hands; they're empty.

Mary is staring at Geoff again. Geoff looks at her but she averts her gaze. He puts his hand on her back.

'Is there anything we can do?' Geoff asks.

'No,' the doctor says, 'not really.'

'What do you mean, not really?' There is hope in this ambiguous answer.

'Well, we could look for a donor, but it'd be difficult, that's something people like to hang onto, keep intact, you know, just in case there's more, after death.'

'No.' Mary is furious. 'Absolutely not.' She shrugs Geoff's arm off her back. 'You're wrong, she has a personality of her own, we've just got to nurture it.'

'Mary,' Geoff says, 'maybe we should listen to the doctor.'

'I am not having our daughter walking around with a second-hand personality. Is that what you want?'

Geoff shakes his head; ashamed. Of course that is not what he wants. He looks over at his baby and wonders if it is his fault. He is, after all, quite a dull man.

---

## Things I Have Done That Were Wrong

**1.**

'Hi,' she said, her teeth wide with too many teeth.

I was at a party. She stretched out a hand.

'Hello,' I said.

She had tiny black eyes and a large flattened nose. I shook the cold, moist hand.

'You're Dave's mate aren't you?'

'Yes.'

'I met you last weekend at the bowling alley, remember?'

'No.'

'Really? I was wearing my purple dress, with the bow.'

'What? No. That was just a child.'

**2.**

'I'm sorry,' I said.

She looked down the sharp slope of her shoulder and curled a lock of hair around her finger. She had bitten the nail down to the quick.

'I guess I just saw the dress, I didn't really notice you, you're so small.'

'You didn't notice me?'

'I mean I only saw the dress, I'm sorry.'

'Well, I'm not wearing the dress now.' She was wearing jeans and a low-cut burgundy top revealing a pale, bony chest. Two lumps were being pushed futilely towards each other by a shiny purple bra. 'But I'm still small, do you notice me now?' She smiled then pouted her greasy lips.

'Yes.'

'And what do you notice?' She angles her face down but looks up at me.

'Well, you're not a child.'

'You don't like what you see? You don't think I'm pretty?'

'I didn't say that.'

'So you think I'm pretty?'

'Yes of course you're pretty.'

**3.**

'Where's Dave?' I asked as she came in with red cheeks. We were at the cinema. It was night and I'd been waiting in the foyer for her and Dave out of the cold.

'He couldn't make it.'

'Oh, we should have rescheduled, tonight wasn't really good for me either.'

'No? A date?'

'Kind of, I could have met up with a girl from work.'

'Well, you've got a date with me now.' She smiled and linked her arm through mine. Her lips were chapped and her clothes smelt damp. 'Let's get popcorn, and hotdogs, and pick-and-mix, the whole shebang.'

'Fine.'

We walked over to the counter. She pointed at what she wanted and hopped up and down on her little feet.

'This is exciting, I haven't done this properly in such a long time,' she said.

We walked over to the pick-and-mix and I held the bag open as she scooped four of each sweet into it with a pink, plastic shovel. The sweets were weighed, the hotdogs, drinks and popcorn were counted and it came to twenty pounds. I handed over my card. Her wallet was in her hand but she turned to me and said, 'What a gent,' then patted my arm.

**4.**

She was crying with her head pressed into the arm of the sofa. I put an arm round her and squeezed her bony shoulder. She turned to me. 'I thought it's what you wanted,' she gasped through the mucus. Her eyes could barely be seen in their puffed-up lids and her whole face was wet. She looked like an amphibian.

'It was a surprise,' I said. 'I'm very flattered.'

'Flattered?' She buried her face back into the sofa and sobbed. 'That's the worst insult of all.' She heaved.

'I'm sorry.'

'Am I that repulsive?' she asks.

'No, you're very pretty, you really are.'

I leant forward to retrieve some tissues from her coffee table. She took them and blew her nose into them with a long, loud honk. She deposited the tissues on the floor and let her hand creep back onto my leg. A tiny shred of tissue was stuck just above her lip.

'So you do like me?'

'Of course I like you.'

I reached up to turn off the lamp. We began to kiss.

**5.**

'I love you,' she said, her gnawed hand curling into mine. She had let her hair down and the sea wind had blown it into a cotton-candy haze, doubling the size of her head. She squeezed my wrist. 'Did you hear me? I said I love you.' The sun was blazing through the café windows and I could see all the way down onto the beach. I was warm with tea and we had just shared a slice of creamy Victoria sponge. 'I love you,' she said again, her eyes peeling open with effort. I squeezed her fingers.

'I love you too,' I said.

*Things I Have Done That Were Wrong*

## *An Occasion*

It was dim and there was some behaviour going on in the other room. I was putting on some clothes I felt suitable for the occasion but I kept pausing to listen to the noises. She came in to look at me, looking like a girl in a painting with her hair and her nose.

'You aren't ready,' she said.

'Neither are you,' I said, which may have been true. She moved away. I did up a couple of buttons. Some singing filtered through the wall. She interjected.

'I'm ready,' I said, standing near them.

We followed each other till the vehicle was located. We waited for it to open. She was further up.

'Jesus, that isn't ours,' she said, one foot already in a different one.

'Yes it is,' I said.

There was a discussion before we went over. We all got in with our bodies. We were very restricted and I realised I was beginning to feel very strongly. The journey started and we began to pass many things; objects and places. There was so much to look at but it was difficult because the view was obscured. So I looked at her hand. It was the most hand-like thing I had ever seen. The journey continued.

'We're almost there,' she said, turning her head.

One of the others said something hilarious that reminded me of my childhood but nothing came of it. I realised the weather was surprising for the season. I looked over and saw her features, then her clothes. She was the only one properly prepared. We stopped moving and stepped out. There were many others arriving at the same time. Some of them were not my relatives.

---

Natalie Butlin was born in the US, lived briefly in the Far East and settled in the UK. She did an Art Foundation course before going to UEA to do her BA in Literature and Creative Writing. She usually writes short stories but has begun work on a novel.

# Tamsin Evans

*Tides*

**M**um is on the phone. She has stretched the telephone cord into the hall and jammed the door closed so she can sit on the stairs to talk, in privacy. I can hear the waves of her voice in the hallway.

The evening is close and stuffy; the air that creeps through the living room windows brings with it the clinging smell of the mudflats. The tide is out, and from the sofa I can see that the estuary sits near-empty, only a sliver of water snaking down its spine. The tired evening sun peeps beneath an eyelid of a cloud. A sea mist is beginning to swallow the view of the opposite shore.

'Doesn't look like there'll be much of a sunset tonight,' Gran says from her armchair, reaching for her mug of tea in its mismatched saucer. She has lived in our cottage for six months now, since she started having falls, but still cannot grow used to the fact that we drink tea from thick-lipped mugs, without saucers. Her own crockery has not been extracted from the boxes in the shed. We haven't got room for all of it, Mum says, when I ask her about bringing them in.

'Lovely cup of tea.' Gran's mug clatters in the saucer as she places it back on the table beside her. She strains to look at my knitting. She's been trying to teach me since I moved back from university, but I'm hopeless. 'Try and keep the stitches slightly looser,' she advises.

'No,' Mum's voice leaks under the door from the hall, 'they didn't really say, I suppose they can't say for certain. There are so many factors, you know. I mean, I'm overweight, I smoked for years, I took the pill for years, I had a late baby, my mother had it –'

She pauses.

'Yes,' she says, 'about fifteen years ago.'

She pauses again, listening.

'Hmmm.'

The stair creaks as she shifts position.

'I think I've dropped a stitch, Gran,' I say.

'Oh, let me have a look.'

'But do you know,' Mum's voice has risen, 'I am absolutely convinced that the stress of the redundancy is to blame for this.'

Gran holds my knitting up, turning her head slightly so she can examine it with her right eye. The left one is blind, the greying-blue iris half covered with a dull opaque skin.

'They're talking about lumpectomies, and removing lymph nodes from my armpit, which can cause lymphoedema –'

'Ah yes,' Gran spots the lost stitch.

'– and then they want me to have bloody radiotherapy, which can have all manner of side effects, like burning your lungs –'

'Can you pass me the other needle?' Gran asks.

'– and after that they want me to take this sodding drug called Tamoxifen, which is supposed to cause menopause-type symptoms and I don't want to go through that again, I mean, once is e-bloody-nough ...'

Gran is trying to fish the dropped stitch from the woollen net.

'And then they have the cheek to tell you you're fucking lucky!'

'Oh dear,' Gran says, 'I do wish she wouldn't swear like that.'

'But I tell you what, it's my body, and I don't want them interfering. In fact, they'll be fucking lucky if I go through with any of it.' Mum's voice pierces through the wall.

'There you are, kid,' Gran hands the knitting back to me. 'Good as new.'

'Thanks.' I stab the needles through the ball of wool and place the knitting on the floor.

'Gran?'

'Yes, dear?'

'Mum said you've got to have a bath tonight.'

'Did she?'

'Yeah.' I smile apologetically. 'Shall we go and get it over with?'

While Gran struggles to her feet I grab a measuring jug from the kitchen and rejoin her in the living room as she heads towards the door. Her walk these days often reminds me of a child taking its first steps. She staggers and stumbles, leaning forwards and reaching out for furniture as she passes. Her progress through the house is invariably stalled by Mum's constant question: 'Where's your bloody stick?'

Gran opens the living room door and stands at the foot of the stairs.

'Just a minute, Lorna.' Mum cups her hand over the receiver. 'What are you two up to?'

'I'm just going to give Gran a bath.'

'Right.' Mum scoots to the side so we can pass. 'Good.' She holds the phone to her ear again. 'Sorry Lorna, carry on.'

Gran climbs the first step, then stops and stoops to clasp Mum's hand before resuming her slow ascent. Mum looks after her, a sad smile warming her lips. Then she looks at me and mouths the words: *Where's her bloody stick?*

The pipes squeak as I turn the taps on. I scatter some lavender-scented bath salts into the running water. Gran plonks onto the old piano stool next to the bath, her breathing ragged from the climb. The piano stool came with Gran when she moved in. The piano couldn't; there wasn't space.

I see her contemplating her feet and the long journey south to untie her laces.

'Here, I'll do those.' Crouching, I undo the bow on her right shoe and loosen it from her foot.

'It's all right, I can manage.'

'It's fine, Gran. Easier if I do it.' I pull the bow on her left shoe.

'I said, I can manage –' she shunts her foot away from me '– dear.' Using her other foot, she kicks the shoe off and, with a stifled grunt, she bends and begins rolling her socks down over her swollen ankles.

While she undresses, I lay the blue mat beside the bath and turn off the taps, then secure Gran's bath seat in the enamel cradle of the tub.

'Ready, Gran?'

'Nearly,' she says, her voice muffled beneath her vest as she struggles to pull it over her head. My eyes linger briefly on the pale scar worming across her chest where her left breast should be. When her head emerges from the vest, I look away. As she climbs awkwardly into the bath, I thread my hands under her armpits to support her.

I was seven when Gran had her operation. I know this because I had been given a nurse's uniform for my seventh birthday and I wore it to visit her in hospital: a blue dress and a gauzy white apron, emblazoned across the chest with a lurid red cross.

'My Granny was a nurse,' I told the nurses on the ward, as they admired my new outfit. Straining on tip-toes, I asked if they would like me to show them how to fold hospital corners.

While we were visiting, the lady in the bed next to Gran was given a bunch of flowers with a green chrysanthemum in it. I was amazed. I'd never even imagined that green flowers could exist. I stared and stared, despite hushed admonishments from Mum, until the lady noticed and beckoned me to her bed.

'Look after this please, nurse,' she said, handing me the flower. 'Be sure to give it plenty of water.'

I carried it home proudly, like a trophy. It didn't last long. I prepared myself to break the news to the lady. But next time we went to the hospital she wasn't in the bed next to Gran any more. Gran placed her hand on my shoulder gently. 'I'm afraid she's gone, sweetheart,' she said.

I was never told why Gran was in hospital, not then and not afterwards. It just gradually dawned on me, as I grew older and began to pick up on her quiet jokes about being lopsided.

'So what are you going to do now you've finished at college, Livvy?' she asks now, sluicing her hands through the water.

'Uni,' I correct her, thinking of the MA offer letter sitting unannounced inside the dictionary on my bookshelf. I dip the measuring jug into the bathtub and slosh the warm water over her upper back, which is rounded, like a whale's hump, the skin across it smooth and tight.

'I don't really know Gran. I'll probably stay at home for a bit. Get a job.'

'Well, it'll be nice to have you around.'

Lathering some soap onto a scrubber, I massage her back in frothy circles. As I stroke the bubbles along the soft thin skin at her shoulder she reaches up and grabs my hand.

'You know she's stubborn.' She squeezes my fingers. 'Always has been. But she'll have the operation, I'm sure of it.'

A muffled thumping creeps into my dream and wakes me. I peer at my bedside clock.

3:25.

My eyes shrink shut. I slide into shallow sleep.

The thumping begins again. My eyelids peel open.

3:27.

A louder thud. Fevered rustling. Snatched, staccato breaths.

I shed my sheets and feel my way through the blackness, pausing on the landing to let my eyes adjust to the grainy charcoal light. The door of Mum's bedroom is slightly ajar. I shuffle towards it and crane my head into the room.

For a moment, I panic: the bed is empty, its surface taut and pale. Then, I see her by the window and the fist in my chest unclenches. I try to nudge the door open further, but it jams against a pillow on the floor.

Mum's back is turned to me and her nightie is a stark white against the blue glow of the glass. Her shoulders are shaking. Suddenly, she starts to slam her palm against the pane repeatedly. Beyond the window, the moon cuts sharp slices of light across the bruised-black water of the estuary.

A floorboard creaks as I turn and pad back across the landing. I lie in bed, watching the digits of the alarm clock change. When the light outside begins to brighten, the herring gulls wail like sirens.

The grumbling of the rubbish truck outside wakes me. I rub the sleep from my eyes and get up to go to the loo. In the bathroom I discover Mum sitting on the piano stool, elbows on knees, head propped in hands, eyes fixed on the floor.

I approach her warily. 'Mum, is everything all right?'

'No.' Her eyes snap up, puffy and bloodshot. 'Your grandmother's gone and crapped in her effing commode again.' She snatches the lid off the commode bucket at her feet, exposing its gut full of urine, muddied with a slick of brown. She stands and pushes past me. Moments later, her bedroom door slams.

I empty and disinfect the bucket and hurry downstairs. From the hallway I can hear Gran has got the radio on in the kitchen. The broadcaster's voice is a soothing hum beneath the sharp clinking of crockery and the rising scream of the kettle.

When I open the front door the heat is already smothering. Bare-footed, I cross the road and stand on the ledge of the estuary wall. The tide has sucked the estuary dry again, leaving its brown belly laid bare for examination by crowds of wading birds. Avocets and oystercatchers pick spindly-legged over its skin, searching for worms and crustaceans to extract from its pores. Dusty-coloured redshanks insert their needle-like beaks into its flesh.

I look upriver, to where the skeletons of rigs clank in conversation around the quay, then cast my gaze in the other direction, far out to where the mouth of the estuary vomits a splurge of reddy-brown into the sea. I walk in that direction until I reach the ladder which leads to the shore. After lowering myself to the sand, I walk to the edge of the flats, where the mud is baked hard and cracked into almost tessellating sections. Further out it becomes wrinkled and wet, covered with fingers of seaweed swollen with fleshy blisters of liquid. In places the gnarled hands of drowned branches protrude from the mire. It will be several hours until the tide turns and creeps towards the shore.

---

**Tamsin Evans** was born in 1983 and trained in contemporary dance at Laban before graduating from the University of Leeds with a BA in English with Development Studies. She has had articles published in *The Guardian* and is currently working on a collection of short stories and her first novel.

# Elisabeth Fairchild

## *The Remodel*

Arnold woke to a shrill alarm in an empty bed. He took a shower. Looking in the mirror he carefully shaved his face, slapped on some aftershave and went back to the bedroom. His wife would be on her way back by now. She was on a business trip and Lyla was staying with her grandparents. Lyla didn't want to be alone with him, he supposed, and he couldn't really blame her. He was glad to have the house to himself for a little while anyway. He dressed himself quickly and chose a tie he hadn't worn in a year or so – it had his initials embroidered in gold thread at the base.

For breakfast he had the usual: oatmeal and black coffee with two sugars. When he had finished he placed his bowl in the sink, grabbed his backpack, and headed for the door. Years ago when Lyla was a baby, she had knocked his coffee into his open briefcase, while he sat holding her. He had started using his wife's backpack from college and had never gotten around to a new briefcase.

Outside it was clear and blustery. His walk to work was a short one: three blocks up, past the crematorium, then another two blocks to the left and he was there.

His office sat above an adult video store with sickly neon signs and painted windows. Keep the voyeurs in, he thought, don't let them look out. The building was designed in such a way that the two businesses shared a foyer. Arnold supposed that to the outside eye he looked like a porn addict. He stuck his key in the bottom lock, then the dead bolt and pushed the door open. At the base of the stairs there was a stack of mail; he hadn't been into the office for several days and things were piling up. He sifted through the letters as he walked up the stairs and then pushed open the office door. As usual there was no good mail: several offers for business credit cards, a bill or two and the usual flyers from the porn shop. He had taken to keeping these in a drawer to the left of his drafting table because he didn't like his clients to see them in the garbage can. Every few months he would put a hefty stack of them in his backpack and throw them in the dumpster behind the pizza place down the street.

Arnold had gone into the porn shop only once, when he and his wife had separated for a little while. At that time he had been sleeping in his office, under his drafting table. The man who worked in the shop was Turkish but his nametag read "Sven". Sven watched everyone in his shop intently. He must get ripped off a lot, Arnold had thought. The whole place smelled heavily of cologne and carpet cleaner and it was stifling in there. On the back wall there was a poster of two naked women chained to a bed. Nearby was a selection of dusty pink and purple dildos. In the corner was a stack of boxed blow-up dolls with a poorly inflated model sitting on the top, legs splayed, head sagging to one side. The rest of the shop contained magazines and DVDs. That is what the men really came for. Arnold looked at Sven and then at the other shoppers. One man was intently 'reading' a *Playboy*, another shamelessly perused a copy of *Asian Dolls*. The magazine rack was overflowing with abused magazines. Each cover looked beaten and torn, and some of them had been left opened on a particularly graphic page. There was a laminated sign above the rack that read 'Buy don't browse,' but this instruction was clearly not enforced. It all made him terribly uncomfortable and he had left without touching a thing. The flyers started coming through the door after that. He felt sick and shamed when the first flyer was slipped into his mail slot, but in time he had become desensitized.

He didn't flip the light on in his office just yet, but moved over to the window and stared out at the leafless trees in the park across the street. It was only seven thirty and the neon sign from the shop below made his window shine with icy blue light. He made himself a pot of coffee in the dark. After a few sips he turned on the light and sat down to work. The project he was working on was a remodel. He was adding an in-law unit and converting a bedroom into a master bathroom. As always, he became mesmerized by the meticulous details: the way his straight lines repeated themselves, or how his hard pencil carved into the drafting paper. He paused for a moment and looked up. His drafting table was neat and orderly. The lamp that was clamped to one side was at just the perfect angle; the table glowed with clean light. He reached for the brass paperweight that lived on the side table next to his desk. When his work tired him he would pick it up and move it cautiously between his hands, feeling its cold flatness and thinking about his wife. She had given it to him twenty years ago when he had received his architectural license.

He looked up at the framed picture he had of her. It was from the seventies, and had that strange sepia glow to it. Her hair was feathered, her expression calm. He couldn't remember taking the photo but she told him he had.

At lunch he walked down the street and bought a sandwich at the corner shop, then went back to his office to eat. In the spring, he would frequently eat in the park across the way. He loved to look at his office from the park, and imagine he didn't know what was inside his own window.

He drank more coffee after he finished his sandwich. His stereo was broken; his office was quiet. Since his business partner had left he had begun to enjoy his job more but he did feel the absence during these silent lunches.

***

When Arnold got home the house was cold and his wife still wasn't there. He lit a fire in the woodstove and put a kettle on the top. He wasn't sure why he did this – he had never liked tea and he used a machine for his coffee. Perhaps he found it disconcerting to have a hot stove with nothing cooking – or maybe he just liked the sound of the water pinging against its cage. He sat down to a book but the words didn't enter him. He read the same page three times before he heard a jiggling in the lock and he stopped trying altogether.

Lyla walked in and the cold air from outside reached across him.

'How was grandpa?' he said. He was a little surprised to see her. She looked tired and her arms were ringed with shopping bags.

'Fine. We played a few games of chess. I won the last game but it didn't count, he let me take back a few moves.' She always seemed to be down on herself and this worried him.

'I'm sure you could beat me. Want a game now?' Her face weakened.

'No,' she said, and trudged up the stairs without another word. He couldn't help but feel that she suspected him of something – something that he was possibly guilty of without even knowing it.

He poured a glass of red wine and waited for his wife. She was not there by ten. She did not call. He imagined himself knocking on Lyla's door and saying something to her, but he couldn't. Not yet. When he went up to bed, her music thumped softly through the bedroom wall. He brushed his teeth and flossed. He placed the aftershave he had left out that morning back in the medicine cabinet and climbed into bed. He thought about his wife. Her body was always cold and when they made love he had always felt a chill pass through him. Now, staring into the darkness, he wrapped his arm around her pillow and with a sigh admitted to himself that she would not be coming back.

The next day he lay in bed longer than usual. When he dressed he put the same tie on from the day before. He looked at all his limp ironed shirts and his khakis and his two pairs of shoes below them. He was a good person goddamn it.

When he got to work there was no mail. At his desk he pulled at the drawer to the left of his drafting table and took out its contents. He picked his paperweight up and, using it as a stencil, carefully drew a circle around part of a flyer. He cut it out and admired his work. The woman's breasts were almost in the center of the circle and the picture ended just above her navel so you could not see that her hand was inside her panties. He pulled drafting dots off their wheel and stuck the picture to the base of the paperweight, slammed it down beside him and went back to work.

---

**Elisabeth Fairchild** was born in San Francisco and grew up in the coastal redwoods of Northern California. She got her Bachelor of Arts in Theatre from Humboldt State University in 2007. Liz is currently working on a collection of short stories titled *The Pacific*.

# Anna Giokas

## *If You Could Be Anything*

Zoë closes the door on the cabin where Sarah is still asleep and begins to pick her way through the olive grove. Her nightshirt sticks and her old school shoes slide on the churned earth. All round her the trees pull their shade close; the grove is a bath of heat and the pounding in her head keeps time with the tze-tze-tze of the cicadas. She is nearing the path to the main house when a snake, white and green, flashes in a scrub of dead thistles and she runs until she reaches the foot of the balcony where a boy is lying with his hands behind his head on Professor Randall's lounger.

'Who's that?' he calls. His voice sounds like he's used to asking questions and getting answers.

'We're not meant to sit on that, the Professor said last night,' she says, eyeing him. He looks older than her but not much, a year, maybe two.

The boy springs up. 'Well, that isn't very friendly.' He leans on a wooden beam holding up the roof and gives her a knowing smile. His eyes are a very light blue. 'I'm Richard. I arrived last night, fucking awful journey.' His hair is thick and dark blond and sticks out from his head at odd angles. 'Are you going to stand out there in the sun all morning or are you coming up?'

She feels the blue eyes flicker over her and is suddenly aware of the stubble on her calves where she hasn't shaved her legs. She pulls on the band holding her ponytail, pushes her fringe back off her face, and reties her hair tighter.

'The plane food was rank, let's get breakfast,' he says.

She bites her top lip. 'We should wait for the others.'

'Sod the others,' he says, jerking himself away from the beam.

She follows him into the kitchen. The bread is in a box on top of the fridge and she has to stretch for it.

'Cut mine thick will you?' he says, flicking cupboards open. He finds marmalade and spreads it generously; he doesn't ask her whether she likes it. They pile the slices onto a plate and go outside. She sits beside him on the lounger and smoothes her nightshirt under her lap as though it were a skirt; an automatic gesture that makes the Greek olive grove seem for a moment like Surrey.

'You've dropped some there,' he says, his eyes on her thigh where a golden bead of marmalade winks up at them, just below the frayed hem of her shirt.

'I know,' she says and turns her knees a little away from him.

'Allow me.' Before she can stop him his thumb is on her thigh, sweeping it clean. It feels strange to be touched there, like that, by a boy. But there is something so confident about the way he does it that she doesn't say anything.

'So how many others are there?' he asks, licking his thumb.

Zoë kicks off her shoes and nudges them under the lounger. 'Um, yesterday when we arrived there was the Professor, obviously, and this boy called Joshua and then me and Sarah.'

Richard leans back and closes his eyes against the sun. 'Sarah?'

'She's my friend from home.' Zoë rubs at the back of her neck where her hair is sticking. 'Joshua is …'

'I met Joshua last night,' Richard interrupts. 'He's in the cabin next to mine, weird set-up this isn't it? My father said it was a summer school, I thought there'd be more of us.'

Zoë shrugs. An ant struggles with a crumb in front of her; she stretches out a toe and flicks it. She had thought there would be more people too, but it's just nice not to be at home.

His knee knocks against hers. 'You've gone quiet,' he says.

'Have I …? I was just thinking I might go for a swim.'

'Brilliant, I'll get my trunks,' he says, jumping up. 'Meet you back here in ten minutes.'

He holds out a hand and lifts her up and for a moment she feels as though her body is light enough to fly.

She rushes to the patio beside the house where her bikini is hanging on the line, shuffles her knickers off and shoves them in her nightshirt pocket. The bikini top is all strings. She has to tie it round her tummy under the shirt and lean forward to get it in place. Richard appears from a side door with a towel as she is making the last adjustments.

They follow a track down the mountain and in a few minutes they are out of the olive trees. Below, the shore stretches in a sweep of white sand that curves with the island. Richard runs down the cliff path and pounces onto the beach. Zoë watches him pull off his shirt, rip at his shoes and run into the sea, a cascade erupting as he goes. He dives under and reappears near where a rowing boat is tethered to a buoy.

'Come on!' he shouts.

Zoë struggles down the path and unbuckles her shoes on the sand. She waits until Richard dives again before she pulls the nightshirt off and rushes into the shallows.

He surfaces close by, rolls on his back and blows a jet of water into the air. He grins, 'Zoë, if you could be anything, what would you be?'

'I think I'd be tall,' she says, dancing her feet along the seabed until her chest is under water.

He laughs. 'You're the perfect height for a girl.'

'No I'm not, I'm short … You don't know what it's like being short. People don't notice you.'

He rolls onto his front and kicks away. 'I would be rich.'

'You already are.' She says it because it's obvious.

'No,' he says, standing up. 'I mean proper stinking rich. I'd buy an Aston Martin and I'd go on a road trip all round Europe, I'd go to all the ancient sites and stay in the best hotels.' He waves a hand in her direction. 'I'd take you with me, of course.'

'You think a lot of yourself, don't you? Anyway, ancient sites are boring.' She floats onto her back, keeping her stomach hidden.

'All right then, I'd take you shopping, we'd go to Milan and I'd buy you the highest heels we could find.'

She laughs, spins round and dives under with her eyes open; a cloud of fish darts away. She turns over holding her nose and sees a bowl of light and blue. This is nice, she thinks. The boys at home either make her embarrassed or they're just weird. Richard's not like that – but then maybe that's because he's more of a man than a boy.

She bobs to the surface, runs a hand through the water and sends a satisfying arc whooshing up and over him. He dives again and yanks her down.

\*\*\*

When Zoë returns to the cabin Sarah is still asleep. Her sheet has wriggled into a knot at the end of her bed, leaving her long naked legs exposed and her hair is spread out over her pillow in gold swirls, rising away from her face as though she were floating. Zoë grabs clothes from her rucksack and creeps into the bathroom. Yesterday Professor Randall gave them vague instructions to meet at eleven in a clearing in the pine forest above the olive groves. It might have been nice, she thinks, yanking off her bikini, if Richard had waited so they could look for it together. She pulls on a T-shirt and skirt and shuffles back into the bedroom where Sarah is beginning to stir. Zoë hurriedly slips on her shoes and rushes across the room. The cabin door swings shut as she runs towards the white scar of a path leading up into the pine forest.

When she arrives in the clearing she sees that Richard has taken the only chair. His elbows are lazily arranged on the bamboo arms. Joshua is doing his best to look comfortable on one of four wooden stools around a stone table.

Joshua stands up, his long arms gangling, then he decides to sit down again. 'Come and sit over this side ... it's shadier,' he says looking at Zoë.

She sits down on the nearest stool. Richard catches her eye and smiles. She feels like they are sharing a joke although she's not exactly sure what it is.

'Did you see the Professor on your way up? Joshie here was just telling me he can't wait to get started,' Richard says.

She shakes her head. Joshua picks up a twig from the ground and draws a circle in the earth. Richard looks amused.

The canopy above Zoë is thin and coins of sunlight make patterns on her hands and arms. It is quiet up here. No birds sing. Even the wind, which whips and whirs further down the mountain, seems to tiptoe here. She straightens her back and tucks a strand of damp hair into her bun, aware that Richard is watching her. She should say something interesting.

There comes a dry rustling and then the sound of heavy breaths. Zoë looks up to see Professor Randall emerging from the forest. He gives the boys a brief wave and walks past her.

'Professor,' Richard says, rising from the chair. 'Please, this must be your seat.'

'Ah, very decent of you,' Professor Randall says, sinking down. He scans the clearing as if something is bothering him. His eyes look very red. Richard sits down on the stool beside Zoë's, closer than he needs to be.

'So we begin,' Professor Randall says. 'Now, it strikes me that it might be rather appropriate to get things going with a smidge of mythology. Echo and Narcissus Anyone?'

There is silence. The Professor pulls himself to his full sitting height and opens his mouth, but whatever he is about to say is lost in a long exhale because at that moment Sarah flits into the clearing, smiling happily. Zoë notices that the outline of her body shows through her white dress.

'Hey everyone ... I'm really sorry I'm late.' Sarah says, pulling an exaggerated frown. 'Oops.'

'Ah, Sarah,' says Professor Randall. Zoë watches his face rearrange into an approving smile. 'We were only just getting started.'

'I didn't set an alarm because I thought Zoë would wake me up,' Sarah says.

'Yeah, I'm sorry about that, I was ...' Zoë begins.

'I didn't mean it like that,' Sarah interrupts her. 'I know you were just being nice and letting me sleep in – it's totally my fault, I'm so lazy aren't I?'

'All right girls, let's get started shall we?' Professor Randall says. 'Just find yourself a seat Sarah.'

'Here, have mine,' Richard says, standing up and sending his stool tumbling. He bends down and rights it. 'I'm Richard by the way, I arrived last night.'

'Hi, nice to meet you ... don't worry, I'll go over the other side,' Sarah says, giving Zoë a private *isn't he funny* smile. Zoë looks away.

'No,' Richard says. 'You sit next to Zoë.'

Sarah shrugs and sits down. Richard strides across the clearing, takes up the remaining stool, carries it over to the spot next to Sarah and pushes it hard into the soft red earth.

'Come on, enough of this procrastination,' Professor Randall says. 'Now, just to reiterate, we are beginning with the myth of Narcissus and Echo. Sarah, any chance you know it?'

Sarah strokes her nose with a thumbnail. 'Um ... I vaguely remember something ...'

'Well,' Professor Randall says, slipping a hand into his pocket. 'Would you care to have a stab?'

Zoë is watching Richard. She sees him grin at Sarah. A strap on Sarah's dress has slipped down to reveal the pink flowers on the cup of her bra. Zoë kicks at the earth and looks away into the dark spaces of the forest; it would be easier if Sarah hadn't come.

*If You Could Be Anything*

**Anna Giokas** was born in 1980. She has worked as a journalist in London and now lives in Norfolk. *If You Could Be Anything* is an extract from the novel she is writing. More information is available from **www.annagiokas.com**.

# Alastair Hadden

## *In Love*

Amity and James walked together across the Fringes of the Arctic. The zoo would soon be closing.

'But what if you get it wrong?' asked Amity.

'I'm not sure I understand.'

'You're going to write down everything I say, yes?'

'Everything,' James said solemnly.

'And you do this often? You come here, and accost people, and ask them questions? To find out about them?'

'Yes.'

'So today you'll find out about me – write about me, I mean – and then we'll go our separate ways.'

'Yes,' said James.

'And tomorrow it'll be someone new.'

'Yes.'

'But what if you wrote our lives down wrong? What if you made a mistake – even the smallest mistake – because you weren't paying attention, even for a moment? It could be the smallest thing of all.'

They settled themselves on a bench near the Amur tiger enclosure. James opened his notebook on his knee and dotted a pencil against the page.

'I don't understand,' he said.

Amity let out a long, low whistle, then drummed at the ground beneath the bench with the toes of her red sneakers.

'Are you cold?' asked James.

'What about her?'

A woman stood nearby with a young boy. They were watching for the tigers. The woman carried a large handbag looped over one arm.

'I don't know her,' said James.

'So let's write about her.'

'I'd have to ask her a few questions first.'

'No questions.'

'But how could I –'

'Her name is Ursula,' Amity said smoothly. 'She has no children of her own, so every weekend she brings her nephew to the zoo. They have a yearly membership. Her nephew is Bernard, aged seven. He likes the prairie dogs.'

James nodded and bent low over his notebook, pencil in hand. Amity watched him, chewing at the corner of her plump lower lip.

'Did you write all that down?'

'Yes,' said James, and he showed her what he had written.

Ursula and her nephew, Bernard, seven, had come to the zoo to see the prairie dogs and the tigers.

'What's in her bag?' asked Amity.

'I don't know,' said James. 'You didn't tell me.'

'Then why don't you ask Ursula?'

'It would be rude to ask.'

Amity laughed, showing her perfect white teeth.

'You're right,' she said. 'It would be terribly rude. The bag is full of the chopped up remains of Ursula's husband.'

'That's ridiculous,' said James.

'Yes,' said Amity, 'it really is – on any other day, it would be utterly ridiculous. But today it happens to be the truth. Today, after six horrible years of marriage, Ursula has finally snapped. That bag is filled with the bits and pieces of her abusive husband. She's planning to sneak it into the wolf enclosure.'

'Why?'

'She thinks they'll gobble all the evidence.'

Ursula and Bernard moved up the path together, towards the wolves. James frowned, and his eyes followed the handbag until it bobbed out of sight.

'It's too small,' he said. 'You're making this up.'

'Of course,' said Amity, 'but that doesn't mean it's a lot less truthful than anything you write. What if people lie to you? What if their memories are faulty? How can you learn anything about anyone just by asking a few blunt questions?'

'It's the most efficient way.'

'That doesn't make it honest,' said Amity. She sighed. 'It's just a little piece of somebody's life. It's just a day at the zoo.'

'The zoo is the safest place.'

'What does that mean?'

'I used to go to the park, or out into the city,' said James, 'but the stories were sadder.'

'So you're already editing them,' sighed Amity.

James thought about this. There was a long silence, during which Amity rooted in her bag for her book and packet of cigarettes.

'Listen,' she said, 'what do you really know about Ursula? I made her name up. That boy is probably her son, not a nephew. But maybe it is her nephew, and she really is childless, but considers it a small price to pay after dodging ovarian cancer. Did you know she fell in love only once, at fifteen? Or perhaps she's never been in love at all. Maybe she married for money, but then her husband gave it all up to become a missionary. He cheated on her, or he died of typhus in South East Asia, leaving her to bring up Bernard by herself. Now she resents the boy because he reminds her of his father.'

James stared at Amity. He opened his mouth as if to speak, then closed it again.

'That's wonderful,' he said eventually, 'but it's not the truth.'

'When she was twelve Ursula came second in a county dance competition. She keeps the medal to this day in a drawer by her bed.'

'It's not true.'

'And why does that matter?' asked Amity. 'What does the truth have to do with it?'

The light was failing, and there was no one around. The afternoon's showers had long since moved on, but the warmth had gone out of everything. Even the enclosures between the paths were empty; all the animals were inside.

'Why are you putting up with me, Amity?' asked James.

'I'm waiting for my boyfriend. He's a zookeeper.'

James crossed a sentence out of his notebook and wrote a few new words in its place.

'What did you write when I told you that?' asked Amity.

'I wrote "zookeeper",' said James. 'Are you in love with him?'

Amity snorted.

'Of course you wrote it like that,' she said. 'Of course you did.'

'Are you?'

'The point,' said Amity, and she prodded James twice in the shoulder, 'is that unless you were omniscient –'

'"Omniscient?"'

'Unless you knew everything there was to know – every last thing – you couldn't write truthfully about anybody. And even if you did know, even if you knew absolutely everything, how could you keep it short enough? What would you dare to leave out? You'd spend all your time writing.'

'I do spend all my time writing,' said James.

Amity rolled her eyes, then flipped open the cigarette packet and lit one. She sheltered the tip out of habit: there was no wind.

'Amity," said James cautiously, 'you're very good at making things up, but I don't think you know much about writing.'

Amity laughed, quite loudly. There was a hole in her jeans at the knee, and the skin there was white.

'I guess not,' she said.

'What's your surname?' asked James.

'Lipton,' said Amity.

'Lipton?'

'Like the tea.'

James made a note.

'What age are you?' he asked.

Amity stared at him. Smoke curled away over her shoulder.

'I'm twenty-eight,' she said. 'I work in a bookshop. There are two freckles on my neck just far enough apart to look like a vampire bite, and when I was younger I wanted to be a dancer.'

James looked at her as she smoked her cigarette. When she was finished she stubbed it out on the side of the bench, then dropped it on the path.

'Do you want to know about me?' asked James.

'Sure,' said Amity. 'Shoot.'

'My name is James,' said James. 'I am twenty-six, and I am a reporter.'

'You call this reporting?'

'Yes.'

'Why call it that and not writing?'

'Because writers write about what never happened, and everything I report on has happened, or is happening now. It's the reality.'

Amity considered this. Her lips twitched.

'Are you going to report on this?'

'"This?"'

'This,' said Amity, and she gestured through the space between them.

'Yes,' said James.

'What are you going to report?'

'Everything I said and did, and everything you said and did.'

'Nothing else?'

'Nothing else.'

'Just the facts,' said Amity. She grinned.

'Just the salient details,' corrected James.

'You don't know what 'omniscient' means, but you know what 'salient' means?'

'I know what "omniscient" means.'

Amity flashed her teeth.

'Well, James, twenty-six, you're awfully cute, but I don't think you know too much about girls.'

The evening sun stretched along the paths. Amity thumbed through a few pages of her book, and then resumed whistling under her breath. Otherwise it was very quiet in the zoo. James folded his notebook and stowed it in the pocket of his raincoat.

'What are you reading?' he asked.

'*Found in Ice*,' said Amity. 'It's a novel by a Norwegian author I like. He wrote it in English – his third language – because he didn't want it to be too beautiful.'

'Is it famous?'

'It's an old book, and one of my favourites. You haven't heard of it? They've made it into a film now.'

'No,' said James firmly. 'I haven't heard of it. Do you know about the bears?'

'Excuse me?'

'Do you know about the polar bears? The zoo used to have two of them.'

Amity blinked twice, and then smiled.

'Tell me about the bears, James,' she said.

'Their names were Spunky and Ootek.'

'No kidding?'

'No kidding,' said James. 'They used to live right here, where the tigers are now, but it was too cramped. The bears were miserable, so they sent them to Sóstó Zoo in Hungary, where there was a bigger enclosure. But before that they lived together here for twenty years, miserably. One time the female bear, Spunky, gave birth in full view of the public, and then she ate her own cubs, in front of everyone.'

'That's horrible.'

'Their whole life was sad,' said James. 'Their parents were shot by hunters. They were found together on a rubbish dump in Canada.'

'A landfill?'

'Yes.'

'I'm from Canada too,' said Amity.

'You sound American.'

'Well, I'm Canadian, James.'

'Where are you from exactly?'

'London, Ontario.'

'Is it nice there?'

'Very. You're not writing this down.'

'Do you miss it?'

'No,' said Amity, and she wrinkled her nose. 'I don't really miss it. I couldn't stand the winters.'

The glass of the enclosure beside them was speckled grey with dust and flecks of dirt. It was like a sheet cut from a glacier that had grown impure during its long grind down a mountain. The day had been cold at times, but it would have been too warm for bears.

'It's five o'clock,' said Amity. 'The zoo's closed.' She stood up from the bench and slung her bag over her shoulder. 'Do you want to walk out with me, James?'

'Don't you have to wait for your boyfriend?'

'No,' said Amity, and she laughed. 'I don't think he's coming.'

Together they went through the zoo. They walked around by the water, past where the tapirs should have been. An attendant opened the gate so they could leave; the entrance booth was closed, and the other visitors had already been ushered out of the zoo. The sun was almost all the way down.

'Aren't you cold?' asked James.

Amity looked up at him and shook her head, smiling. She twined her arm through his and held it tight against her side.

'I want to know why you write about people, James.'

'What's there to say about it?'

'Let's just get some dinner.'

'Where do you want to go?'

'I don't mind,' said Amity. 'It's not Valentine's Day until tomorrow.'

Arm in arm they walked past the zoo sign where it stood out from the even white slabs of the wall. Behind the railings of the Phoenix Park the tea rooms were closed. James and Amity went on towards the city with the last of the sun at their backs, until they came to the quays. The evening was light and open, and the Liffey below them flowed on freely into the sea.

---

**Alastair Hadden** was born and raised in Dublin, where he received a Bachelor's degree in Philosophy from Trinity College. Later he worked in a wine shop. He was awarded the *Seth Donaldson Memorial Trust Bursary* in 2007, and is currently completing a book of short stories entitled *Fairground*.

# Ben Harvey

## Smoking
*An extract from a short story*

Excuse me mate, have you got a cigarette? Ah, thanks. Thanks a lot – I left mine at home. Sorry, have you got a lighter as well?

So, you having a good night? Yeah, it's all right. Not great though. Not like it used to be, do you remember when this place was the Ferry Boat? It was great. It was kind of rougher, but cheap and a good crowd. Nothing like this. I don't really know why I come here anymore – I always hate it. The music's shit. Well yeah, the dubstep's all right, yeah. They used to have funk nights here, when it was the Ferry Boat.

The lights, I hate them as well. They're always in your face, you know? You can't see a fucking thing. But where else is there to go in this town? The funny thing is I hate it here, but I always end up staying the whole night. It's like smoking – I don't even know why I do it any more. It's probably a good thing, the ban. Probably loads of people can't be arsed to smoke out here in the cold. Doesn't put me off though. I know it's shit, I don't even enjoy it, I know it's killing me – but I do it anyway. It's because it kills you slowly, I reckon. That's what I think, anyway. If it was one cigarette and then you've got cancer, then you wouldn't smoke that cigarette, would you? But whenever you light one up it's like 'well, it won't be this one that kills me.'

Yeah, I'll be here all night. I got here at ten o'clock, and when does it shut, two? I'll be here at the end, I always am. Fuck. Ten 'til two, what's that, four hours? That's like two feature length films. And I hate it here, so it's like two really shit films, like *Wild Wild West* and then *Jurassic Park 2*, or *What Women Want* and then *Tron* – I don't care what anyone says, that film's shit. It's boring.

I shouldn't be drinking to be honest mate, but I've been having a shit time recently. When I drink, right, I wake up in the mornings and I can't remember a thing, I mean not a fucking single thing. The guy I used to live with, Jack, he had to fill in the gaps for me. I've done some pretty terrible things. Once I chased this kid down the street. In the daytime – Jack told me about it afterwards. I've got no fucking idea why I chased him. Jack didn't know either; he said the kid didn't do anything. And I can't remember a thing about it, not a single thing.

I tried to shave off Jack's moustache once. He grew this really big one, right. Yeah, I know, they look shit don't they? Nobody looks good with a moustache. Except Stalin, maybe. So when he starts growing it, I think: he's going to look shit with this moustache, right? And I ask his girlfriend Emily, I'm like 'What do you think about Jack growing a moustache?' And she says 'I don't know, we'll wait and see what it looks like.' So he grows it anyway, and I'm watching it grow, like thinking this is going to look awful, right? And then one day I come downstairs and he's sitting there and it's fully grown, and it looks fucking great, doesn't it, all thick and handsome, he looks like an RAF fighter pilot or a circus ringmaster, or something. I'm telling you mate – Jack can pull off a moustache. Nobody can pull off a moustache. But Jack can. And Stalin, yeah, he looked pretty good didn't he, with that big bushy thing on his face.

So then I'm completely hammered, and I go into Jack's room, he's in there asleep, and I get on his bed like this, right, and I get the electric shaver on him. I can't remember a fucking thing about it, but it must've happened because he showed me where there was a great big patch missing in the morning. Yeah, he woke up as soon as I started doing it and he had to fight me off the bed. Fuck knows why I did it, I was off my face. I mean I must've been completely gone. He had to shave the whole thing, because of the mess I made of it. I know. Nuts. That's why I shouldn't be drinking. I mean I'm not an aggressive guy or anything, but when I'm drunk I do shit like that and then I can't remember it afterwards.

You got a girlfriend, mate? She in here? No, I haven't, not right now. I'm sworn off girls as well at the moment. I had a girlfriend for ages when I was a teenager. I'm twenty-six, so that's years ago now. She changed though. Girls realise about eighteen what they can turn themselves into, that they can become these sexual stimulants, you know? That's the worst thing about this place, the girls. They all know what they're doing. They're those really annoying girls – you know, those really annoying like pretty girls. You know the ones I mean.

I was friends with these girls before, they loved coming down here. They're probably in here somewhere right now, actually. Anyway, I had to come down with them every weekend and watch them get off with some black guy – or half-black, you know – I'm not being racist, that's what happened, every single weekend. His greeting would always be like pumping my chest with his fist, like this, and I'd say something like 'Having a good night?' and he says 'yeah mate,' and then there's more pumping, and I know it's just to get in with one of the girls I'm with, and with all the pumping I just want to shout 'take whichever girl you want! I don't care! They're not mine!'

Is it all right if I pinch another cigarette? Thanks a lot, mate. Are these from America? Yeah, you can tell by the white tip. I like these.

Anyway, I was in here once with Jack – that's the guy I used to live with. I said to him 'Jack, I'm really into Marilyn.' Marilyn Monroe, right? I said 'Jack, I'm really into Marilyn.' Yeah, I know she's dead mate, I've seen the pictures of her corpse on the internet, have you seen them? They're sick, she's all like white and rotting. Anyway, I said to Jack that I'm really into Marilyn, and he goes to me, 'she's out of your league.' I was gutted. I know. Marilyn Monroe.

Jesus, look at that guy over there. What a fucking meat-head. There's something basically stupid about the way a guy like that moves. Yeah, a muscle-man. I don't mean just like a guy in good shape, I mean like that, a fucking hulk-man, all fucking stiff with steroids. He can't touch his sides for all that meat, it's like he's still got the clothes hanger in his shirt. It's like the bouncers as well. It's all right, they can't hear me. Look at that one though, the one on the left, his skin's all lumpy, it looks like a trifle that's gone off or something, with the tattoos showing through the custard. His tattoos are shit as well, it looks like he drew them on there himself when he should have been paying attention at school.

Sorry, I sound like a bit of a wanker don't I? But I'm not a wanker, honestly. Everything's just been going a bit shit for me lately, you know? Yeah, of course a girl. How did you guess? This girl, Emily – Jack's girlfriend. Yeah, I know: 'fallen for your best friend's girlfriend.' Classic.

He found her at the art gallery. You know the one at the bottom of St. Martha's Hill, is it called St. Martha's Gallery? I don't know, I never go in there. I went in there once, it was rubbish. They're always rubbish aren't they, small galleries? I mean yeah, if you go to the big ones, the Tate Modern or whatever, they're great, I like them. Have you seen that video thing of a clown, in the Tate Modern? It's fucking great. It's these two TVs right, and they're playing the same film, but one of them is upside down. And the film's this really creepy clown, and he's jumping up and down like he's having a tantrum, with his fists clenched like this, right, and he's shouting 'NO! NO! NO! NO! NO! NO! NO! NO! NO!' I know, it's fucking weird, man, but it's cool. It's fucking creepy. But St. Martha's Gallery was all just pictures of hills and horses and flowers and fucking cats, by 'local artists', and you know they're just these old duffers, just doing a bit of painting before they get put in the ground. Part-timers, you know?

Anyway, Jack goes there all the time, to pick up girls. He says it's easy to pull at galleries, because when girls are looking at paintings they're open to attacks from the side. I'm like, 'really?' Because I can't imagine doing that, can you? Some girl's looking at a picture and you go up to her and you're like 'Do you like that picture? Yeah? Do you want to come back to my place?' Jack always makes out that he's into the art as well, but I'm not sure mate, I'm not so sure.

But get this, right, when I first met Emily, when he brings her round the house for the first time, I see her and I'm like man, she's fucking beautiful, you know, she's beautiful. And I go to Jack, 'Do you like her?' and he says 'I don't know, mate. She doesn't know much about art.' Can you believe that? 'She doesn't know much about art!' I mean, this girl! And then in the end he went out with her anyway. That's what Jack's like though, mate.

Oh right, are you going back inside? Okay then – I'll catch you in a bit.

---

**Ben Harvey** was born in Basingstoke. He has lived for four years in Norwich, where he took his undergraduate degree in English Literature and Creative Writing.

# Eli Herman

## Abundant

*An extract from a novel-in-progress*

I was invited to Jen's sister's birthday and I really don't know why. With my family there had to be a steady backlog of less consequential meetings and drinks; that was an introduction, you were being tested out. Jen's family, however, liked to put people on stage from the outset and see if they floundered, which, if they did, said a lot about their personality. It was mingling under force, just ridiculous.

The invite happened in the usual way where casual prodding about our relationship during a phone conversation with her mother (Yes, we're still together. Yes, everything is fine) had become Jen's assurance that I would love to come. I didn't want to go. I'd met Jen's parents or other members of her family a few times, it was large compared to mine. They were people who bred at an early age and Jen was the only one who had passed twenty-three without a child of her own. The women were also astonishingly attractive: luminescent eyes, bursting blouses, but always the same tangled unruly hair. They dealt with it in different ways: by bleaching, dyeing, straightening or just surrendering to a ponytail.

We arrived at their house on the eastern limits of the city. We took Broadway till it ended and curved onto a dusty washboard road with a driveway every hundred feet or so. The house was large and employed a Tex-Mex restaurant rustic look with corrugated steel on the porch and the odd splintered rocking horse or pair of cowboy boots placed around. It reeked of effort and too many days spent at antique shops. Once inside, it was obvious that Jen's parents had not known what to do with their money and decided to put the contractor through his paces by building up and out until they were satisfied. The ceilings were over twenty feet high and the whole property felt more like a large U-shaped municipal building than a house.

'Hi Luke! You finally made it out here huh?' Jen's mom said to me, flanked by Jen's dad who was involved with hugging her and smoothing out her collar.

'Yeah, you guys are really out here. Do you get any javelinas out here?'

'Jen told me you like the javelinas.'

'I do. I think I do, I haven't actually seen any yet.'

'No? Well they come through here almost every night'

I had wanted to see the javelinas since I came to Tucson. The idea that there were feral pigs running around the city causing trouble in their small way by turning over garbage cans and snorting into sheds intrigued me. They had always eluded me on my drives at night though. I was told that the best time was dusk, when things were cooling down. When I got off work, instead of going straight home, I would head out to the foothills and scan the valleys outside my window. If they were there they'd be hard to spot, like grains of pepper sliding across sandpaper. They moved in herds of thirty and trotted at walking pace across the desert in semi-residential areas. One night when Jen was watching her aunt's place up in the foothills I had gotten a call at about two a.m.

'What's wrong?'

'Nothing's wrong, there's javelinas outside.'

'Really! Get one for me.'

'I'm not going to get one for you, you can't keep them as pets,' Jen said.

'I don't want to keep it. Just put one in the bathroom and I'll come over. I want to touch one or take a picture of it.'

'That's not happening. They're mean.'

'They are? I thought they just snorted around and knocked shit over.'

'Yeah. They're leaving already though. Never mind.'

'Wait, get a picture of one for me.'

"Ok, I'll try. I gotta go if you want a picture," she said hanging up the phone as I said bye. When the picture came back a few days later it was a murky blur with just a bit of hoof and sand. They fascinated me. I don't know why.

The birthday celebrations were going along as anyone would expect. This was the obligatory family get-together for Carly before she had her own, far more secularly debauched occasion on the weekend. I spent most of the party trying to avoid the party by museum-walking in and out of rooms and visiting the beer cooler every twenty minutes or so. Uncle Brian was on a similar rotation. Every now and again Jen would be in mid-conversation and start to glance around and look for me, wondering where I'd gone or who I was talking to. She was not drinking and as I circulated there were more frequent stops at her hip and shoulder. I think she began to like the feeling too and leaned back into me when I would come over.

I wore that hip down for the next half hour. She was standing with one arm on the counter exposing just enough flesh between shirt and pants. There's a level of decorum involved in stroking someone's daughter and I nearly went past it playing my fingers over the jut of the bone rubbing away at an invisible stain. I went outside for a cigarette, another cigarette, and saw that the sun had gone behind the mountains and soaked the ground and cholla in peach. After only a couple drags Jen burst out of the front door and came to me walking low and grinning.

"You have to come out back."

"Hang on, I just lit this …"

"No, you have to come out back right now," she said grabbing my hand. I tossed my cigarette and she led me through the house to the back sliding glass window where everyone was gathered. Outside there were about forty-five brownish-black pigs spread out across the back property biting at weeds and trotting along.

"There are your javelinas Luke," Uncle Brian said.

"Yeah, there they are. They're smaller than I thought." I opened the door a little and Jen's mom held her hand in the air before my chest.

"You aren't gonna go out there are you?"

"Why not, what are they gonna do? It's OK." I opened the glass and quickly slid the door back. The pigs noticed me with their sideways glances, craning their snouts my way. There was a stream of them coming from fifty feet behind me and then down the hill extending into the valley. There were more of them than I thought. To my right, on the ground was a heavily rusted sword with a broken plastic handle. It was probably some addition to the house's aesthetic that didn't make the grade. At the time it didn't seem curious that it was there; more like the right tool for the job. I picked it up and looked at the family lined against the windows. Uncle Brian smiled, Jen's father pursed his lips and Jen arched an eyebrow. As I tried to walk down the hill and into the midst of them, they bullied each other away from me. They smelled strongly of garbage and sweat. A group of three of them were at the dog house putting their snouts into the dog bowl and shuffling around it. They let me get close and I extended the sword trying to graze the sprig of hair along one's back. As I held the sword up they scattered and galloped away. I tried walking at them now, then running to catch them. They were fast and I was beginning to sweat and feel slightly concussed from the beer and heavy smoking. I was running from one corner of the big dust lawn to the other with the sword extended towards the hirsute pigs, getting nowhere. The herd quickly thinned and I watched them scrabble through the brush towards the next house and then walked back. The family was watching me through the window mouthing words at each other. I looked down at the dust and saw hundreds of miniature hoof prints in nonsensical lines across the yard and tossed the sword to the side.

"You finally got to see them!" Jen said as I closed the door.

"Yeah. They smelled."

"They're pigs."

"They were afraid of me though, I couldn't even touch them."

"What is it with you and touching the javelinas?" she said. I said I didn't know and went to the beer cooler again and swished my hand in with the ice and water looking for the red and white cans of beer.

---

**Eli Herman** is from Ann Arbor, Michigan. He was born in 1980. He graduated from the University of Arizona with a BA in Creative Writing. He is currently working on his first novel.

# Anjali Joseph

## Don't Touch Me
### Extract from a short story

'**Y**ou'll like the place,' I told her. 'It's beautiful, it's not like Bombay.' She frowned. 'You've been there already?' Shadows moved across her face; they were from the tassels on the Sai Baba picture hanging off the rear-view mirror. The windows were open and the picture waved in the breeze.

'No, but Ramesh told me about it and I spoke to them.'

I wanted to say that I'd made a reservation, but felt shy about using the word. A new song came on the radio and I put on my gold-rimmed sunglasses, the ones from Colaba Causeway; they made me look like an air force pilot in a film. I started humming along and Leela smiled. But when we reached the toll booth she went quiet.

The men in the kiosk looked at us curiously: such a pretty girl, and a taxi driver who wasn't in uniform. Leela kept her eyes fixed on the Sai Baba picture; it was like she was having a conversation with the saint. Old men and young girls always get on well. I took the toll receipt and let out the clutch.

The landscape had changed after Vasai: next to the road were grey stone hills, bare apart from green scrub here and there. People who looked like farmers walked barefoot in the sun. They seemed undisturbed, as though they hadn't yet noticed the three-lane highway that cut through their land.

I knew the place I was looking for – it was on the other side, just after a big hotel.

'See if you can see the sign,' I said.

'Radha Krishna Resort.'

'That's it.'

I parked outside and took her small bag. The taxi looked far from home. I'd washed it in the morning, but it was dusty again from the mud roads outside the city. I wound up the windows and left the meter turned to the side; the usual sign was painted on it in English: Don't Touch Me.

The reception office was air-conditioned and cold. I almost wondered if I should take my sandals off at the door, but I didn't. I walked straight up to the desk.

'I called earlier about the room,' I said. 'My name's Shaan – Shantanu Kumar.' Leela lingered behind my shoulder. I could feel that she, like me, was waiting for the man in the shirt and tie to ask if we had a marriage certificate or a *mangal sutra*. All he did was open a book and look in it.

'One night only?'

'Yes,' I said.

He pushed the book towards me. 'Write your full name and address. The rate is eight hundred rupees, air-conditioned.'

I had to give the pen to Leela and he looked surprised. She frowned, wrote in the book and gave it back to him. He read it over. By now I wanted to hit him. My hands were beginning to feel cold. I waited for something to go wrong.

He nodded. 'Eight hundred rupees.'

I took the roll of notes out of my pocket and counted it out. I'd been saving since last year, as well as sending money home, but except for things like rent and licence fees and *hafta* I'd never spent so much at any one time since I came to Bombay. But it was good. I had more money, so we could eat well and wouldn't have to worry about anything.

The reception guy took out a key and called a boy who would show us to the room. We walked behind him through a garden with that rough grass they always have outside wedding halls, and unfired red pots waiting for plants, and white statues of girls, like the ones in temples but with fewer clothes. The swimming pool wasn't finished; it was a hole with open sacks of cement lying next to it.

'Pool will be ready in August only, that's why the rate is less,' the boy told me over his shoulder. 'We're making a full water resort. For families.'

The room was on the first floor and faced the highway. The boy put on the lights, the television and the air-conditioner to show they worked. I gave him five rupees and asked him to get some water. Leela and I stood far from each other and looked around the room, and out of the window. You could hear the truck horns even through the glass.

'It's nice, isn't it?' I said. There was a lot of furniture: the bed, with a pink cover, then tables, a mirror, chairs near the window.

Leela glanced at the chairs and tables, at the roaring air-conditioner, and then at the window. She drew the ends of her dupatta about her arms, and nodded.

The boy came back with the water. He was careful not to stare at Leela. I took the jug, closed and locked the door after him, pulled the curtains shut, stepped out of my sandals and sat on the bed. The carpet was soft and unexpected under my feet. Leela looked terrified. I was sort of nervous myself.

'Won't you come and sit next to me?' I asked. She came, very carefully, and sat on the bed. She looked pretty; she was wearing a new salwar kameez, sky blue.

I took her hand in mine. 'Want to watch some TV?' The boy had given me the remote when he left but the sound was off. She shook her head. 'Want some water?' I said.

'Mm,' she said. I got up and filled one of the glasses, spilled some water, tried to wipe it with my sleeve, and gave her the glass. She drank a little and sat looking at the rest.

'Should I order some food or something?' I said.

'If you want.'

'Are you hungry?'

She looked up. 'Not yet. But if you're hungry –'

'Is it the place? You don't like it?'

She put the glass down on the floor. 'It's nice,' she said quietly. 'But it's weird as well – so far from everywhere. I feel bad about lying to my brother.'

'But it's just so that we can be together,' I said. 'It won't be like this for long.'

She nodded but she still looked anxious. I felt so tender, and also turned on. I drew her to me, and kissed her mouth. It was soft, just as you'd imagine a girl's mouth is. It was almost strange, after imagining it for so long, actually to kiss her. I smiled at her and pinched her cheek gently, as though she were a child. She rolled her eyes, but she smiled too. I bent my face to kiss her again; a strand of her hair brushed my nose. The room was half dark.

'Shaan.'

'Mm.'

'Wait, I have to say something.'

I waited.

'I can't –' She looked away.

'It's OK, we don't have to. We can just hold each other,' I said. I rubbed her back. I was disappointed, but almost relieved, too.

'No, that's not what I meant. My brother –'

'What about him?' I was tired, in truth, of her brother. She was always afraid of him and what he'd think or say. When we were married, his opinion would be less important; he'd have to stop telling her what to do all the time.

She looked up at the air-conditioner. 'He's getting me married in a month.'

'What are you saying?'

She turned to face me. 'He's found a boy and he's getting me married.'

'Then tell him!' Maybe I'd tightened my hold on her hand; her fingers moved.

'He told me he knows there's someone I've been meeting. He said he doesn't want me spending time with any dirty north Indians and if he finds out for sure who it is he'll make sure that person –' She looked down at her right hand, which was in her lap, clutching the end of her dupatta.

'I'm not afraid of him. If you want we'll just go and get married before you tell him. Then that'll be the end of it.' I could hear traffic noises outside. We could leave right then, go home to Agra, and get married in a temple. You heard of people doing things like that all the time. I saw us doing it, though in my mind it became slightly confused, as though it were a scene from a film; but it was a beautiful image.

She took her hand out of mine.

'I can't.'

'Why not?'

'What if I don't fit into your family,' she mumbled. 'I'm from here, you're from there.'

I got up and started walking around.

'Don't get angry.'

'How am I getting angry? I thought we were going to get married, we come out here, and then you tell me you're getting married to someone your brother's found? What's there to get angry about?' I looked at her; suddenly I saw her seeing me differently too. For me all this was new, but she'd known what was coming, and thought about how I'd react. 'Stop looking so frightened. What kind of person do you think I am? Do you expect me to kill you, out here, miles from Bombay? Or throw acid on your face? Is that what you think I'm like?' I went to the window and opened the curtains, threw myself in the armchair and put my head in my hands. The sun came through onto the back of my neck. Don't shout, I thought. Don't overdo it. But I couldn't believe what was happening. I felt queasy, as though I'd been in the sun for hours and forgotten to eat. Things were less solid than before.

After a little while I got up. She was still sitting in the same place, looking anxious but determined. I looked around at all the pink and white furniture. There was too much of it.

'Don't be worried,' I said. 'I'll take you back any time you want to go. If you want we could stay here for a little bit first, lie on the bed and talk. If you have time.' Once we left the room, I knew, things would have changed. It was like driving at night, when you sense something coming at you before you can see it.

She hesitated.

'You don't have to,' I said. 'It's fine.'

There was a small effort in her face; then it softened, and she said, 'No, there's time.'

I sat on the bed and then lay down, propping up my elbow and resting my head on my hand. I could see my shadow, low and lumpy, on the wall. The foil packet in my front trouser pocket cut into my leg. The room was really cold now; the air-conditioner had been on all the time we'd been there. It was strange to feel cold like this in summer. Leela came to lie down next to me, but I could tell from the way she moved, and folded her dupatta so that it wouldn't crease, that she was already thinking about getting home in time; her mind was on the next thing.

---

Anjali Joseph was born in Bombay in 1978. She read English at Trinity College, Cambridge, taught English at the Sorbonne, and was a senior feature writer for the *Times of India*. She is working on a novel and a collection of stories, both set in Bombay.

# Tadzio Koelb

## Bad of Country
### Extract from a novel

At last, she lives with me, in my apartment. She travels gently from room to room and looks from all the windows. When it is cool the straight, rough hair on her bare skin stands from the gooseflesh as if shocked. Then she will drop lazily on the pile of rugs by the poisonous little gas heater I took from Michael's apartment, or boil water in the kitchen, carrying the steaming pots to the tub one by one, her face a comic blank of concentration framed by a heavy veil of dirty hair. The bath's electric boiler is weak. She smiles with sudden self-awareness when she sees me following her progress with my gaze.

'It's got to be hot!' she says in the burly gruff of a jazz musician, eyes wide with exaggeration. The floor sounds the short, flat-footed walk of the naked. From the bathroom she will call for me to come wash her. There is a preference we neither of us admit aloud for being in the same room. Sometimes while she washes her face she swallows a little water and coughs, mouth open and tongue exposed like a child. Every couple of days she shaves carefully: under her arms, the length of her legs, the tops of her biggest toes, the thin line of dark hair that rises towards her navel. To gain access to the elusive crease inside her thigh she lies low in the water and twists, first one way, then the other, her leg a torn antenna, her head partially immersed beneath the grey soapy water, but even this she does swiftly and with the ease of practice.

'Did I get everything?'

I nod. Where it has been submerged her skin is reddened. The bath was scalding hot when she stepped into it, steam drew figures that lingered across the surface, and she lowered herself very gently, letting herself grow accustomed to the heat: first standing, then squatting with her arms around her knees, then lying slowly back, all the time making faces of discomfort. I sit and watch the otherworldly swaying stillness of a body under water, the spreading blemish of soap. I wash her back, dragging my nails through the slippery film; red lines appear. She wraps the towel around her and wears it for a time, finally discards it on the floor or over a chair-back. Her nipples and smallest hairs bloom stiffly into the chill. She lies on the shapeless heap of carpets, hands crossed demurely, a mortician's pose.

The rugs I keep for my models, but I hardly work from life anymore. Instead I have taken to painting entirely from memory (or from the imagination, if you prefer; I don't know which is more accurate, or even if imagination is really anything other than memory tellingly manipulated), painting portraits that have no express originals outside my mind, figurative allegories whose meanings even I don't care to guess.

In my sketchbooks I draw only May, her frank features and relaxed poses. In the studio she half-naps in a small patch of sun, and I draw her as she slips in and out of sleep.

She also keeps a sketchbook these days, in which she pastes images carefully cut from magazines that people throw away or leave in parks and cafés. It is especially pleasing to her to find pornography, part of the vast genus of charged material she calls 'the good stuff', and it will take days of careful consideration to decide which figures are to be sacrificed so that those on the other sides of pages may be outlined with the scissors and made part of the strange story she is shaping over the thick paper. May keeps these things in a cardboard box, all loose and confused, like a diary written in any order: like memory. She ponders them, sifts the contents regularly, familiarly.

Sometimes I wonder if I wouldn't do better to work as she does, borrowing whatever I can, having it on hand to consider exhaustively before use. Lowell Rank told me that to rely too much on oneself for creativity is 'an injudicious over-exploitation of a limited natural resource: the usual Romantic miscalculation', or as Peter Achurch puts it, 'Sometimes the crap is important. You have to learn to recycle.' I say the word over to myself and observe how my accent emphasizes the first syllable. In Achurch's gentle Blackpuddlian the stress is on 'cycle'. I think about it as May sorts her plunder in quiet, contented admiration.

This detailed attention is not for the scrap box alone. When we talk about her day she always describes for me exactly what she has worn when she goes out, and often remembers to the centime what was paid for each item, or if it was found, or a gift. She is proud of her bargains, no matter how long ago she achieved them.

There's a sound at the door, and she names it: 'Peter.'

Achurch's skin is the temperature of the outdoors, his narrow eyes watery, a damp smell of stale tobacco mingling with the cold stab of the weather in his clothes. I accept his thick, chapped fingers at the door. He says my name, "Alex," then shows himself shyly over the threshold.

'All right with you?' he says.

'And with you?'

He nods. In the short hallway I am suddenly aware of how much dust there is in the corners, how dirty the doors are around the handles. It's not that Achurch will mind. He's famously untidy himself; but I want to be neater than he is, to impress him with our gentility, however shabby, to prove that I am, after all, taking good care of things. May gives a wave, a quick smile, and runs her funny run, right foot always forward, one arm across her little breasts to stop them showing. She will go and cover up for Achurch, protect him from embarrassment; she knows it would be unfair to risk alarming him with her sheet-etched thighs and floor-blacked feet. She returns wearing my clothes, trousers rolled at the ankle and waist, shirtsleeves swallowing her arms. It's a compromise: this isn't really clothing. She has a relationship with her every belonging with which mine cannot compete. If I were to lean close to her at this very moment, as I am tempted to do, and by a few words make them hers, whether because they suit her simple shape or even for no reason at all, their significance would be immediately altered; suddenly she would be dressed, really dressed, in clothes of her own. She would always recall the moment they became hers and at some point they would hold, if only for a short time, the ceaselessly rotating honour of being her favourite this and favourite that, a long, detailed roster that I sometimes imagine includes in its elaborate and infinitely flexible sub-categories the entire narrow span of her worldly possessions. She would note just as solemnly the moment she gave them to someone else, or left them clean and neatly folded in an open paper bag on the street for a passing student or other needy soul to take home.

'Now they can think they've found something good, or even that they are stealing it,' she will whisper. 'They'll never have to thank me.' This is the blessing she wishes most earnestly on strangers. She herself thanks people unreservedly, but I can't help thinking it isn't without some reluctance, or else why would she try so hard to spare others? I think that with the first words I heard her speak, she thanked me. She was dancing and twice fell against me, first gently and then again more deeply, her shoulder in my stomach as she tried to find her balance in the crowd. I grabbed her roughly, blindly, and while the pain passed from my gut held her suspended above the floor, left hand against the moist skin of her underarm, the other around the corrugated tube of her rib cage, slipping slowly over the easy swell of her breast. Cloth bunching in my fingers exposed her belly. She tipped and swung, put a hand to the ground.

'Thank you. That must have looked very graceful on both of us.'

'Don't mention it. In fact when you fell into me I didn't really have a choice.' To overcome the music we bowed closer when we spoke, each addressing the side of the other's head, then straightened again, an automatic return to the normal pose of conversation. All around the edge of the room people bobbed as we did: a bend of the waist, a turn of the neck, then back, heads nodding. Shoulders met and lips brushed cheeks, seeking the ear. She moved close again and I leaned forward to listen.

'Are you all right?' She craned her neck around to confront me; I became aware that I had avoided looking her straight in the face. She smiled with her mouth open and hoisted her heavy eyebrows. I could just make out a faint scar, a pair of fragile furrows traced across her cheek.

'Of course.' She nodded and bit gently at her lower lip. I felt something more was expected of me. 'Sorry, by the way, that I ...'

'Groped?'

'Oh. I guess so, yes.'

'Well, for helping a stranger you deserve a shot at the good stuff.' She gave her body a showgirl shake.

'Then we're all square?'

'A breast in hand is worth two on the floor.' The slick odour of her perspiration clung to my fingers.

Achurch accepts my invitation of toast and tea at the kitchen table. Strangely I have assumed the habits of the English, or at least Achurch's habits, and I find comfort in them although my conversion seems inexplicable to me even now, as the ritual commences: the gas lit, kettle filled, four spoonfuls of the pungent black leaf spilt into the largest pot, the butter brought out of the cupboard. I haven't made my own coffee in years although I drink it sometimes with my students, standing at the bar in the café by the school. When I hear the water sing its shrill hymn there will be pouring, and then steeping, and then more pouring, an offertory rite. Achurch's sparse ginger hair is a little greasy, a little wet from the drizzle outside.

He sits and I sit and there is the table between us. I look carefully at my cup. I rise to fetch the sugar bowl, but find it is already there, so the movement is wasted, or almost, and I sit again.

The chill radiates from him, from his skin and clothes. He doesn't take his coat off. I say, 'It's cold out.' Achurch makes me think of Brussels the way a policeman makes me think of crime, or a priest of sin. In the end Brussels was Achurch's city, not because he cared for it, which he didn't, but because he never tried to impose himself on it. It was his city, and he is its nuncio; against the smell of him the memory is struck and ignites.

'Cold, yeah,' Achurch says as if it has just dawned on him, and suddenly laughs. 'It's really cold, yeah.' Achurch's mild features focus sharply when he laughs, the upper lip curling towards his nose and the lower cupping wetly. I could count his teeth, small, yellow, and sharp, and give each one a name. There is something both reassuring and overwhelming about Peter Achurch's quiet laugh, as if it were a profession of faith, an acknowledgement of the absurdity that is always with us, the constant intercession of 'dumb fucking luck', as May likes to put it.

We don't speak again until the water boils.

---

Tadzio Koelb's first manuscript, *Fate's Lieutenant*, was a finalist for the Faulkner Society's *William Faulkner/William Wisdom Award*. His art and book reviews have appeared in a number of publications, including *The Times Literary Supplement* and the *New Statesman*. He is currently working on a novel, *Bad of Country*.

# Jesse Kuiken

## *Malcolm*
*The first chapter of a novel in progress*

The crossroads at the center of Astora is empty. A single pair of headlights glide through, lighting vacant windows and buildings. At the crossroads, the pick-up turns down Blackwater Road, passing dim, quiet houses. The blue house with brown shutters is near the end, where the sidewalk crumbles and gives way to a field, then the gray silhouette of the old railway bridge. The wild wheat that grows in the field during the summer is crushed by an inch of hard snow.

Dylan Siestra is only just up, his alarm clock still buzzing in the air. Dragged from sleep, a dream with the scent of old, creased leather and something sweet. Lying on his side, he squints out the window, watching red tail-lights dwindle into the blue dark. Grunting, he pulls himself from bed, limb by limb.

Cold air floods bare skin, making scars on his chest, still shiny-soft, pucker. Shivering, he pulls on jeans, a T-shirt, flannel with holes worn in the elbows. It's all cursory, no chafing his arms or chest to warm himself. He jams his feet into a pair of workman's boots, puts on his watch, his jacket, and thuds down the stairs. They creak around him in the dark. Dylan's been up and down these stairs so many times since he was a child he doesn't need light.

He cups a yawn in his palm as he enters the kitchen. Putting the coffeepot on, he picks up a few slices of bread and an apple. He pockets the apple, eats the bread. Swallowing, he pours the coffee into a large metal thermos, screws the cap on. He walks out the front door, inhaling as frozen air scrapes over his face like a blade. His breath billows, trailing his broad shoulders. He walks down and across the front yard, to the detached blue garage, passing the cottonwood tree. The rope that used to have a tire tied to it swings, frayed and empty, like a snapped noose. With Tom, his little brother, he slid up and down, backwards and sideways through that tree as a child. Their dad, Malcolm, kept watch from the kitchen window or the front porch, always there, in the periphery. Tom liked to pretend they were astronauts in a spaceship, looking down on the earth. Dylan liked to play Robin Hood, waiting to ambush the Sheriff of Nottingham. Tom always said Dylan should play Maid Marian, because, well, duh. Dylan would smirk, saying Tom should be Maid Marian; he was always whining and crying like a girl anyways. They'd grapple, nearly falling from the tree until Malcolm snarled: 'Knock it off!' That tone of Malcolm's voice, Dylan insists to Tom, put the fear of God into him as a child.

A morning dove coos, woo-oo, woo-oo, breathy exhale. Dylan realizes he's stopped halfway to the garage.

He unlocks the garage. The aluminum door rattles up, vanishing. Stepping in, he pulls the door down behind him, shutting out watery pre-dawn light. In the dark, he sighs. A cold, wet smell in the air. He turns on an electric lamp, light bright hot in the small, greasy space. Metal – shovels, axes, saws, hung on the wall – glistens. He places the thermos and apple on a workbench and kicks on the heater. The air throbs with the machine's low murmurs. He rummages through the tall, red toolchest, big as a dresser. The toolchest's drawers are crammed: pliers, wrenches, coils of wire, electrical tape. Only Malcolm knew exactly everything in the toolchest, knew where he'd last left an obscure bolt or screwhead. Dylan still finds things in back corners, under familiar piles. Once, it was a new pair of gloves, tucked away as if awaiting Malcolm's return. When Dylan had put them on they were too big, his fingertips a knucklelength too short to fill out the gloves. He'd felt disappointed by this in a way he couldn't explain with words.

Dylan fishes out a can of penetrating oil. He turns to the center of the garage and a large black tarp. Peeling the tarp away, he exposes dinted, scuffed metal, flaking paint, a blind tail-light and twisted rear-view. The car stands wheel-less, on rises. Angled awkwardly, Dylan spent the last three mornings removing the wheels and suspension, wrestling rusted bolts free until sweat wetted his spine. Now, Dylan runs calloused, cracked hands lightly across the hood, leaving misty fingertips. He takes the penetrating oil, a couple of socket wrenches and extensions and places everything carefully on the ground. Opening the passenger side door, he climbs in with the electric lamp. Battered leather upholstery gives gently under his weight, cupping him. He aims the light over the door, from the rusted hinges down to the jam. He scratches the jam with a fingernail, scraping up rust. He shakes his head.

Climbing out, he catches a whiff – an echo, the memory of the fresh, new leather the upholstery had been, rather than mildew-eaten, sun and wind-scorched leather it has become – which makes every tiny hair down his spine ripple. The same smell he dreamt of. Dylan stops. He runs his tongue over and over his teeth, as if he can pick the bits of his dream that he can't remember out of his gums.

It nags him, the thing he can't get to, can't wheedle out, though he's sure he knows what it is. It paces around the back of his mind as he starts spraying hinges and bolts of the door with penetrating oil. Fetching his thermos and the apple, he eats and drinks as he waits for the oil to seep in. Leaving the apple core, he goes to work, massaging the oil into the bolts and hinges, taking his time, watching rust flake away. He catches himself humming 'Can't Fight This Feeling' under his breath at one point, clears his throat nosily. If Dad were here, he thinks.

'Sometimes, it's like I don't even know you,' he might've said. The Malcolm from last summer might've said, smiling just a little, just enough to tell Dylan he was teasing.

He lifts a socket wrench and fits it over one of the heavy bolts in the upper hinge of the door. He leans his whole shoulder, his whole right side into it, pressing against the bolt. The bolt, the hinge, squeals, doesn't move, jammed with grime and rust. He pushes, thick muscles in his arms, shoulders and neck taut. He breaks off, swearing, sonofabitch. He drinks the rest of his coffee, shedding his jacket and flannel. He pushes again, groaning, stopping. Sitting on his haunches, he eyes the bolt.

'Coax,' Malcolm might say. Dylan grimaces, thinking, Malcolm should be the last person to use the word 'coax' – after the last six years between them – using words to bruise and bloody one another.

Dylan pushes against the wrench, then pulls gently back. He works the bolt, patiently, rocking it back and forth, slowly, a stiff swaying half-dance, him and the car. With every push, pull, the bolt gives a little more, gives until it's loose. He puts the bolt in a plastic bag, scribbling DRIVER'S SIDE, HINGE 1 on a piece of paper. He lays the bagged and labeled bolt on a clean workbench behind him.

The second hinge takes nearly as long to ease out, and, when it does, it too is bagged, labeled and set next to its brother. Both bottom bolts are quicker, less rusted, and Dylan is fast, aware of the strain on the single hinge holding the door. As the last bolt spins free, Dylan braces the whole door with his body, letting it rest against him as he eases out the stop pin. Carefully, trying not to drop or drag the door, he carries it backwards a few steps, laying it out on a makeshift mat of clean cardboard. He looks down at the door, then the space where it had been. Slashes of rust color his arms; his shirt is damp between his shoulderblades, under the armpits. He wipes his face, limbs trembling, but he's smiling. If he could see himself, he'd see his smile radiating into the tips of his ears and nose, softening his blunted features, his whole body relaxing.

Dylan checks his watch, exhales crap under his breath. Gathering his tools, he stops to polish grit and rust off, puts them back. He throws the hollow can of penetrating oil in the trash. He hangs the electric lamp on its peg. He kicks off the heater. He pulls the tarp over the car, seeing the space where the driver's door had been again. Taking a broom down from the wall, he sweeps debris, dust. In the silence, without the heater's hum, the bristly rasp on the concrete floor is loud. He puts the broom away, picks up his thermos, apple core, his jacket and flannel. He switches off the electric light.

Outside the sky is bright, like a robin's egg with a flashlight held inside it. The sun isn't up yet, but it's coming, casting a thin golden band ahead of itself in the east. Dylan trudges through his front yard.

The sound of the front door closing reverberates. Dylan squints. After the garage, the house is bright and cold and empty. He's already going through the things he has to do at the store. A pile of inventory sheets. Cleaning off the bulletin board, he dumps his jacket, the thermos on the kitchen table. The bulletin board'll be easy. He turns the kitchen faucet. There's nothing on the bulletin board. No one in town has pinned any sheets, notices, cards, signs. He stretches his shoulders and neck, squeezing dish soap into his palm. He works grease and oil off his hands under the faucet. Stocking. There's always a fine black rime leftover, seaming his knuckles, under his nails, he can never scrub out. Dylan's looking at his watch again, scowling. The usual, cleaning, sweeping, upkeep. He's thinking of asking Malcolm about inventory. Soap foams into a cut in his right palm he didn't remember getting. He hisses as it burns. He runs water over the cut. Turning off the faucet, he looks at it: pale jagged edges of skin, blood seeping, a small mouth spitting blood down the sink.

The memory collides with him suddenly. He remembers childhood days of late summer heat sizzling. Skin turning dark pink before peeling, like a snake shedding. Waiting on the front porch one evening as the sun sank, feeling the air cool, telling Tom to stop whining, stoppit, and don't pick your nose doofus, shoving him around because he just wouldn't pay attention. His heart crammed in his mouth when he saw that long, loping silhouette coming down the street from the crossroads. Rocketing off the patio, shrilling: 'Dad!' Malcolm's deep laugh shaking the low stars. Being caught by his dad mid-bounce, legs and arms thrashing excitedly for a minute. Dylan remembers pushing cheeks into the crook of his dad's neck; the smell of sweet aftershave, his dad's old leather jacket. Clinging to the worn lapels with soft child's hands, his dad was solid. The same feeling as lying against the earth, which never seemed to move like teachers at school said.

'Hey kiddo.'

Dylan can't ask Malcolm about inventory. The thought cleaves through him and he feels halved, like whole parts of his body are gone. His breath is quick, right in his ears. He wants Malcolm to come in, pull him back, clasp his shoulders in his hands. He wants to hear Malcolm say it's OK and know he's right, like knowing the solidness and surety of the earth below.

Dylan stays at the sink.

He forces his breathing to slow. He straightens. He looks at his watch. And turns to go upstairs, ignoring his own faint, raw-eyed reflection in the kitchen window.

---

**Jesse Kuiken** grew up in Elizabeth, Colorado. Her work has been published in the *University of Colorado Honors Journal* and the now-defunct **worldqueerdomination.com**. Her current project is a series of short stories set in the American West, focusing on rural life from a queer (primarily transgender) perspective.

# Georgina MacArthur

## Currents

*Extract from a novel*

On his first day, he was brought to our class by Mr Lambert. I think that we were all shocked by his appearance. None of the lectures or videos or question-and- answer sessions had prepared us for what it would be like to see someone with cerebral palsy in the flesh; none of it had taught us how we might begin to respond. To be honest, I think we'd listened with a sort of detachment as Mr Lambert had described the disfigurement of the limbs, the awkwardness of the speech. As Matthew stumbled into the room, we were stunned. Although he was walking by himself, Mr Lambert stood close beside him with his hand reaching forwards, just in case. Matthew looked like a broken puppet, abandoned by his puppeteer. His legs wobbled dangerously, and his feet hit the floor at strange and unlikely angles. He had a leather strap beneath each knee, attached to which were two metal poles that joined at the edges of his shoes: these were presumably designed to reduce the drunken swingings of his legs or, at least, to attempt to provide a possibility of balance, but they just made him look weirdly mechanical. His clothing was the same as ours but it sat differently on him: the jumper spiralled uncomfortably around his twisted frame so that the school logo, instead of sitting on the left-hand side of his chest, was somewhere near his lower back; the flies of his trousers seemed to shy away from our gazes too, crawling around his left thigh in embarrassment. His arms swung wildly as he walked, his hands like small, white doves fluttering around him as he tried to point excitedly at us, at this classroom, at this world of apparent normality which he so much wanted to be a part of. He beamed ecstatically and saliva dribbled from his mouth, collecting in the chin-strap of what was, to us, the pièce de résistance of his spectacularly bizarre appearance: on his head he wore a helmet – it looked like a leather cage, all straps and gaps from which his mousy brown hair stuck out anarchically, not a helmet so much as a strange kind of basket. We'd been told about this: it was to protect his head and his healthy brain because he couldn't control the movements of his body. It was hard to believe that there wasn't something wrong with his brain too, though; it didn't look like just a physical disability, like seeing someone in a wheelchair. You think you know what to expect with that. But Matthew moved weirdly, his *face* moved weirdly. His eyes were bright but he drooled all over himself and didn't wipe it away; when he shouted 'Har-ooooh!' at us and tried a wave, the word completely mangled by his tongue, it was just too much for some of the class to deal with. Some of the kids giggled. Some of the naughtier and more confident ones wildly waved their own arms above their heads and echoed him: 'Har-ooooh!' they copied. 'Har-ooooh!'

A few of the girls eventually got out of their seats and went over to him.

'Hello Matthew,' one said kindly, although she spoke to him as if his hearing was impaired (which, Mr Lambert had told us quite clearly, it was not). 'I'm Elizabeth. You can call me Liz. Not because I don't think you can't manage Elizabeth, it's just that everyone calls me Liz. So I should've just said, 'I'm Liz', really. I'm sorry, I don't mean ...' And on and on she went, so desperate to be kind and to do the right thing. She was a nice girl, Liz.

Matthew ended up sitting at my table. I don't remember feeling uncomfortable. I don't know how it was that I could respond so easily to everything; I suppose I just have a knack. And I suppose that I already knew what it was to be different, not to be accepted.

'Hi, I'm Andrew,' I said to him.

'Ah kner,' he smiled. And then, in response to what must've been a questioning look from me, 'Your naihm-ta's hangi ow o your yumpah!'

We became good friends, me and Matthew. I admired him in the classroom. He was so clever; it was all the more impressive because it was so unexpected. It didn't matter that Mr Lambert had already explained it to us before he'd arrived. Seeing Matthew for the first time made it impossible to square the things that we'd been told with this broken, disabled body. But he was *so* clever: he knew about stuff I didn't and picked up concepts far more quickly than I ever could. He was a great addition to our class for all kinds of reasons, but lots of the other children resented him. They didn't like the fact that they expected him to be mentally disabled but that he actually outshone them. They got annoyed by the way that his hands would flutter up so quickly, the wings of those birds beating at the air in the classroom, crowing out their owner's intellectual superiority, but that it would then take him so long to articulate the answer. They'd sigh impatiently, hanging their heads on their hands in despair. Mrs Brown, our teacher, eventually lost patience too. She seemed to enjoy the challenge at first, but as time passed you could tell that she was beginning to feel it was all a bit beyond what could reasonably be expected of her. She started to call on him less and less just so she wouldn't have to stand there in the silences that filled the room as he formed his words with such an intense effort.

Then he began to be alienated in small and subtle ways. The children who had once mimicked him began, instead, to ignore him. The girls who had, at first, made such an effort to be kind and helpful grew tired and resentful; they were particularly unsettled by Matthew's romantic attentions towards some of them. They hadn't expected someone with his difficulties to have the same interests and obsessions as us, the 'normal' boys of the class. When he gave Liz a Valentine's card that declared: 'I really think you're so divine, you have to be my Valentine' and which was signed not with a mysterious question mark but with Matthew's sprawling signature, she smiled uncomfortably and said, 'Let's just keep being friends, OK?' Matthew just said 'OK' back, with a cheerful grin, and worked his way over to Lucy, handing her another card with an identical rhyme and signature. She turned him down too, but both girls ended up being outraged – Liz because Matthew had taken her rejection so well, and Lucy because she was his second choice. The boys of the class resented the way that he could be so confident and they didn't think it right. He was nice to them and was clever; in a strange way that they couldn't understand, they had begun to envy him, and they resented him for that, too.

He only lasted until December. He had a bike with stabilisers attached to it, the ones we'd all outgrown years before. He always cycled to school on it, his mother walking beside him from their house up to the giant oak tree that stood guard across the road from the school gates. I used to see him as I made my own way to school sometimes and I always wondered how he managed to stay upright. He looked so unstable when he cycled, just like he did when he walked, but his mother would always stroll beside him with her hands in her pockets, never letting them hover nervously behind his back. When they got to school she would smile and wave as Daphne, our lollipop lady, directed him across the road. In the afternoons she'd stand waiting beneath that tree, always looking anxious until he was safely by her side once more. I used to wonder if she stood out there all day, biting her fingernails from the moment she waved goodbye until the moment when she could walk home beside him again. I sometimes wished that my mum had time to drop me off in the morning, that she would be standing under the oak tree, eagerly awaiting my arrival, in the afternoon. That sort of thing stops being acceptable when you're a certain age though, doesn't it? And when you don't have any kind of disability. It's weird to think that I could have been jealous of Matthew's condition, but maybe I was, in a way.

I remember the last time he left school. I was watching some of the boys playing football on the playground after lessons had finished. I think it was Joe who first called a stop to the game.

'Come on!' he whispered urgently, picking up the ball to prevent further play. 'He's just left.'

I like to think I wasn't the only one who didn't know. There were plenty of boys who claimed not to have done, but I'm sure some of them were just worried about being suspended, about what their parents would say. I never did quite work out exactly who had been in on it. Joe was primarily responsible, that much was obvious. He beckoned to us to follow him, tip-toeing elaborately and making urgent hand signals so that we knew to keep quiet. From the corner of the boys' toilets, if you craned your neck around the wall, you could have a decent view of the bikesheds and the car park. It was quite empty apart from Matthew. I spotted his mother across the road as she waved to her son. He waved back and teetered over to where his bike stood. He pulled it into a clearing in the car park, then swung his right leg and grabbed at it with both hands so that he could get into position.

'This is going to be *so* funny!' Joe giggled.

For a moment, I thought that he was just getting ready to mock Matthew in the way that some of them usually did. The exact mechanics of what happened are not entirely clear in my mind; the whole horrendous episode seems to have happened all at once rather than developing in any kind of order. At some point between settling himself onto the seat of his bike and forcing one of the pedals forward, the whole thing collapsed beneath him and he crumpled onto the ground with the sound of crisps being crushed. He let out an almighty wail and his mother, wanting only to be beside him, screamed his name and ran into the road, straight into the path of an oncoming car. All I remember then is silence, a profound silence filled periodically by Matthew's cries as I swayed in and out of conscious observation. I didn't hear the panicked exclamations of the driver as she got out of the car, holding her chest as though her heart might force its way out in an attempt to escape the horror of what she'd just done; did not hear Daphne as she ran towards us, presumably urging us to get help; did not hear anything that the other boys might have said as they witnessed the disaster they had caused. I was conscious only of Matthew and his pain – the pain he must have been experiencing right then, and that which I feared might be coming as an ambulance was called and Mr Lambert ran out into the road to attend to Matthew's mother until it arrived. I tumbled over to Matthew and knelt down beside him, taking his hand and wiping the tears from his face; I knew that I shouldn't move him, so I just spoke to him and smiled at him, as his friend.

'It's all right, Matthew. Help is coming, you'll be all right.'

---

**Georgina MacArthur** graduated from Cambridge in 1998. For the last seven years she has been teaching English Literature, most recently in Manila. She is currently working on her first novel, a story about a careworker who undertakes what he considers to be the mercy killing of a disabled young man.

# Tammer Mahdy

## *Put Out The Sun*
*Extract from a work-in-progress*

A ll night the snow had been relentless, thick flakes that dipped and curtsied with the wind, glared against the headlights then settled in low dunes along the deserted highway. He drove with an eye on his speed, keeping it slow while steering the pick-up under a loose hand and sometimes persuading it back into the lane whenever a rut lurched the vehicle toward the edge. Some time around midnight the snow began to let up and still he went on, with little else to do than drink cold coffee and listen to the wash of static on the radio.

And he dozed. In cycles: torn awake, blinking hard, stared at where the headlights plowed a path in the darkness, then squinted in the pale dusk of the dashboard until the light receded again. A bump shook him and he opened his eyes to see that he was headed for the guardrail. The pick-up swerved and slid, somehow the tires caught and he made it back to the road. He gave the inside of his lip a bite and let out a heavy breath. An oncoming truck flashed its high-beams, lowed its horn.

'I get it, asshole,' he said to the fading sound. He rolled down the window and let the cold cut across his face. The rush of wind, the hum of the engine. Little snow devils scurried across the light.

A road sign leapt out of the dark; he was twenty-seven miles from Cheyenne. From the top of a hill he could see yellow on the clouds, hopefully the lights of a motel, maybe a rest stop. He rolled the window down some more and stepped on the accelerator.

When he got there, he found the place to be a careworn gas station on the outside of a bend in the road; a weathered sign advertising souvenirs, the pumps, a shop and a small house at the end of a short driveway. He filled his pick-up and stretched, glad to be standing. The wind ran against his legs like cold water. In the shop window he could see a red-haired lady watching him from behind the counter. He went in.

'Evening,' she said, rising to her feet. He glanced at her and answered with an almost imperceptible nod. 'Surprised to see anyone driving in weather like this,' she said. 'And here I thought the highway was closed.'

She spoke in the slow, measured manner of someone who was used to waiting and no longer held much hope. He didn't remember seeing another house for miles and now imagined her waiting, day and night, just watching traffic go by. And yet there was a spark, a glimmer in the way she addressed and looked at him.

But without so much as a shrug he wandered into an aisle. The shelves did not seem to be arranged in any particular order: boxes of candy bars next to maps, fuel containers next to Indian dream catchers and different types of jewelry – most likely the souvenirs. Whether they were homemade he didn't know. With his head lowered, he also studied her; a plump woman with sagging cheeks, checking her reflection in the window, patting at her hair, tucking strands of it behind her ears with casual movements. The idea that this grooming was for him entertained him. Then he let it go. He raised his head and she stopped fidgeting, smiled. He passed a slow gaze over the store.

'There a bathroom here?' he said.

'All the way in the back and on the left. You can't see the –'

But he had already walked off and when she stopped talking, the thump of his boots was the only sound in the neon-lit silence.

When he came out he found the coffee pot by the back window. There was a hot-dog broiler next to it and, with a quick glance over his shoulder, he snuck one out and ate it unseen. Outside, the snow had almost stopped. The lights of the gas station pushed the night back onto itself so that it seemed darker, and in the distance a truck's lights appeared to hover just in front of him in the parking lot. He finished chewing, poured himself a cup of coffee and brought it up front.

'You'll like that,' she said. 'It's a fresh pot. Put it on just before you showed up, so I guess I got lucky you walked in, wouldn't you say?'

'There a motel anywhere near here?'

'Are you always this fun to talk to?' she said. She put a fist against her hip, bent a knee so that the hip stuck out, and heaved a suppressive sigh. 'The nearest one that I know of is in Cheyenne. Twenty-five miles, give or take.'

His stubble bristled as he ran his hand down his face. He didn't know what to do. He paused his breath on an intake and opened his mouth to speak when a gust sent a spray of snow and ice against the window. They both turned to look just as the truck rounded the bend and they stood blinking in the sweep of its headlights. Its turn signal was on and the engine brake sputtered loudly as the truck decelerated. Then, just before the gas station entrance, it shifted back into gear and the turn signal went dark again. He heard a faint 'hm', turned to see her lowering her eyes from the window and then turned back. Grinned, watched the fleeting truck, hidden behind the glowing mist that fanned up in its tail-lights.

'Huh,' he said.

'Excuse me?'

He faced her again and she unleaned herself from the counter. Right then – and it was in the way she raised her eyebrows, he decided – there was an air of youthful innocence about her. The wind rattled the door. But for that, the shop was still.

'I was just saying it must be nice out here cuz it's so quiet.'

'So you do talk. Well, yeah, it's nice but it's always nicer when people are willing to pass a bit of time. You'd be surprised at some of the characters I meet.' She took a step towards the cash register. 'You paying for the gas now too?'

'I take it you live in the house back there.'

'Yes I do. It makes the walk home a lot shorter.' She laughed in a way that suggested she told the joke often. 'And that's a good thing in this weather, right?' she said. 'It hasn't iced over this bad in years.'

'Is it just you?'

'Yep. Now, you want me to ring up the gas too, or just the coffee?'

He raised the cup to his lips, drank and tightened his mouth, nodding his head with approval. Took another sip then put it back down.

'You were right,' he said, pointing at his drink. 'That's one helluva coffee. You know'– he leaned his elbows on the counter – 'I didn't mean to be short there earlier, but being on the road and all ...'

'Oh, don't worry,' she said, coming back from the register. 'It wasn't really that bad.'

'You sure there's not a place to stay that's closer than Cheyenne? I've got this real important meeting there in the morning, you see, and I want to be fresh for it.'

The lady plucked at the neck of her shirt with her middle finger and thumb, holding the bent elbow in her opposite hand, and looked out the window, concentrated before facing him again, preparing to speak.

'Just needs to be close,' he said. 'It's just that I'm already dozing at the wheel, you know, so...'

There came another silence and a brief moment where he saw her eyes flicker back and forth as though she were reading something in his face. She managed a smile that didn't make it all the way up to her eyes. Something about the stillness, albeit punctuated with rattles and gusts, made him want to clear his throat. But then he stopped himself, conscious that any noise from him now would sound too alien, might lose him his advantage.

'I guess you could stay at the house,' she said, turning as she spoke to look in that direction then back. 'There's the spare room.'

'Really? I ... you know what?' – he dropped his gaze and watched the toe of his boot push into the floor – 'That would be really helpful and I appreciate it, but you don't seem too sure. Besides, I wouldn't want to impose.'

'No, you wouldn't be,' she said with more conviction than he guessed she felt. 'I mean, the room's never being used and anyway it sounds like you really need it.'

Over the next fifteen minutes they talked while she cleaned and locked the place up. They introduced themselves; her name was Lucille. He was Sam Hatch.

Soon they stood in a narrow hallway under a naked light bulb. Over the stale air, the house smelled of onion and damp. Jaundiced flower-print wallpaper fell away from the corners in limp lashes, uncovering age rings of mold. 'Would you like something to eat?' she asked him and he said no thanks. 'A drink?' He didn't see why not so he accepted and surprised her by asking for alcohol. Drank a pour of whiskey in a single pull before asking for another. Tiredness had left him, no longer washing over him in dull waves but replaced by a sense of excitement. He had felt it as a child, stronger then, games of hide-and-seek. They sat talking for another while and he kept refilling their drinks. He liked the way she let her hair down, unyarning it with her fingers with a look of relief and unburdening. Liked the way her eyes shone the more she drank, the way her little breasts squeezed under her shirt. With both hands she held the glass like a child and sipped quickly. When the bottle was empty, they rose to go to sleep though she fell back into her chair the first time she tried to stand. Sam went to the spare bedroom where he lay listening through the open door. It wasn't long before he heard the soft revving of Lucille's snoring.

The wind died down in the earlymorning hours and the storm had moved on. When the sun came out it did so into a sky of hard blue and found Sam speeding away from the gas station, thirty odd miles past Cheyenne, never having stopped there. He was headed south on Interstate 25, through Colorado then on to Oklahoma, his real destination.

---

**Tammer Mahdy** was born in Orange, New Jersey, in 1976 then moved to Liège, Belgium where he grew up. He served in the US military before joining the Creative Writing MA at the University of East Anglia and is currently working on his first novel.

# Justine Mann

## MooshMoosh
### Extract from a short story

At first all you know is that he's French. She tells you this, otherwise nothing. Any questions are misfires, met with contempt no matter how cleverly disguised.

Other fragments are dropped into phonecalls with her best friend, Nancy, as you chauffeur her from school-to-home and to her job at the hotel restaurant. He arrived from Normandy in a car with a foreign number plate, carrying only a holdall and a bag of knives. He argues with the Head Chef and once stormed out mid-shift. He was found smoking under a tree. Her laugh bubbles up.

'Not that hard to find some angry, French bloke in chef-whites, even in the dark.'

You fill the gaps with the body parts of French actors until you see an intense man, lean and medium height, in a dark poloneck, a mane of shoulder length hair that he flicks to show disdain.

She's sitting on a stool at the kitchen bench wrapped in a hot-pink bathrobe and you're reminded of her as a baby, lying naked on a towel. How she kicked and grabbed her toes, gazing up at you and already hungry for the world beyond your shoulder.

One bare leg is hugged to her chest revealing a triangular glimpse of purple underwear you don't recognise from her laundry. Head down she watches everything through lashes flaked with yesterday's mascara. She eats her piece of toast as she always has, from middle out. Picking random sections with dirty fingers, the burgundy nail varnish chipped and bitten.

It's the Easter holidays and you're marking mock exam papers. When not working at the restaurant she lives like a recluse, only leaving her room to spend time in the bathroom or to visit Nancy. She's saving for their trip to Spain. The one you agreed to, thinking it would never come off. After savings she spends her remaining earnings on pizza delivery, bargain store chic and designer cosmetics you could never afford.

You're back to doing all your own housework because her pay from the restaurant is more competitive. At fifteen she's already moved up the corporate ladder. Blood warms your face as you vacuum and she leaves her room running, calling something over her shoulder you can't make out above the suction. You yell after her:

'Claire!' and the front door slams: the cliché that's become her signature or perhaps another of those unpredictable, hormoneshifts that have come to tyrannise you. Maybe she'll live at home long enough to suffer your menopause. A smile steals over your lips.

From the hall window you see her talking to the geeky pizzaboy. He's helping put on her helmet so she can ride on that death-trap scooter. You bang on the window but they've already taken off. Two perfect bottoms perched together.

You use the Hoover head like a bayonet, forcing open her bedroom door and cursing what you find on the floor. Tights with dirty knickers still entwined. Every shoe she owns discarded in a heap beside the mirror. You throw them onto her unmade bed and spy a pretty necklace on the bedpost: a string of shiny purple stones threaded on navy ribbon. You put them over your head and turn to the mirror, then remove them immediately. Skin is gathering at your throat like a turkey. You don't belong in these.

There's something about this room. Alone you feel closer to her. You can glance at things without her tsking. You learn more looking at these walls than you do spending time with her.

There's a computer ping from the corner and you glance towards her laptop. Ping-ping, it comes again like rapid machinegun fire. You walk over to her desk. There's still time for a retreat but you don't. You flick a finger over the mouse. A document is open with an essay title:

'What is meant by the following phrase in Carol Ann Duffy's poem? "We Remember Your Childhood Well": "No, nobody left the skidmarks of sin on your soul and laid you wide open for Hell." '

And underneath:

'Er, how about denial/blatant lie?'

In a separate window, a Web browser is open in a chatroom. Your eyes fish out words and phrases:

'keep the rhythm regular/ it's soo uncool to gag/ use your hand to stroke it/ hold it at the base and stretch his skin, he'll LOVE it'

Who are these unknowables? You conjure her mouth: that smooth, red, shock of skin that's not even finished growing yet.

There's another ping as you pull up the chair.

'work with the natural downward angle of your throat/ start slow then speed it up/ lips down over teeth/ ask what French boys like, then tell us!'

You're thinking of the hot-pink bathrobe on the floor, with strands of her hair on the shoulder and the toast crusts still lying on the plate in the kitchen. You're wondering why she broke off and left so quickly. You're wondering why the people in this chat room have chosen the names they have:

Pyrotechnica7228

Lashes99

'I knw some1 who did it wth a brace, just b xtra carefl.'

Pyrotechnica7228: u still there MooshMoosh?

MooshMoosh? You Google for a definition, hoping moosh still means 'friend'.

The UrbanDictionary.com translates it as 'Take off your clothes or I'll do it for you.' They give other, innocent sounding definitions but this is the only one you remember.

You imagine that right now she's undressing him in the restaurant's wine cellar or perhaps in a parked Renault Clio.

Lashes99: May b she's practising on her hairbrush LOL.


You turn up at her work an hour before you're due to collect her and tell the head waiter you'd like a table for one. Her hair's pinned up in a beehive and the shade of her red lipstick catches your breath. She's serving a customer from the dessert trolley and isn't pleased to see you. You skip the starter and wait for your-chef-for-this-evening-is-Philippe to appear at the carvery. To avoid looking conspicuous as you stand alone, you feign interest in the horseradish. The kitchen's open plan and your eyes meet over the hotplate then dart away: a squat bear of a man, late twenties, perhaps. There's thick dark hair on his hands and he shares with you that telltale edge of disappointment.

He emerges through a saloon door and makes for the trolley of joints politely asking do you lick your meat pink? You consider wrestling the carving fork from his hairy hand and holding it to his throat but instead you smile, yes, and feel him watching as you ladle more gravy from the serve-yourself-station.

Behind her hand, in a corner of the restaurant, she's bitching about you with the other waitresses. Avoiding your eye, she strides across the room, or as best she can in platform shoes, and you notice at other tables men's eyes follow, then drop away.

The blood mixes with your gravy and turns it burgundy. In the open plan kitchen Philippe is laughing with her over something. She's leaning into him and her face is lit. He isn't hers quite yet.

Over a single espresso you fill in the customer response form and circle very poor for the food. Comments: cold and undercooked but the waitress service is excellent.

On the way home she asks what you were doing having dinner on your own like a complete saddo.

You ring her father. He doesn't see any reason to get into a state. He actually laughs.

'In Holland they don't make such a big deal of teenage sex. Britain is so prudish.'

Perhaps he means you. In the background you hear the sound of dinner being cleared away and wonder if his new wife, Gertrude, indulges in transgender role play with strap-on accessories.

You see a light under Claire's door. Maybe she's reading the thread of her chat. You pour wine and fire up your PC. You don't mean to intrude. It's worry that drives you. The username you create is something you give little thought to. There's no need to add a number to the one you choose. The registration process confirms you're just plain StrapOn: the one and only. MooshMoosh is not in the chat room and the earlier thread is gone. You linger awhile in case she signs in. Having gone to the effort of creating a covert identity you want to say something.

Ping! Ping!

Lashes99: So?

MooshMoosh: He likes this wmn that wks on reception a ginger that gt implants 4 her 30th.

Pyrotechnica7228: Yeh bt he wants U 2 honey!

Lashes99: Didn't u say e ws bitng ur ear and sayng ur name over and over and stuff.

StrapOn: When was this? Where was this?

Lashes99: Keep up nu grl. The other nght.

MooshMoosh: Just want 2 gt the 1st time over with.

StrapOn: But why the rush? How old are you? Where would you even do it?

CHATROOM_SUPERVISER: REMINDING USER StrapOn OF RULES. NO EXCHANGE OF PERSONAL/CONTACT INFORMATION.

Lashes99: Duh. So she knws the moves for the nxt guy, isn't it?

You pull out the broadband cable. Soon there's movement upstairs. It only takes a moment for her to appear. You tell her something's up with the modem. Her eyes narrow.

'Have you called someone?'

'Not yet, it just happened.'

'Can I look? I need it for my essay.'

'I told you it's not working.'

You're speaking in the tight little voice of your mother.

In bed you imagine Philippe's furry hands inside your blouse, greedy for every inch of flesh. He feels along each rib. Like a rack of lamb. In return, you tease him. Holding him back from the brink until, sweating and faux-angry, he promises: of course he'll stay away from her; what's she to him; only some kid with spots? It's you he wants, stupid: a woman who has lived and touched all of life. You want to rewind and see his sexy little mouth repeat this but suddenly Claire appears in the doorway in the hot-pink bathrobe.

'The cable was out.'

***

The restaurant is quiet. The carvery lights are off and the trolley stands gleaming and empty. The head waiter leaves his staff in a corner, shining glasses.

'Can I help you?' He's holding the bookings diary in front of him.

'I've an appointment with Philippe.'

He pauses, wanting more, and you smile sweetly, letting him know that's all he's getting. When Philippe appears, you're sitting in reception peeking at the redhead's new breasts. His chef's trousers hang past his boots. He's shorter and squatter than you remember and those hairy hands were not meant for caressing food.

Blushing, you say:

'We spoke on the phone…'

He smiles and gestures to a corridor:

'Shall we?'

***

At dinner you ask Claire:

'Why so miserable?'

'Why so happy?' She snaps back.

'Well, I found some caterers for your birthday. There're some menus on the side.' You carry your plate to the sink and turn on the tap.

'Did you talk to Philippe about it?'

'Not yet.' Your face glows. 'Anyway, what did you do today?'

She shrugs.

'Marc came over.'

'You mean pizzaboy?'

'I mean Marc.'

Your nail breaks in the water.

'Do you have a nail-file?'

'Top right drawer in my room.'

'My hands are wet.'

'You always tell me not to leave the table till I finish.'

Her room is stuffy. It's on your way to open the window that you spot it in the waste bin: the discarded rubber sack with its neat little knot at the end. Your heart skitters in your chest and hearing her feet heavy on the stairs you stop yourself from reaching for it.

In the doorway, she folds her arms and raises an eyebrow but her chin is trembling.

'Is everything alright?'

'Philippe just called.'

'Oh?' You try to swallow.

'Yeh.' Her voice shakes. 'He says he wants to speak to you.' And you notice her platform shoe is tapping the floor like a drum.

---

**Justine Mann** is writing *Cargo*, a thriller set amongst a community of trafficked immigrants. Her stories have been anthologised by Apis Books, Tell Tales and Fish Publishing. In 2008 she was awarded second prize in the *Fish International Short Story Competition*.

# Tracy Maylath

## Kwik Save

You wander into Starbucks loving that the statistical possibilities of all the beverage combinations make you as jittery as a caffeine buzz. Tall, grande, venti? Peruvian, Ethiopian, Kona? Extra shot? Iced or hot? Room for cream? You could ask for a pre-made concoction but the simplicity of the act would defeat the purpose in coming here.

The ersatz jazz twangs like a frayed nerve. It breaks your concentration on ordering yet another combination you've never had before, a sad fucking record to be proud of.

Still it's an ambition and let's face it, you need one. It hasn't been necessary to get up in the morning since you got fired from your cosy Wall Street position leaving behind the busyness. You keep your nametag with, Carlton F Yale, Financial Adviser, engraved on it like an affirmation. The size of a credit card it fits in your wallet, under the clear plastic, so that it can be seen whenever you pay for something.

It's why you hang out in Starbucks, the watering hole for the terminally ambitious. This coffee a self-reward for the business they took care of that a.m. before filing over to Starbucks where they can multi-task with a grande, soy, double mocha, no whip.

You have a notion that, by hanging out with the high-fliers, you will contract full-blown enthusiasm in some vague osmotic process involving WiFi and the sound of frothing milk.

The itch of your coffee craving forces a decision on a dry caramel cappuccino, grande, no make that venti, you're not in a hurry. You flick your AmEx gold card at the barista 'cause you're short on cash and she needs to know you've got the number one in credit cards. It's your dad's and he's dead but what the hell, you've got the same initials and no one's cottoned on yet.

The card must be nearly maxed. Withdrawing cash means clenching your butt cheeks during that interminable pause before the ATM spews out the requested amount. You'd just purchased your BMW Silver 6 Series convertible a month before you got fired. The enormous monthly payments are depleting the tiny inheritance remaining after taxation tore through most of it like a brush fire. Checking your savings this morning you were smacked in the face with the figure $42.60.

Despite what your ex said, putting on her best charity worker's worthy voice, the job had to be accessorised. The silver car and the platinum Rolex. The B&O sound system and the Armani wardrobe. She earned a pittance and left you when your dad got sick.

Prising the lid off the cup at the coffee station, you whack three packets of sugar on the counter, tear off the corners in one motion with your teeth and pour them in from a height. You stir the scalding liquid with a wooden stick but it drowns in the too-tall cup and you burn your fingers and say 'fuck, fuck' aloud while you fish it out. You cram the lid back on say 'fuck' again. There are no empty tables.

Deciding who to share a table with makes your dry mouth drier. The guy wearing the suit with cowboy boots is bound to try to sell you something. The woman with football-mom hair, to tell you about her overachieving children.

You strategise that an improvement to this monolith of a coffee institution would be those plastic, rectangular dividers supermarkets provide imbued with the responsibility of keeping your stuff separate from the loser's next to you in line. Used so that the minimum-waged doofus, who is bleeping away his career, can make an uncontaminated judgement of you based on your purchases as they roll up on the conveyor belt:

6-pack = alcoholic

TV Guide = lazy alcoholic

Lean Cuisine meal for one = fat, lonely alcoholic

3-ply toilet paper with aloe vera = deluded alcoholic who figures he may as well be kind to his ass

You want one of those rectangles now. Then you could walk over to a singly occupied table, plonk it down in the middle and negate any need for:

'I need to sit here but don't want to engage in any pseudo-conversation, wage a surreptitious battle under the table for leg space or exchange inane social pleasantries.'

Coming back to the dilemma, minus the option of plastic table dividers, you consider your options.

\*\*\*

The Polynesian family, occupying the other half of the room where your dad is dying, is having a luau. Their bodies bulge through the curtain which splices the room in two. Their shoes static in the gap between floor and fabric. The cooking smells, as they peel tinfoil off trays of steaming food, mask those of drugs, latex, urine. They tsk tsk between bouts of singing as your dad groans and the nurse squeezes past them to up his morphine dose.

As the family behind the curtain celebrates, you and your mother agonise over the decision to withdraw liquids. At least that way, the doctor says, you can see an end in sight.

The sound of laughter soothes as your dad's tongue dries and cracks like a leather shoe abandoned in the baking sun.

\*\*\*

She is wearing a green, Kwik Save uniform. Her nametag, emblazoned with 'Donna', has four brass stars pinned in it and an empty hole waiting for the fifth. Her legs crossed tight, she grips her steaming mug on one knee, her other hand, spidery, splaying the book open in front of her face displaying its title: *The Tyranny of Freedom*. She might be OK to share with and doesn't look up as you yank the empty chair away from her table.

'Shit', you mouth as you pull your library book from your plastic bag. The *Black Dog* of the title would give Donna obvious insight. It's a year overdue now but you need to browse the section on symptoms each day. You put it back in the bag.

Everyone wants to label you. Giving you a moniker, 'depressed', 'underachiever', 'lazy', 'loser', they go away satisfied, a conundrum solved.

\*\*\*

Your colleagues engage in a continuous battle of self-improvement. Borrowing books from each other with some toothy-bright executive on the back promising that you could reach self-actualisation.

They become devotees of 'Regress Your Way Forward' and 'Breathwork for Professionals' seminars. Armed with a new stock of labels, eager to paste them on you when you cross their righteous path.

'You know what you are, Carlton?' One of them asks, waving the pack of flyers filched from the latest personal development orgy, 'you're an RTFI.'

'A what?'

'An RTFI.'

'OK, I'll play your silly game, what's an RTFI?'

'A Reflective, Thinking, Feeling, Introvert.'

'Oh.'

'See now you're reflecting on what I just said and you'll go away and think about how you feel about it.'

'You think? Well maybe I'll go away and think about how you're an SSSA.'

'What?' He looks alarmed at this gap in his knowledge of acronyms.

'A Smug, Self-Satisfied Asshole.'

'Now you're just acting out because you can't deal with the truth.'

You storm out.

\*\*\*

You rush from Manhattan at five each day to sit and listen to your dad wheeze and your mother cry and the Polynesians sing. If you told anyone they would label you grief-stricken, scared of death. And if you rejected their labels they would chalk it up as a typical response and walk away, smug as a doctor whose patient was living up, or dying up, to his prognosis.

\*\*\*

At the height of your career you become a neo-Machiavelli. You capitalise 'Me', 'Myself' in memos as if you have divine right, but type 'i' in lower case in some cummings-esque strategy to draw attention to it. You peer at both your cell phones during meetings even when it's you speaking and ignore them when you're alone.

When your dad dies your boss sends a card and a wreath to the funeral and fires you a month later after you lose a prized client a five-figure sum. You leave taking only your nametag and your mug which says, "Old investment bankers never die, they just trade up".

Your dad hadn't been an investment banker. His massive heart attack three weeks after his retirement is a cliché you toast with a bottle of scotch.

'Donna', lowers her book, peers at you through tinted, aviator-style glasses and asks 'you go there?' pointing at your sweatshirt, which says 'Yale' across it.

'Where? Oh … no … I don't, didn't.'

'Oh?'

'It's my name. My last name. Yale.'

'You're your own brand then are you? Hilfiger, Versace … Yale.' She laughs.

You shift in your seat. Focus on the flyers sticking out of the coffee station, which urge you to answer, 'how are we doing?'

\*\*\*

The doctors ask you, 'how are we doing today?'

The Polynesian roommate and his family leave. The curtain pushed back reveals the crisp, empty bed. So your dad wastes two days wandering through his morphine haze without musical accompaniment until he kicks life like a habit.

When the doctor calls to tell you the news, waking you from your own sweaty bed, he says, 'Dad died 20 minutes ago.' As if your dad were an all-Dad, an omniscient Dad.

After you get fired your mom confesses to her own cancer in some half-assed act of supreme martyrdom. Giving up her life for your dad in some fucking act of charity. Selfish. Like your ex. Charity is a mask for your own pathetic needs.

\*\*\*

'I go there,' Donna says.

'What? Where?'

'Yale. I go to Yale. Just getting some money to pay for it.'

'Good for you.'

'Thought you might be interested.'

'Well I'm not OK?'

'Suit yourself. So what do you do?'

You sigh, 'nothing. I'm booked solid making small talk with over-qualified, grocery store workers in Starbucks.'

'Thought you might be.'

Stumped, you slurp foam through the plastic lid like a toddler.

Maybe it's the caffeine that causes the disintegration of all the plastic rectangles between your thoughts so you can't separate them. Your dad kicking it and making the same decisions about your mom a few months later. The silence while she died. No one sending wreaths to the funeral.

Prising the lid off the cup again, you gulp the still-steaming coffee. The burn leaves your tongue feeling like cotton but it's better than the idea of being an orphan. You laugh out loud. Not some Dickensian urchin with a snot nose, but a 38 year old with no buffer now between him and the great Starbucks in the sky. The two people who had been in front of you in line, now all paid up.

'What's funny?' Donna asks.

'God you don't give up do you? Nothing. Nothing's funny.'

'Whoa there, Cowboy, I was just trying to be nice. You look like you've spent way too much time on your own. I can see why now.' She lifts her book in front of her face again.

'Listen,' you want to make good. This stranger being pissed off at you seems important. 'You work over there? At the Kwik Save?'

'Yeah, genius, what gave it away?'

You don't smile. You ask, 'any jobs going?'

'Might be. Guy like you deserves to work in a hellhole.'

\*\*\*

Sometimes you balance all the plastic dividers up on their ends to see if the people in line will notice. Sometimes you pass them to Donna. Smirking she slaps them down on her conveyor belt at odd intervals between items; a bulb of fennel, a jar of marshmallow fluff, a box of straws. You laugh at the perplexed shoppers in your line trying to keep their stuff in neat, separate piles.

The manager at Kwik Save tells you that you could be next up for promotion if you earn a fifth, brass star. You tell her you're not in a hurry.

You and Donna go to Starbucks together when you're not working. You stick to filter: black, medium.

7 facts about **Tracy Maylath**: ex-performance poet, Londoner via Denver, Colorado, short story published in *The Illustrated Ape* magazine, regular reader at Tales of the Decongested short fiction event, working on a collection of connected short stories including *Kwik Save*, seeking fame and fortune, suffers from exuberant daydreams.

# Lauren Owen

### *Death and The Girl*
### *Extract from a novel*

## Chapter One

Too many tales. Too many fancies strange
Flit through her thoughts like moon-faced owls, who cry
Rather to fright their prey than to forewarn.
Up starts the milk-soft innocent, and hears
The cold man's footsteps quicken in the dusk.
Oh, far too close, the shadow, far too strong!
**James Millis Norbury**, *Gondoline*

W ell, duh, Sophie had said, when Lucy asked if St Helen's was haunted. Schools were always haunted, everyone knew that. And a school like St Helen's – so large and echoing in the holidays, the corridors lined with red cloaks and layered in dust, the gates so high and black and scrolling – a school like that was bound to have ghosts.

Even their school, which was not St Helen's but the village primary school down the road, had two ghosts of its own. There was the Green Lady, who would appear if you got a lit candle and something green and stood in front of a mirror at midnight and chanted 'Green lady, green lady, green lady'. Then she'd come into your bedroom and kill you. The other ghost was a girl who used to go to the school years before. She'd decided to hang herself in the toilet using the toilet chain. When you pull the chain, a Year Six told Sophie on her first day, that's her screaming.

Sophie didn't know if she believed it or not. Sometimes she almost thought she might – but then, when she'd told her mother, her mother had laughed like she hadn't for a long while, and said thanks, Soph, I needed that.

But she hated the toilets anyway: they were outside, you had to cross the playground to get to them, and it always seemed to be raining when Sophie needed to go. They smelled weird, too, and there were spiders and moths living there – and once an enterprising family of toads.

The boys' toilets were worse, though. They smelled much weirder, and probably had far more spiders, too. Once, after school, Sophie and Gloria (who had dark gold hair and was fearless and Sophie's best friend) had climbed onto a dustbin and peered over the wall, just to have a look. She had seen cubicle doors, painted green like those in the girls' toilet but marked all over with footprints, like someone had been kicking them again and again.

'D'you think –?' she began, but then she abruptly lost her balance and toppled from the dustbin, knocking Gloria over as she fell. They landed badly, snarled together, and the black tarmac smacked painfully against Sophie's knees and the palms of her hands.

She struggled to her feet and inspected the damage: her hands were bleeding, tiny black bits of grit sticking to the cuts.

'Moron,' Gloria said – not maliciously – hopping on one leg to inspect a gash to her shin.

'Cow,' Sophie parried. She raised her right hand to her mouth and ran her tongue curiously over the graze. 'I didn't mean to.'

'Yeah, well.' Gloria's gaze returned to the toilet wall. 'We could go in,' she said.

'Yeah,' said Sophie.

'D'you want to?'

'No.' If you went into the boys' toilets you would be gammy, besmirched, as if being a boy was catching. (She liked that word, besmirched: saying it felt like biting into an apple).

'OK,' Gloria said (relieved, perhaps, despite her proven courage), and they had gone back to Gloria's house to watch TV, and that had been the end of the expedition.

There was one girl at school that everyone hated. Her name was Jackie, and she was shadow-thin and greasy-haired, and there was a rumour that all her clothes came from Oxfam. One day someone scrawled

jacki sux dogz dix

on the cloakroom wall in poison-green felt tip. No one seemed to know who was responsible, so they had a Don't Do Graffiti Assembly and Mr Fellowes, the caretaker, was despatched to remove the libel from existence with a tin of white emulsion. It showed through, though, a phantom scribble right above Jackie's peg where she hung her horrible pink coat every morning. After a while the words, like the pink coat, seemed to belong to Jackie somehow. They followed her around like a curse, chanted or whispered or scrawled into people's rough jotters. And sometimes Sophie wondered if it wasn't Jackie's fault in some way, that people wrote things about her.

One day Jackie was chased round the playground and pushed inside one of the cubicles in the boys' toilet. Some people thought it would be a good idea to stuff her head down, but nobody wanted to be the one who actually did it, and in the end they only kept her in there for ten minutes or so – only until someone watching thought to get Mrs Jessop, the Head. It wasn't Sophie: she had been watching at the edge of the crowd, excitement burning her insides like sherbet. It was awful, though, she'd thought. People shouldn't be mean like that. Poor Jackie.

Jackie had shrieked and yelled abuse during the hunt, but once inside she'd gone quiet; she didn't say anything for the rest of the day, in fact. Some of the boys were given lines to do, and they had a Don't Bully People Assembly that Friday afternoon. After that, the girls in Sophie's class started being very nice to Jackie. They said 'hi!' to her in a special, bright sort of way, and said how much they liked her hair, and asked her where she'd bought her fake designer pencil case. It was horrible, Sophie thought. She hadn't realized kindness could be so horrible. Afterwards, when she thought about the girl who'd hanged herself, she always imagined her with Jackie's face. But she kept telling the tale, because she thought it might be nice for the hanged girl to be talked about. It might make her feel less lonely. Besides, it was a shame to waste a good story.

Ghosts could be trouble, though: Sophie remembered one school trip to Scarborough, to the hostel that everyone said was bound to be haunted. After three nights of terror, Briony Upwood had finally become hysterical and began demanding to be sent home, and there was a meeting in the hostel canteen.

'You've let me down,' Mrs Jessop said.

Mrs Jessop was tall, and in spite of her beige tights and angora cardigans she had an inescapably military air. She reminded Sophie of Boudicca: it was quite easy to imagine her on a chariot in the midst of battle, cleaving her enemies' skulls in twain.

Mrs Jessop said that they were representatives for the school, and should know better than to be telling each other such silly stories. She spoke in a tone of dignified regret, as if they were her troops and had disappointed her by fleeing before the invading Romans or getting back late from a pillaging expedition. The class were humbled.

Mr Kinnick, their form teacher, had added that they ought to be ashamed of themselves. Mr Kinnick wore grey leather shoes with little tassels and had a beard which looked like it had crawled onto his face whilst he was asleep. Nobody really cared what he thought.

Perhaps he realized this, because he asked sharply who had been spreading the rumours of ghosts, anyway, and everyone – the traitors – pointed to Sophie.

Mr Kinnick said several cutting things about people whose imaginations ran away with them, and gave Sophie lines to do: she had to write

I will not scare others with made-up stories

a hundred times. And until she was finished she would stay in during the afternoons whilst the others went down to the beach.

She knew about writing lines: the best way was to write the first word a hundred times, and then go back to the top and do the second word the same way, and so on. She sat down on the first afternoon and began to write 'I' over and over, until the word looked strange and lost all meaning. She heard the seagulls screeching to one another over the bay, and was miserable.

The next afternoon, she would have started writing 'will'. But that morning the trip was abruptly broken off and the children minibussed home without any explanation.

'Ghosts, probably,' Sophie said to her mother with some satisfaction.

'What?' Her mother looked up sharply from the letter the school had sent. She'd been smoking that morning, the smell of it followed her everywhere. Sophie could taste it at the back of her throat as she crunched her cornflakes.

'The ghost. There was a ghost where we were staying, you know. There was this really high staircase, and sometimes you'd hear it creaking, but there was nobody walking up it. That's why Mrs Jessop's so weird at the moment, probably. She went ballistic at Harriet yesterday, and normally she loves Harriet, she's her favourite.'

'It wasn't a ghost, Soph,' Sophie's mother said.

But she refused to elaborate further, leaving Sophie to draw her own conclusions. And Mr Kinnick left very shortly afterwards, which just went to show.

***

There was only one ghost at St Helen's, Sophie said, and he was all right as long as you kept on his good side.

They were sitting in the school theatre, where they should not have been. Just because we live here, Sophie's mother (Headmistress to the Lower Sixth) had said, doesn't mean you can treat the place like a hotel. Some places are out of bounds. In the holidays, Sophie had her birthday parties in the school cafeteria and roller-skated up and down the corridors, and sometimes she heeded her mother and sometimes she did not.

There were four of them in the theatre: Sophie, Gloria, and Gloria's two sisters, Lucy and Kit. And that afternoon, the afternoon when Lucy had asked whether the school was haunted, Sophie told them the story of St. Helen's Ghost.

'OK, so there was this Roman Army, right? They were staying here before the school was built.'

'Why?' asked Lucy. Lucy was the middle sister: sweet-faced, a collector of semi-precious stones. She was the one who was the most interested in motivation.

'They were invading Britain,' said Sophie. 'Like on that Roman Day we went to last term.' The Roman Day was brilliant. Gloria and Sophie had been together in the duelling workshop, and Sophie had nearly lost an ear. 'Anyway, one of the soldiers had six fingers on his right hand.'

'Six fingers? That's impossible,' said Kit. Kit was the youngest of the three. She was red-headed and belligerent and had a knack for maths. She was also a fierce stickler for realism.

'No, it's not. I saw a documentary,' said Gloria.

'Fine, whatever,' Kit said, rolling her eyes. 'He had six fingers. Then what?'

'Well,' said Sophie, 'all the soldiers made fun of him for having an extra finger, so he cut it off.'

'How?' asked Gloria, who was going to be a doctor.

'With his sword.'

'It would've gone septic,' Gloria said, with calm conviction. 'His whole arm would have gone black and fallen off.'

'Well, it didn't,' said Sophie.

'It must have!'

'It didn't. Anyway, the soldiers made fun of the stump where his finger used to be, so he chopped off his hand.'

'Why didn't he just tell them to leave him alone?' asked Lucy.

Sophie considered. 'He wanted them to be his friends, I suppose. But they just made fun of him for only having one hand. So he cut off his arm. But then they laughed at him for only having one arm, so he chopped off his head.'

The Mundys exchanged glances.

'He chopped off his own head?' said Gloria.

Sophie raised an imaginary sword, twisted her arm behind her head, and demonstrated. 'Like that.'

'Oh.' Lucy looked slightly queasy.

'And so they buried him, and they thought that was the end of it ...' She paused for a moment, enjoying herself. 'But some say that his spirit still lingers here, forever vengeful and alone, a fell creature of the night. And woe betide any who incur his wrath.'

'What?' said Kit.

Sophie sighed. 'He haunts the school forever.'

'Oh.'

'And that,' Sophie concluded, impressively, 'is why there's that statue by the Tuck Shop. Of the soldier without a head or an arm: The Headless Roman.' Nobody said anything. 'The End,' she prompted, crossly.

'Oh. Cool,' said Lucy, who had very good manners.

But Kit sneered. 'You just made that up,' she said, accusingly.

'Yeah, well, that's what you think,' said Sophie. 'Don't blame me if he's angry with you for saying he's made up and comes and gets you tonight.'

A small pause. And then –

'Why would he care?' said Kit.

---

**Lauren Owen** graduated from St Hilda's College Oxford in 2006 with a degree in English Literature, and subsequently achieved an MA in Victorian Literature from the University of Leeds. She currently lives in Yorkshire, and is working on her first novel.

# Salman Shaheen

## Children of the Sunset

An extract from a novel-in-progress

## Chapter One:

### The End of History and The Last Man's Last Laugh

C all me what you will. After all, names are just a choice. And they say there's a world in every choice. A divergent reality. I was there for most of them. It might not have been me riding that tank while they fought a war with lightning and a generation of Germans, but I was there in 1924, sitting in number 11 Landsberg Prison whilst my cellmate dictated a different kind of struggle. I didn't stick around long in St Petersburg after they painted the town red and saw it was time for a change in name, but I was there in the heady days of '48 when Karl and Friedrich set it all in motion. I wasn't waiting in the wings when they nailed the son of a carpenter up because the Holy Land had one too many prophets as it was, but I was around when they came to write about it later, not because history is written by the victors, but because it is written by me. And yes, I was there in 1967, in the tiny Bolivian village of La Higuera, when The Doctor's Son came upon the schoolhouse.

They build a statue here later. A monument to the greatness of a great man. Or the petrification of the petrified. That's always the way isn't it? It stands, in your time, beside a humble cross in the shadow of rolling moss-green peaks thick with foliage. I suppose, one could say it is my time too, for all time is my time. But enough of me.

Emerging from the shade of the tree-line into the heat of the semi-tropical spring sun, the boy wiped a little hand across his bronzed mestizo forehead and drew a darker line of sweat and dirt behind it. It had not rained here in some days. The sun burnt a bright suspended discus high overhead in the white-wisp-flecked blue bowl that stretched out over the hills and trees and squat single-storey houses with their run-down roofs of chipped tiles and thatch and walls of brittle brick and brown baked mud. His clumpy shoes, still half a size too big for his still-growing feet, scuffed little dust storms as he picked his way as quietly as he could along the track of parched earth cracked in an atlas of lines. The village seemed dead to him. The brush around though – the bushes in hundreds, thousands of shades of green – was alive with chirping cicada song. Somewhere not too far away he heard a dog barking. Gruff rolled r rrrooofs. And a man's muffled cry.

The Doctor's Son stopped a moment, sat down on a heated half-shaded slab of grey stone next to a rickety roadside shack leaning over him in a perilous parallelogram. There he sighed and pulled off his shoes and socks, releasing the footsmell of sweat into the gentle breeze that brushed the mess of his soggy black hair. Rubbing his aching soles, he willed the blisters back into his feet. He had walked far. Through the warmth of a milder yesterday, through the night and morning. Far from the comfort of home, far from the safety of the sleepy cobbled town in which his father chose to practise his medicine, miles over rough terrain, through the jungle, along dirt tracks into the hills. Brought by a dream. A vision in a dream: nothing more than an idea in its most abstract. It was not until he was nearing this isolated campesino backwater, until, hiding in the bushes, he had overheard the passing soldiers bragging of their new prisoner, the limping Argentine, that he had truly understood.

There was a rustle in the thicket behind, a glint of red. The boy turned and that was when he might have seen me, had the first and vaguest of impressions that I might have been close by, but I had not come to him yet. Not fully. No doubt he doubted his eyes, keen and wide and dark and full of wonder as they were. He removed his glasses – those thick black rectangles with their great wedges of convex glass that covered a full third of his face – and with a pinched corner of his T-shirt, brown and ripped by forest thorns, wiped the steam from the lenses. The squawk of a passing macaw turned to another, more human, screech and something told him then he didn't have much time. Reaching into his pack, he pulled out his knife and ran, barefoot, straight for the sound.

That was how The Doctor's Son came upon the dilapidated old schoolhouse – a long and low building of crumbling mud bricks, with a flimsy wooden door, that looked as though the Bolivian soil wanted it back and would soon have taken it back without a fuss were it not for the structure's famous prisoner and its future pre-eminence – and that was how he came upon the uniformed soldiers and a man he recognised, one Sergeant Carlos Domingo Lozada. Peering around the corner, one hand on the sun-warmed wall, he could see the four soldiers, rifles slung over their backs, standing in a tense square fifty yards or so away by the entrance to the schoolhouse, speaking in raised voices, shaking heads, pointing fingers, arguing about something. He could not make out what they were saying, but he thought he knew. Keeping low, keeping to the shade, he ducked behind a stone wall and ran along its length. From where he was now, he could no longer see their faces, but he could hear Domingo talking.

'No, Mario, that is not fair,' Domingo was saying. 'Why should you be the one to do it?'

'Carlos, Carlos,' the one called Mario replied. 'Have you ever executed a man before?'

'I am a soldier, I know how to kill.'

'It is not the same. Killing in battle, their bullets flying at you, your bullets flying at them, you or them, them or you: there is no time to think. Killing a man in cold blood, you have time to see his face, time to hear his words, and both will stay with you.'

'I do not see why we have to kill him anyway,' a third soldier said. 'Surely he is worth more to us alive than dead. He said so himself when we took him.'

'These are our orders, José. They come from President Barrientos himself. Five Hundred, Six Hundred, that is what Felix said. The President says he wants his head on a spike in downtown La Paz and that is where it will be.'

'I do not trust any of this, Mario,' José said. 'Why are we doing the bidding of the Americans against our own brothers? Sons of the South.'

'The Argentine? Goes to whip up his hate in some tottering state, then comes here? To fight in our Bolivia? That is called an invasion. He is an invader. And we must follow orders. I understand if you do not want to do it.'

'I never said that!'

'Mario, you are talking this up!' Domingo said. 'I know you. You want to be the one to do it because he is famous. Because you will go down in history, your name a footnote to his.'

Mario laughed. 'Can you say any different, Carlos?'

'No.'

'Well then, how do we decide? Do we flip a coin?'

'Sí.'

'No!' the fourth soldier interjected. 'That is not fair either! I want to do it.'

'Wait,' José said, and after some consideration added, 'me too!'

'Then we draw straws,' Mario decided. 'Whoever gets the shortest gets to be the one.'

'Straws?' Carlos groaned. 'We always draw straws. Who gets the last cigar? Straws. Who gets the whore with the biggest pechos? Straws. Who gets –'

'To kill the world's most famous revolutionary?'

'Straws,' the soldiers chimed together.

'Then it is agreed.'

'Agreed.'

'Sí.'

Peering over the wall, The Doctor's Son saw the soldiers distractedly searching the dirt for suitable pieces of straw. Their backs were turned. This was his chance. Without stopping to think or look round, he dashed the few feet across open ground to the door of the old schoolhouse. Hurriedly pushing his way in, he closed the door behind him, placed his back to it and let out a sigh of relief. That was when he heard another sigh. A gasp, a moan, a pained whimper. At first all the boy could see through the dingy gloom of the interior were two points of red that could have been hot glowing embers in a hearth in the far corner. Training his eyes, he could soon make out other things. Shapes. A table. A chair. Some piping. A man handcuffed to it.

'Che!' The Prisoner exclaimed in that Argentine way for which he was well known. 'Che!'

Looking upon him, The Doctor's Son knew then that he was now a part of history. The Prisoner looked so different from his iconic photographs – the one that would later come to decorate student bedrooms all across the world – sprawled out on the floor, crumpled in a hurting heap, bleeding from a bullet wound in the leg, his beret gone, his hair, his beard, unkempt and overgrown, his face pale and frightened.

'Che!' he said again. 'Who are you?'

'I –' The Doctor's Son began.

'What are you doing here?'

'I do not know, señor.'

'You do not know?'

'I think I came to help you.'

'There is nothing you can do for me.'

'There is, there is!' the boy cried and he ran to The Prisoner, dropped to his knees on the floor beside him, drew his hunting knife and began to saw its serrated edge against the handcuffs. It was no use. Frustrated, the boy raised his hand to try to slash at the cuffs, but The Prisoner stopped him.

'Stop,' the man croaked.

'There must be something I can do.'

'Water. Do you have any water?'

'Sí.' The boy reached into his pack, took out a flask of water, unscrewed the lid and brought it to the man's lips.

Tilting back his head, the man drank greedily until the flask was empty. 'Gracias,' he said. 'Now you must go before the soldiers find you.'

'But they will kill you.'

'It is better this way, I should have died in combat.'

A tear rolled down the boy's cheek and he wiped it away.

'Do not be sad,' said The Prisoner. 'I will tell you something. Years ago, I set off across this continent, a young doctor in the making, full of dreams, ready to heal the world. The things I saw, the things I wanted to be, I thought then that great men could make great changes. But what are we? Just flesh and bone, weak and brittle. Fragile. Look at me. You can patch it up for a time, but only a time. Maybe I should have stuck to treating lepers. The world is too sick for me, for one man alone. But it was never about one man. I will pass. Into history, into obscurity, it does not matter. Legends do die. But ideas, ideas do not.'

The Doctor's Son nodded. He opened his mouth to speak, but at that moment he heard footsteps approaching, voices drawing closer.

"Hide!" The Prisoner hissed.

The Doctor's Son had only just managed to scurry under the table when the door opened. There in the patch of sunlight he saw Mario: a piece of straw in one hand, a Kalashnikov in the other.

The Prisoner laughed.

'I know you are here to kill me. Shoot, coward, you are only going to kill a man!'

A burst of gunfire and another a minute later.

The Doctor's Son was not looking as the shots rang out – as The Prisoner gurgled his last bloody breath – and I came to him.

**Salman Shaheen** was born in Norwich in 1984 and graduated with a First in Social and Political Sciences from Jesus College, Cambridge, where he was Literature Editor of *Varsity*. He was a co-host, alongside Jon Snow, on the Channel 4 series *First Edition* and has appeared on various television programmes.

Page/blog: **www.myspace.com/salmanshaheen**

# Kelly Smith

## *On the Plus Side:*

You don't have to shave your legs every day, standing up in the bath, face flushed from water so hot it's your own private steam room; arching your back, contorting your body into yoga positions, checking behind your knees for stray hairs. You don't have to slap on the wax because you must be hairless and smooth in every conceivable place and there is no way on God's green earth that his tongue, in delicate flicking motions, must be allowed to feel stubble down there or anywhere. God no. Now you let it grow, you watch dark hair return, you'll call it liberation for a little while. You give your body a break. On the plus side.

You don't have to apply moisturizing make-up for that translucent 'I still have teenage skin at 33' glow. You're worth it, so you paid for it, you paid through the nose for it. You don't have to have plump perfect moisturized lips, lipglosstastic, smacking together as though covered in pink sticky glue. You don't have to prime your face as part of your 'skincare regime'. You don't have to high-beam your cheeks with a wash of light-reflecting particles in order for your best side to sparkle as candlelight catches your 'maybe she's born with it' features across the table over dinner. You splash water on your face, pinch your cheeks and realize you look lovely without your mask. You see freckles you'd long forgotten. Freckles the boys in school ached after. Pulled your hair for. You give your face a break. On the plus side.

You don't have to spray perfume in those 'where I want to be kissed' places. You don't bronze your body with shimmering pearls that sheen your shoulder blades and the plunge of your breasts. You don't paint your toenails in short sharp strokes of chip-resistant polish so that they will look pretty as they are flung over his shoulders in those 'how to have an orgasm every time! Guaranteed!' positions, even though you're the only one who can see your feet from that angle anyway. Now you pull on thick socks and your favourite worn-in Levis, an over-sized T-shirt you wore in school. You spritz your neck and wrists with no intention of going anywhere. You smell good for you, grab a cushion to cuddle up to, the one that still smells of his aftershave; the cushion you were held against and loved against and that you can now just about bear to have close. Now it smells of you. You give your heart a break. On the plus side.

You don't have to wear matching lingerie that will thrust up your bust, a must, or hold-ups that let cold air blast you on the streets as you long for your 90 denier tights and winter boots that would keep you the hell warm instead. You don't have to worry he'll show up unexpected and put on a full-face of make-up 'just in case' or wear the perfect 'daytime to nightime' outfit to the office. You don't have to stow away your everyday knickers at the back of the drawer, the ones you look perfectly fine in and you've been adored in before. Now you stand in front of the mirror, your naked body looking back at you in the cold morning light of your room. Your stomach is flat and you run your hands across hips that are childbearing and strong. You stand on your tiptoes to watch your calf muscles flex. Not bad, not bad at all. Now you shake your hair and raise your hands above your head, watch your breasts rise and your curls fall across the nipples. His loss, you think. You give yourself a break. On the plus side.

You don't have to share a bed, share your space. You don't have to create 'mood lighting', you don't have to pick up clothes strewn all over the floor. Your room is once again your boudoir. Your retreat from the world. You drape necklaces over mirrors and rummage through old photos in shoeboxes stored under the bed.

You don't have to look at his sleeping face on the pillow across from you as you fall asleep, the crow's feet beginning to appear at the corners of his restful eyes. His lips, that you could kiss right now right now slightly parted. You don't have to stroke his hair away from his forehead and trace his neck and shoulder, his brown skin tanned from summer sun. You don't have to turn around and nestle your back against his chest as he wraps night-time arms beneath you and over you, drawing you to him, your bangles and bracelets gathering at his wrist as you hold his hand in your own. You don't have to fall asleep to the sound of his breath, to the feel of his kiss on the back of your neck, to his thumb stroking your palm, your hair brushing against his face, falling down your back. You don't have to want to stay this way for always for always, never to leave this moment. Now you can just about cope with the absence you feel, with the loss and the hurt. You

*On the Plus Side:*

stick to your side, have a glass of wine on the nightstand and light candles in the grate of the fireplace just for you. You watch the walls flicker with light and wonder what he is doing right now right now. You fall asleep with your favourite book in your hand, and his presence on the periphery of your dreams. Words blur on pale pages and you are falling but not falling. Your heart doesn't break, after all. On the plus side.

---

## Lie.

You don't lie awake at night wanting to be anywhere but here, anywhere but next to this man. It must be the moon that wakes you; it's too bright. The curtains never keep it out. You take a trip to IKEA at the weekend. You enjoy watching him put all those pieces together, turning the screw, filling your house with disposable furniture. You wonder if that's why it's so popular. It can be dismantled quickly. You say this out loud and he asks you what you mean. I don't know, you say, I don't know. You imagine buying antique chests for each child you'll have together, their names engraved on the lids, their first things stored inside, lined up in the attic like the ones in *Little Women*. You read too much, he says. And you don't read enough, you think. You're a romantic, he tells you. I suppose I am, you say, and you shake your head, laughing at yourself.

All marriages are like this, or end up like this, you can't keep the passion forever, you settle, routine takes over; life takes over. Or is life taken over? You forget that thought, you stick it in the filing pile with the bills and the junk mail your son brings home from school in his book bag. You don't feel like your life's been hijacked; don't feel like a prisoner in your own home. You load the dishwasher and imagine a grainy video recording of you at the kitchen table, a masked man pointing a kitchen roll at your head: 'Please do anything they ask.'

You wonder if you're going mad. You get angry for no reason and for every reason. You tell him it's over, that you're walking. He looks at you with a pained expression, and you go over to him. I didn't mean it, I didn't mean it, you say. He strokes your hair, and watery mascara stains his shirt at the shoulder. You gave it all up to be with him. You want to shout at him, remind him, but you feel ridiculous. You'd have done anything, followed him anywhere. There was a gaping, empty space when he wasn't near. You craved for him. Pined for his body.

You wrote love letters on airmail paper, you sprayed perfume and made the ink smudge. He kept them all. You talked for hours on the phone, fell asleep cradling the receiver. *Where you go I go*. It was your choice, you weren't taken by force, you weren't bundled into a van with a hood over your head as tyres screeched and kicked up dust in the street as they sped you away. There weren't televised appeals for your return.

Now you crave and pine for that old apartment in the town that you loved before you loved him, the distant sea view; falling asleep to the sound of pounding bass beats from the pub up the road, shafts of light against wooden floorboards and the blue painting over the old butler sink. You search for the canvas in the garage; you open boxes and find things you'd forgotten. I don't feel fulfilled, you say to him over dinner. I don't feel anything. You're just having a bad time baby, he says. He smiles. Don't worry, you'll shake out of it, you always do. You nod, you twist spaghetti on your fork and watch it slide back off on to your plate.

You don't long for the time before he loved you. You have a child who clings to his neck and who he carries on his shoulders. You are the one taking the photos. You see them both through your lens; you twist it into focus. Smile, you say, smile. They are your beautiful boys. You are imagining it all. You can't be so selfish. You fill your time with things. You buy things. Organise things. See things. Book a holiday, a change of scenery is what you all need. You feel the Mediterranean heat on your face. You tan and you smile. You feel alone as you sit in familiar silence. You take yourself with you, wasn't that what your Mum used to say? This is comfortable, you tell yourself. This is knowing someone so well you don't have to say anything. I know your every thought, he says. You don't, you think.

You chose him for a reason. You don't ache inside for conversation, for laughter. You don't question why you are happier alone. You can't have everything in one person. You laugh with Rachel when she calls, you get drunk and talk for hours; you can get what you need from other people. You reassure yourself of this. That's the way life is. He tells you he loves you, and you smile. Say it back, he says, and you spin the ring on your finger over and over. Don't worry. Don't fret, he says.

He's so supportive, you tell anyone who will listen. He's always there, he wants me to succeed, you tell all your friends. *I don't know what I would do without him.* You imagine what you would do without him. A parallel existence runs real-time in your head. You're both so tired. He used to take you to bed in the middle of the afternoon; you'd forget the cleaning and the dismembered

*Lie.*

socks and weekend jeans in a pile by the washing machine. You want him to take you out; you want him to bring you home. You want him to pull you into the hallway in the dark, laughing together and then not laughing. You want someone to want you so badly that they have to have you. You fantasize. You banish the thought. You blush inside. Get a grip. You can't have that. You love the same old moves, the reliable orgasm, the spooning. You take the course of least resistance because there are worse things. He doesn't hit you. He perseveres. He's the one you stood and said you'd stay with, no matter what. You have his name; you gave him his son. You wished he hit you. You'd have a reason to go. You wonder if he wishes the same thing.

You go to work; days pass by, you plan meals and wash laundry. You probably need pills, he says, despairing. You go to the doctor and you tell him you cry, sometimes uncontrollably. He hands you a green slip and signs it with a steady hand. You stand in line at Boots and can't look the pharmacist in the eye. You take the packet home and put it in the medicine cupboard unopened. You pull a clean cup from the dishwasher. You make yourself a coffee. You wonder where the answer lies.

---

**Kelly Smith** was born in 1974. She read English as a mature student at Lucy Cavendish College, University of Cambridge and is now working on her first novel and a collection of short fiction. She lives in the city of Cambridge with her three children and likes to wear killer heels.

# Alistair South

## *Avoid Me Not*
*An excerpt from a short story*

**M**y father visits me in the hospital every day. Sometimes I hear him crying; sometimes he just asks me, very softly, why I've allowed this to happen. I never want him to know the truth. It's the only counsel I have with myself these days.

I will die soon: the doctors have told me so. My heart is very weak and my liver has rotted through. Dad tells me more often now how proud I used to make him. He says that he keeps a photograph of me in his wallet from the day I went to university. It was, he tells me, the proudest moment of all. I become angry then, and tell him to live his own life. I'll never see that photograph now, so perhaps I'll never appreciate what it means for him to hold it up against my face and see how I have changed. I was beautiful then. But now my hair has fallen out, and it seems my skin has taken on a dull metallic sheen. It was something I always thought might happen. I'm glad to have lost my eyesight; to see myself like this would destroy me.

It strikes me now that the picture my father carries – spilling over, so I'm told, with the vitality of youth – was my silent, unseen companion through the year of my life which enriched and ultimately destroyed me. I dream of it often: imagine it in a frame, set on a window ledge with a view out onto the sea. Sterling silver, the frame. You can almost see your face in it.

If I had to summarise the last year in one word, it would be absence. Absence of the only human being I had ever been close to; absence of the one thing I was looking for; and, perhaps most pertinently in my attempts to resolve the first two issues, my own absence from the majority of the Part 1A Natural Sciences Tripos.

Genius doesn't come along very often, which is why, I think, my Director of Studies was so reluctant to have me sent down from university. He even admitted, just before the end of year exams, that the faculty had given me every opportunity to keep my place on the course. It was somewhat insulting of him then to suggest that I would fail the exams if I didn't do some work. 'Work' is not a concept that sits well with minds such as mine. For the previous nine months I had achieved outstanding results in progress tests without having to attend a class. What infuriated my Director of Studies most of all, though, was that I'd been attending lectures and seminars in other faculties all year.

It had seemed a perfectly reasonable thing to do. The first year Natural Sciences syllabus was tired and unoriginal. I'd mastered the several methods of spectroscopy while I was still at school, and the quantum mechanics they taught for evaluating molecular structure wasn't worthy of the name. So I obtained a listing of all the available classes in the university, and set to work devising a programme of learning. I think this was the first time I felt Echo's presence, guiding me towards my destiny. I could sense her hand at work.

I never mentioned Echo to my Director of Studies, despite his repeated requests that I explain myself. He was a difficult, impatient man who seemed already to think that I was mentally imbalanced; I didn't want to give him another reason to refer me to the student counsellor.

Don't get me wrong: Echo wasn't just a voice in my head. I really had known her once, before I went off to university. We first met in her psychology class, at the start of the sixth form. She was sitting on her own, so I put my books down next to her. Even then I felt some kind of attraction – not sexual, but the ineluctable drag of polarised charges. The kind of intense empathy that can only exist between perfect opposites. It was probably the sight of all those sex-starved male eyes on her, this slender blonde-haired girl, submerged in a pool of libido. They would look at me that way sometimes, until I'd catch their eye and they'd turn away embarrassed. I've always had a knack for confusing boys. I smiled at Echo as warmly as I could. I think she appreciated that.

I was never one to make friends. People are changed by friendship; they steal away parts of each other until they become composites; an amalgam of corrupted identities. But after a few minutes of the class, when I was asked by the teacher to leave, I was surprised to find myself tearing a scrap from my jotter and writing: 'Naz – Common Room 4pm'. I slid it across the desk to Echo and left the room without looking back.

When I arrived that afternoon, Echo was already waiting. I bought her coffee in a plastic cup from the machine and then waited for her to say something.

There was a long silence.

Naz?

Yes.

Why did you do it? she asked.

What?

What? You know what. Skip your maths class just to sit through psychology. It doesn't make sense.

I told her; she seemed impressed.

Genius? she repeated, with a puzzled smile. Well, I've never met a genius before. I let her study my face; I watched her come under my thrall.

Echo didn't tell me a great deal about herself that day, and I don't recall being very much inclined to ask. But I became tired of answering questions about myself, and so I asked her about the rest of the class that I'd missed.

She had very little to say on this subject. They hadn't apparently learned any psychology at all in that first lesson, and had instead discussed the course outline for the year. I was becoming impatient with Echo; disappointed in myself for having given time to one so vacuous. I wanted to end the conversation, and so I asked a question to which she would surely be incapable of reply.

Tell me your thoughts, I said, on Jung's theory of the collective unconscious.

It was immediately clear that I had been mistaken. Echo had plenty to say for herself.

The Jungian collective unconscious, she began, is a primal species-wide substructure which –

I saw what she was doing.

– provides an archetype for the activities of the individual psyche? The composure visibly drained from her expression. Yes, I said, I've read the same textbook. But what do you think about it?

She avoided my eyes, looking instead at the plastic cup which she now held in both hands. It was empty, but for the pale foam that had dried into a sticky film against the sides. She squeezed until the cup split open, and I saw in her face a look of sadness, of vulnerability.

I don't know, she said.

I recognised something in her that afternoon that fascinated me. I made our coffee meetings in the common room a regular appointment, and despite her apparent humiliation on that first occasion she seemed to thrive on them. The conversations weren't limited to her psychology class, but covered literature, philosophy, science, even mathematics. Echo was tremendously well-read, almost on a level with me, but with a dearth of originality that I found simply mesmerising. I think she realised that I could teach her something no textbook ever could.

As the conversations went on, week by week, I watched the dynamic of our relationship crystallise. Whatever topic we discussed, she would provide a perfect reformulation of the arguments she had read in this article or that journal. I would let her speak, listen approvingly as she regurgitated some rote-learned theory. Descartes, she might tell me, failed in his Cogito to provide a cogent theory of self.

But he only failed, I might reply, if self and body must be coterminous.

And Echo would pause for a moment, rolling the words around in her mouth. Self and body ... Coterminous ... Yes, I think you must be right.


I came to realise that this was the only friendship which could ever sustain me. We spent evenings together, weekends. When the long vacations came around our meetings became more infrequent, but more precious. Often Echo would visit my house and we would walk along the stream at the bottom of the fields; she seemed rather to enjoy that, until, one evening late in August, I telephoned her at home and insisted that she come round at once.

She did, of course. I had known that she would.

We walked. The sky had the milky luminescence of a sunset's afterglow: a porcelain-blue shell bound to the dark earth by a brushstroke of sepia. I took Echo's hand in mine.

I had to call, I said after a while. One's own company can become so tiresome.

Echo's face was fragile in the half-light, translucent. Tiresome, she said. Yes, I suppose I do know what you mean.

I laid down the blanket I had carried under my arm and took out the glass tumblers which were rolled up inside it. The moon watched down blindly on us through its vast, empty-socketed eye.

Echo poured out some whisky, and then hesitated.

You don't find me tiresome, do you? She gave me a solemn, vulnerable look.

I filled the glasses to the brim with coke until they were quite black in the dimness of the night, and only the faintest of moonbeams played upon their surface.

Of course not, I said at last. No one understands me the way you do, Echo.

A smile broke out across her pale face; a single teardrop caught the light, skipped off her mouth. She wiped it away and wrapped her arms around me.

Can I tell you something? she asked.

What?

I didn't come because you asked me to. I came because I love you.

Moments passed; she pressed her body against mine.

Naz, she whispered, and I felt her breath upon my mouth. Naz, I said I love you.

I know, I said. I know.

I held her cheek in my hand and stroked away another tear with my thumb. She closed her eyes, and I felt the warmth of her skin near mine. Her lashes brushed my cheek; I let her lips caress blindly until they found my own and opened out, soft and moist.

I pulled away from her.

No, I said.

No? she asked, with a look more of bewilderment than despair. Why no?

I stared into her eyes, shimmering pools of darkness; in them the outline of my face loomed large, distorted.

Because it would be like fucking myself.

Echo recoiled.

Fucking myself, Naz? she repeated grimly through the tears. Fucking myself? Never have I seen a face collapse so utterly.

She struggled away from me and ran, ghosting through the fields until her silhouette had faded into the night. It was the last time I would ever see her.

I wrapped the blanket around my shoulders and looked up into the heavens. Alone upon a coruscating tapestry of stars the moon returned my gaze, and somewhere in the darkness an owl called out its mournful requiem:

Who? Who?

It was the most beautiful evening.

---

**Alistair South** was born in Northamptonshire in 1982. He read Classics at Christ's College, Cambridge before training as a chartered accountant. He is currently writing his first novel.

# Christie Watson

## White Gold
*Extract from a novel*

*B*lessing is twelve years old when her Mama brings home her white oil company *worker boyfriend, Dan. Her brother Ezikiel stays away, her Grandma ignores Dan, and her grandfather, Alhaji, and his second wife, Celestine, are desperate to impress. But Snap the dog has the most extreme reaction.*

It was late afternoon when Alhaji returned from the Executive Club. He climbed out of the Peugeot 405 to find Dan sitting on his veranda chair, reading an old copy of *The Pointer*. When Dan lowered the newspaper and revealed his white face, Alhaji's jaw dropped open.

'Welcome, welcome,' he said, after closing his jaw.

As he walked towards the veranda, Alhaji made no other sign that he was not expecting to see a white man sitting on his chair.

'Hello. Pleased to meet you, sir,' Dan said, shaking Alhaji's hand instead of kneeling or even saying, 'Doh.'

Alhaji kept his eyes on Dan the whole time, but I could feel the questions leaking from his skin:

Who is this oyibo?

Has he been sent from the Western Oil Company to interview me?

Do they have a crisis in quality management that requires my urgent attention?

Do they want my help in a diplomatic matter involving the fighting between Izons and Itsekiris?

Has Tony Blair or George Bush sent this man to deliver their personal reply to my letter (which I wrote some weeks ago)?

I giggled, causing the eye contact between them to disappear. Mama stepped forward and opened her mouth to speak just as Celestine said, 'This is Timi's boyfriend. Dam.'

'Actually it's Dan,' said Dan, but nobody was listening.

We just watched as Alhaji took his Marmite out from his medicine bag and unscrewed the lid. Dan frowned and looked at Mama. Then Alhaji sat in the chair, and applied some Marmite to both of his temples, rubbing slowly, closing his eyes. It was not a good sign.

We all sat down. Celestine served tea from a chipped china tea set that I had not seen before. My cup and saucer clanked together as though they did not fit.

I did not look Dan directly in the eyes, but I could feel him looking at me. I moved my arm slightly to cover a tiny hole in my T-shirt. 'Are you enjoying school, Blessing?'

I looked up at Mama. She nodded very slightly.

'I like school, sir.' I watched them all to see if I had given the right answer.

Mama sat back into her chair, and smiled. 'She's a good student, straight As, but not interested in books. I keep trying to encourage her.'

I relaxed. My body felt more comfortable with Mama talking about me, than with Dan talking to me. But I still had my arms crossed. Alhaji stopped rubbing Marmite onto his temples. He turned his good ear towards Dan.

'What's your favourite subject?' Dan asked.

I saw the shadow of Grandma in the doorway. I felt brave at once. 'I am training to be a birth attendant. That is my favourite subject.'

Dan nodded his head politely. Mama groaned and put her hand over her eyes. Celestine sucked her teeth. The shadow of Grandma became taller and bigger, and filled the doorway.

I watched Dan for the rest of the time. He did not say much. He listened to Celestine's stories about European Fashions and Professional Town Mourning and Giving Birth to Twins, and he listened to Alhaji, who was hushing Celestine to bring the conversation back to Petroleum Engineering. Nobody mentioned politics. Or religion. Or Grandma's shadow in the doorway.

'What are your interests, Dam?' Alhaji eventually asked. 'What team do you support?' His voice sounded squeaky and high as if it was being pushed out too quickly.

Dan looked at the sky and I thought religion would come up, after all, but it did not. 'Oh, I'm not a football fan,' he said.

Alhaji looked puzzled. 'You prefer MBA?'

'No, no,' Dan laughed. 'Ornithology,' he said. 'Birds.'

We all fell quiet. We waited for an explanation but none came.

Eventually Mama spoke, 'Dan's a keen bird-watcher.'

Alhaji scratched his chin. 'What do you watch them for?' he said.

Dan's smile increased. 'I've always been fascinated with birds since I had my first binoculars when I was four. You know, I watch their habits, record the unusual species. It's really a fascinating hobby. Really fascinating. But of course, I don't get much time at home. Never enough hours in the day.' Dan laughed. He looked around at us all. We had our mouths wide open. Except Mama. She was smiling and nodding, smiling and nodding.

'It sounds funny when you try and explain it,' said Dan.

Nobody spoke. Alhaji had stopped rubbing his chin. A large frown between his eyebrows was splitting his head into two. Eventually a bird flew over us.

Alhaji jumped up. 'Look! There's one!' He pointed to the sky excitedly. Dan smiled. 'Do you need a pen and paper to record it?' Alhaji asked.

'Oh no. Thanks.'

A few seconds later and another bird flew over us. Then another. 'There! Two birds! Get a pen for him. Quick!'

'Please, no, no, thank you. No, honestly. No, no thank you,' said Dan. 'I only record the unusual species.'

Alhaji sat down, and folded his arms. 'Well, why say something when you mean something else? You said you like to record the birds. Most species here are unusual. You are in Nigeria.' Alhaji said Nigeria as in three parts: Ni ge ria. His shoulders shrugged up slightly, and did not unshrug for the rest of the day.

Celestine refilled our cups, and we all slurped our tea. All except Dan. Dan was a silent tea drinker. But I did notice his cup and saucer were also clanking together.

The Twins suddenly screamed from the Boys' Quarters.

Celestine tutted loudly then smiled at Dan, before walking away so slowly and with such hip movement that she reminded me of a riverboat during a storm. Grandma walked past with a bucket and went back to her garden area where she started pouring water on her herbs and cacti, while she whistled loudly. I had never heard her whistle before.

Dan was still smiling until Snap came running towards us, and saw him. He growled for the first time in his life and ran at Dan's leg, which was uncovered by his very short trousers.

Snap opened his mouth and bit.

Dan cried out, but not very loudly. Twin One could still be heard above him from the Boys' Quarters.

***

Ezikiel had returned very late, long after Dan had left. 'I don't want to hear about the oyibo,' he said. He touched his face where Mama had slapped him. But he remained nearby while Celestine gave the day's details, and he played with the basketball, weaving it in and out of his long legs as he listened. I kept my hula-hoop on my lap. I did not want to upset Grandma further, but I could not wait to put it around my middle.

Snap was lying pining and wailing under the veranda. Boneboy was with him, stroking him and singing to him as if Snap was a baby. Alhaji had had to kick Snap to get him off Dan's leg. Snap was not a dog used to being kicked.

'He bit him hard,' Celestine said.

We all shook our heads. 'Poor man,' we all muttered. 'Terrible thing to happen.'

Then Grandma leaned forward. 'I bet he thought it was a bone.'

'What?' said Alhaji.

'Well. That oyibo's leg,' continued Grandma. 'All white and thin. I bet poor Snap thought he was lucky to find such a bone.'

A few seconds passed while we looked at one another. Then Celestine let out a laugh. Then Grandma. Then Alhaji. Then me. The laughter built up so much, tears were running down our faces. We laughed so hard we had to hold our bellies. We could not stop even when Ezikiel said, 'I wish Snap had bitten him harder, and broken his leg.'

We could not stop even when Mama stood up then stormed into the house.

---

**Christie Watson** won the *Malcolm Bradbury Bursary* at UEA, where she recently completed her first novel. She has previously published in *Mslexia* and *Wasafiri*.

# Naomi Wood

## *The Godless Boys*

*Note: England has deported its atheists; the Malraux family have interred themselves in an attic.*

\*\*\*

At night Granny played tag with her grandsons and confused it for kiss-catch. Nights like this descended into bawdy-horror and Mother would have to pull her off by the shoulders while Granny's lips were all lust-leery and wet and Mother would say, 'No! Not on the lips! Not with the boys, Clare!' Granny even did the same thing to Margaret, spurred by all this demented lust popping up in her veins. Later in the night she might slip into bed with any grandchild she could find, or rattle at the bolted door: 'Please. Please. Let me go, Malraux, it's time to get these threads, you see these threads they won't thread themselves and it's my lungs they're getting squashed in here and my eyes, I'm going blind! Can't you see I can't see you? And there's a man out there who's waiting for me with flowers who I quite urgently need to get to, if only, Mr Malraux, to organize a rendezvous. I've got to get the thread because it was he I was knitting the scarf for. It's the colour of grass though it doesn't smell of it. And music! I need music! I'm off to the vaudeville. I'm off to the vaudeville with Henry Agonistes and you're making me late!'

Margaret's father would stand in front of the doorway and let her push her fingers into his stomach and when she had stopped babbling the air was empty of noise for a bit while Granny prodded her fingers into him until he took her hands in his and curled them up like small doves. 'Not now, Mother. We're not allowed out yet. Shh now. Please quieten down, the children are frightened.'

Margaret sometimes heard her father crying. Before, especially last year, it had always been her mother, but since they had moved into the attic it was always her father crying now. Her father cried and it sounded horrible coming from a man like that because he couldn't do it quietly. And then Granny would shout, 'Oh do be quiet, Bernard! You are making such a fuss!' Sometimes Margaret heard her parents making love, or at least, even when they did manage to cover the sound, watch her father discreetly thrust against her mother under the too-thin blanket. She could tell her brothers were watching too.

Sanity was the stupid thing in the attic. The other Malrauxs lusted for the release Granny was allowed: to be mad, to be crazy, to be at their wits' end; but they all went placidly enough. 'I am not an animal, Bernard,' Granny often said, 'I should not be asked to be kept like one.' This was Granny Malraux, who had brought up her sons on pleasures and kickshaws and on the muscle of it; who loved the vaudeville, and music; who saw the trees on the avenues and wanted to climb them right to the top; who loved warmth and summer, ginger and figs; who spat at them when they spat at her; who bared her breasts once in a church service (wrinkled old dugs and the children sniggered); who carried placards; who was slaked by the fists and the vigour and the crowds, pushing up and pushing against each other – boots into shins and shanks and thrown punches and women and men pushing up and pushing against each other and leering for the good fight! Rather she should die! Rather she should spar for a rise, for rocks, for batons, water cannon, effigies burnt, an eyelid caught and bloody and ribs stamped by a boot! At least this! At least a bursting forth! To end up like this, an old husk in a twenty square foot attic, forbidden to go to a world she loved and feasted on and saw. Now she did not even see! Rather she should die! Rather she should go mad!

Margaret woke one night and saw the amber light curve across Granny's face. She had the gun pointing through two of the slats, whispering 'Marauding holy bastards'. The gun was cocked, and Granny's eyes squinted over the barrel, her mouth fallen open in expectation. 'Dad,' Margaret said, 'Granny's got the gun.' Her father prised the gun from her hands and led Granny back to her sleeping bag. When she started snoring, her father placed the gun under the loose floorboard.

The seasons snapped, and the Malrauxs found themselves in heat. There was the sweat, the fungal infections, the problems of damp. Spores appeared on the ceiling. Inside a book Margaret discovered a mould had started to climb. It was *The Adventures of Heron Murphy*, by Angela Black, and Margaret wanted to cry when she saw the grey bloom on the pages.

By summer, Granny's memory had become a shipwreck, a home for dark, unnameable things. Granny called the family the names of lost friends or sweethearts or any name she plucked out of the air. More than once, Margaret was called Henry Agonistes. Granny slept by Margaret's sleeping-bag, because she menaced the boys so with her misplaced lust, but still she would slip an arm around Margaret, insidious, like a squid's tentacle. She would draw her body closer and whisper into her ear. 'Henry. I need out of here. England's greatest Decimalist, interred in an attic! Come and get me, Henry. The thread for your scarf is nearly ready, but Mr Malraux believes we're turtling up in here and it will all come to fruit, though I don't believe him. I had a boy before him. It took me four days to push him out of me, and then they fed him to the fires and I never saw his face. How! Richard! There. I'd knit a scarf for him if I could but then I don't know where they put him. His neck is cold. Please help me find him.'

Sometimes she sat at the windowsill and murmured and it was as if her whispers might bring down empires.

Margaret prayed nightly, but did not put the words into the dark, since she was not sure what her family might think of this. But, she thought, if there was doing nothing and doing something, even if the something wasn't even there, then the doing something was better than the doing nothing. On the outside, she had worn the black cloth spine, but on the inside she didn't know whether she didn't believe.

The only space in the attic was in time. Margaret tried just to watch her thoughts, watch them bud and blossom and then die, like the sped-up footage of flowers she had seen in her biology class. Time-lapse photography, that was what it was called. The attic was lapsed time, it had slipped into slowness. In fact, time was almost dead dead dead. In the space of hours, she watched her thoughts, and watched her thoughts watching her. Sometimes, she listened for something else. Occasionally, she thought she detected something: some drift of belief; the caress of God in her ears. It was never in words but in a feeling, like when her father stroked her hair, a feeling of being protected by someone far greater than herself. If God was anything he was her father's hands.

That hot noon in June, when the Calverts had left the lunch through the letterbox door, that was when all their backs were turned on Granny, who had been sitting at her sill all day, staring out between the slats. All night she had been murmuring conspiracies; all day she continued. That morning Margaret watched her wet mouth and the dark hair on the upper lip and wondered if she would get dark hair there when she was an old woman. To become an old woman seemed impossible to her; she could not imagine herself transforming into someone who looked like Granny. She could not imagine living sixty more years; how long would sixty years take to get there?

'If there wasn't a place to go for him,' Granny said, 'I would have gone, it would have been simple. I could have gone there in place of him. An outrage! That will never happen again but it did because all of them were lost, and why was it, it was because I wasn't like them. They never would have had me. I am all blood and bone and none of what is mine is his.' Her hands fluttered about her head about the air like birds. She had a fat tear dribbling down her cheek. Suddenly Granny stood up and shouted, 'Why is it there is no way out until the sea comes up to your EARS?!' and she strode the three or four paces necessary to get to the floorboard, dislodged the black French handgun and discharged the bullet into the vault of her skull.

In Margaret's mind darkness comes and it closes the ear that hears the word. This ear is shot or submerged or clogged with algal blooms and a ringing sound comes in instead and it closes down the drift of the words so that all she hears is a huge and resounding whirr. Her flesh is of fish. God is a bubble leaving her mouth and popping on the surface of things. She hears Granny and sees her again put the gun to her temple, 'Why is it there is no way out until the sea comes up to your EARS?!' and she sees it all again as if Granny has fractured time and put in an echo of herself. Granny is the loop of the flower – the bud and the bloom and the rot – budding and blooming and rotting, over and over again – Margaret sees the gun, hears the EARS, the fall, the red bloom at the temple. Now Granny has lapsed from time. 'All the way up to your EARS!' and the ear itself inside Margaret closes; the world is put dark; and the soft drift of words will not come again.

Her mother said, 'It is finished, then.' And then the light comes.

The door is smashed open. Her father held the gun but his shakes shook the gun and when the police appeared he did nothing but drop it and it dropped with a tinny sound to the attic's floorboards. They hooded their heads. Her wrist was grabbed by her mother, it felt like her mother's fingers. 'Do not let go of them, Christine!' That was her father speaking. They were hurried down the stairs and Margaret, despite the terror, felt a small joy at the strangeness of movement and dustless air. Outside, even beneath the hoods, the new light was unbearable. They were put in a van, her mother and Margaret and her brothers, and outside she could hear people hitting the metal with their fists. Margaret stayed close to her mother who had not let go of her wrist and so she assumed she had not let go of her brothers' either. The engine was gunned. There was a woman's voice, it sounded like it belonged to a very thin woman, it sounded crazy and wolfish, and she shouted, 'Get ye gone! Across the seas with yous! Get yous gone, ye godless ones!'

When the van stopped, hours later, they were at the pier. The sun was coming down. The sea took in the colours and carved them up on the waves and the waves scissored the dying lights so that the sea was the colour of autumn up on its surface. Even with Granny, even with the wait for her father, Margaret stood and watched and was over-whelmed by the astonishing colour of it all.

---

**Naomi Wood** grew up in Hong Kong and has lived in England and France. This extract is from her first novel, *The Godless Boys*.

# Poetry

*Introduction by* **George Szirtes**

*Janani Ambikapathy*

*Catherine M. Brennan*

*James E.C. Buxton*

*Mark Harrell*

*Aundi Howerton*

*Meirion Jordan*

*Kelly Kanayama*

*Nicole Lyn Lawrence*

*Ben Parker*

*Genevieve Schiffenhaus*

*Sarah Wallis*

Poetry is not forensic science though poets have been called scientists of the emotions. Their task, as such, is to explore and name new states of being in the world. It is language that takes them beyond the known, the purely subjective – for the world for a poet is, and has to be to a great extent, that which presents itself in, and as, language. But it need not be particularly difficult or abstruse; it needs, rather, to be a 'full' language, one filled to near-bursting, somehow straining against life.

There are an infinite number of ways of achieving this, some, apparently, very simple, some highly formal, some swirling their way towards us as fractures of various sorts. Since poetry at UEA does not set out to teach any one of these specific ways, it relies on intelligence, on intense reading, and on the sixth sense at the very edge of language to act as both maker and editor.

This year is a bumper crop for poetry. Some here have already written a first book, or have a book about to appear, or are ready for the world of books. Beyond that of course is the setting out on a fruitful, exciting voyage, and they have all done that, from the carved historical sonnets of Mark Harrell, through the restless narratives of Aundi Howerton, the off-centre anecdotal narratives of Ben Parker, the hybrid historical-speculative fiction-novelistic prose and verse poems of Meirion Jordan, the gripping humane lyricism of Gena Schiffenhaus, the wit and intensity of Catherine Brennan, the eloquent, troubled, meditative poems of Kelly Kanayama, the bright abrasive points of tension in the work of Nicole Lyn Lawrence, the cultural crossover electricity of Janani Ambikapthay, the observation and playfulness of Sarah Wallis and the equally playful part-documentary, part-state-of-the-moment narratives of James Buxton.

Each one of them is moving down a trajectory of his or her own. The only demand is that they should be intelligent, sensitive, informed and properly adventurous trajectories. And so they are.

GS

# Janani Ambikapathy

*Shine, East Coast Road*
*Sky crawler's soporific treatise*
*Krishna Biraha*
*Muse*
*The Quick Fix*
*Silk City, East Coast Road*

### Shine, East Coast Road

We who were clusters of beedi haze,
grating and dis-
integrating
small puffs, expert rings,
white dwarfs and
        *endless*
milky whites of scaly wings.

We who brought up Buddha,
at street corner tea shops,
the sooty dogs were howling
skinny for biscuits. Our flip-flops of
Zen, almost never right fitting.

We who stretched in tangled labyrinths,
contorted into peace perfect shapes
of sun scape.
Curled up, old curses squealed dark,
interest free karmic debts were unfolding.

We who were sequentially
appearing and dis-
appearing in bits,
occurring elsewhere in part blemishes.

We who one day froze in the stark yellow gas light, feeding the scavengers dead
moth bits.

**Sky crawler's soporific treatise**

He crawled the skies with trekking gear and a paint brush between his teeth. He kneaded one fistful of cloud at a time, eroded their volatile cores, drained them of their silly fluffy exuberance and pulled out the excessive white of summer, until lean, long black sticks of clouds remained. He steadily hinged these pieces together and piled skeletons across the sky.

Nobody looked up and guessed shapes anymore. Kids screamed, too many deaf dogs roamed the streets. People started living with a lower perspective.

Then one day someone saw god on the moon. That was it, he quit. He hung up his boots over a pair of pallid limbs and retired to Iggy Pop and scotch.

**Krishna Biraha**

On her couch, the emptied halo hovered, Krishna!
She burned. Still yearning embers, whispered Krishna!

She drove all night, to reach the ever nearing flute
notes. Sudden peacock plumes clattered, Krishna!

Tears leaned over to peek at her dead memories
A tiny apparition ran to her – Amma! she heard, Krishna!

Her whisky fingers sang husky on his tender spine;
His blue on her breasts lingered, Krishna.

His darkness waited in the parking lot, juggling his
chakra, barely visible, her pining, feathered Krishna.

A rotting mould of cells in the ICU, she danced at
dusk in naked orchards, with her sculptured Krishna.

**Muse**

'Suicide calculated well in advance, I thought, no spontaneous act of desperation.'
**Thomas Bernhard**, *The Loser (2006, Vintage)*

Today, when you woke
did you find sprightly red gashes, tiny bleeds,
a scratched belly, little scorched fissures?
I was as careful as I could be.
No traces, no permanant scars.
It is never easy stealing lives.

I had to gently pull it from under your

Duvet,
fear, skin
blood, pain, bones
spasms, sinews
breath.

**The Quick Fix**

She was a oneminutegoddess
(in times when noodles take two)
I didn't ask. Too grateful for the
instant redemption.

A snoring priest, flies and
my mother's faith hummed
at low frequencies, like
gentle tremors from the earth.

An after hours crowd of
bearded tramps raked
the muddy yard for
cigarette butts.

I peered through rusty bars
into their sacred darkness and musty chambers.
The gods were sleeping, convuluted.
Mouths agape. Eyes soldered open –
by lids and lashes.

## Silk City, East Coast Road

The sounds emerged from their
lithe bones,
from under the water.
A damp and salty undersong.
Fishes licked the crevices of
their sculpted bodies.

Sanctum bells washed
ashore accepted as
unheard scraps of silence.
Domes that peeked hushed
beneath furtive boats.

Until the comfortable coastline
moved,
swallowing what existed,
spewing what was denied.

Walls turned up at crest ends
too tall for now,
too awkward for reason.

The half-eaten city now had
an upright lion, an eroded king
and six more temples below.

---

**Janani Ambikapathy** was born in Kolkata in 1984. She graduated in English and journalism from Christ College, Bangalore and has worked as a freelance writer, documentary editor, and theatre actor. She is currently working on a sequence of poems that follow a journey down the East Coast Road from Chennai.

# Catherine M. Brennan

*Hell Raising*
*Elysian Fields Employment Agency*
*Shooting the dogs, 1915*
*Skin (v)*
*Darkness: marked time*
*High Chapeaurelle*

## Hell Raising

*In August 2006, the International Astronomical Union*
*decided that Pluto was no longer a planet.*

Last orders at the Lethean Lounge,
and he's asking for some concoction
the bartender's never heard of, a cocktail
based on pomegranate juice, but the whole
of it, pips and pith, the lot: any second now,
he'll be raising a glass
to the memory of his ex-wife.

A stranger makes the mistake
of asking for a light, it sparks
a flood of invective: the magnificence
of Phlegethon, great rolling currents of fire
he once commanded, the days
when he was a contender.

They've heard it before.
Saturn gestures to Mars, Venus rises
in the hopes of stopping Pluto before
it's too late: but it is too late,

he grips his listener's lapels,
promises him an experience
he'll never forget, a hell of a time,
it'll be out of this world....

This can only end one way: Saturn rings
for a taxi to take them further along the belt
of bars spread out along the waterfront
in a last ditch effort to preserve the reputation
of at least some of the Olympians.

Mercury's quick to divert the stranger,
and somehow it's enough and they're out
of there, like bats out of hell, as Neptune
remarks, unleashing a sea
of unhappy memories.

It will be dark hours yet before Pluto reaches
the softer side of nostalgia, starts reminiscing
to anyone he can corner
about what it was like in the days when Cerberus
was a pup, all lolloping limbs and slaver,
but if you knew how to handle him,
loyal to the core.

The Olympiad heave a galactic
shudder. After this, he'll go from karaoke
to verse: from *Highway to Hell* to *Dante's Inferno*,
each Canto broken by a pause for personal digression,
and his usual refrains: to have the best of intentions,
and *What is now proved was once only imagin'd*
which seems to give him comfort
in ways they never understand.

### Elysian Fields Employment Agency

*There Charon stands, who rules the dreary coast –*
*A sordid god: down from his hoary chin*
*A length of beard descends, uncomb'd, unclean;*
*His eyes, like hollow furnaces on fire;*
*A girdle, foul with grease, binds his obscene attire.*
**Virgil**, *Aeneid Book 6*


She's coldly polite, inflexible. He is, after all,
the last client of the week. There are procedures
to be followed if he seriously wants a job, which
she somehow Doubts Very Much. But it's not her place
to cast judgement: she'll find a vacancy
to match his skills base, give him the address.
After that it's down to him.

His references are dubious: non-committal statements
from customers who'd tipped him in the past;
the odd long-haul traveller claiming enjoyment
of the return journey. Nothing from his actual company,
Underworld Incorporated. Apparently
the Chief Executive's in a state of deep depression
since they folded, has taken redundancy hard.
No such thing as a job for life any more, she thinks.

He's mumbling now, making her lean forward,
strain to hear the words. So unclear, he might as well
be speaking Greek. Her smile freezes, rictus like.
He's asking her to go with him: absurd. Really,
she can't be expected to ferry him around town
in search of cash and a quick pint at the Golden Bough.

*Catherine M. Brennan*

His arrogance is breathtaking. As if the job
were more than a temporary cab driving gig. She's not
even sure of his licence. Not that he'll get one foot in the door
with that beard, those clothes. Honestly, you'd think
he was past caring.

And the dog: frankly, the dog will have to go.
It sprawls, monstrously lazy. Looks as if it would snap
more than sticks in any game of fetch. Deeply lidded eyes
fixed on her the whole time, fiery saucers drawing her in,
great pools of darkness from which there can be no return.........
no, it has to go.

The clock is poised: 16.59. She smiles brightly,
terminates the interview. Time and tide...

**Shooting the dogs, 1915**

There is nothing painful in the grind
of white, as ice embraces the hull.

Nights creak and groan as a ridge
settles. The Endurance keels.

Gun shots fracture, echo the crack
of the mast as it splits, falls. Forget

sensation: rough heat of a red tongue,
brush of frozen particles on wiry fur.

Let cold paralyse until the black days
break with the swell of warmer currents,

the floe disintegrates. Then, the thaw
begins of what has been compact

as pack ice: the place where trust
and fear lie tethered to the same spike.

**Skin (v)**

Unknown
It's a gamble, with uneven odds,
and the outlook doesn't look favourable
from this side of the track. It might have
been better to back a different horse,
but you can't always tell until they race
whether the outsiders have it in them.

One thing's for certain: when the last nag
has stumbled across the finishing line,
at least one of us will taste regret,
dig hands deep into empty pockets,
rummage for a coin that isn't there.

We may well wish we'd stayed at home,
or placed the money elsewhere,
given more thought to the choices
before making the commitments. As if
the day could dawn when an honest bookie
would give advice and we'd soberly listen.

We take these chances, push the season
to the limit. Ignore the shade, and burn.

### Darkness: marked time

Finally, let me kill you honestly
on the winter shores of Brobdingnag, where
you may claim your proper form, all flesh
and sweating bulk as you obscure the sky

and sun. In your shade I'll draw my right arm,
strain sinews, pluck the last arrow
from the quiver. I'll aim true,
seize this one chance to skewer the muscle

that pumps dark blood through your curses
of veins. You'll dance an airless stagger,
pierced at the heart of the matter
by something small and unexpected.

You'll fall. A blaze of sky will arch above.
I'll wipe my brow. Unclench my fist. Drop the bow.

*Catherine M. Brennan*

## High Chapeaurelle

It was six hats at dawn. Theodore Fedora shivered
into centre position, arbiter of what was to follow.
Dust obscured the polished shoes of the first arrivals:
Trilby & Bowler, punctual as ever, rolled newspapers
tucked beneath their arms, only the headlines visible.
Gloved hands turned pages in unison, flickers of impatience
restrained. Still no sign of an adversary on the horizon.
The waiting crowd milled, uncertain. No honour
in concession, this duel had to be fought to its bloody
conclusion. Meanwhile, on the other side of town,
Lacey Feathers dropped a hail spot veil into place, took
a last deadly look in the mirror. Her pistols might
fail, but she would remain ahead in immeasurable
ways: fashionably late, and dressed to kill.

---

**Catherine M. Brennan** was born in Dublin and lives in London. Her first collection, *Beneath the Deluge*, was published by *Cinnamon Press* in February 2008, after receiving their *Collection Award*. Her work has appeared in *Iota*, *The New Writer*, *Envoi*, *Smoke*, *Other Poetry*, *Pulsar* and *Dream Catcher*.

# James E.C. Buxton

*Ex am*
*You Never Keep Your Word*
*Section 32 or Putting Words in Your Mouth*
*Payphone*
*Marathon*
*Soulmates*

**Ex am**

Sweat slopes the smudged nib
He presses so hard his thumb slips
He wants to push himself away

All words written endure
The curved angular graft
Stitches the silence

Ticks encompass the class
The needle needs a point

The nib glints through a passage
Penned in he gulps in a cul-de-sac

Wood splinters beneath the page
So strong he embosses the back

Tiny scores on the grainy table
Notches on a tally stick

**You Never Keep Your Word**

What is my word the word I never keep?
Is it a word that causes me restless sleep?

Did I lose my word between another's sheets?
Or was it not actions but the word I repeat?

And was it really your word meaning mine
Or was it our word I did malign?

Never? But did I ever have forever
I see too many times means never

Unreliable, is this my name?
Should I not speak but walk in shame?

And this excuse it falters inside
Will this make your anger subside?

No, I know it is my word I should keep
But I gave it to you and now you weep

What can I do as it no longer belongs to me?
Now I see it is not my word but what I did agree.

**Section 32 or Putting Words in Your Mouth**

You have the right to remain silent
You have been charged with a criminal offence
And you are guilty till proven innocent

You have been accused of possession with intent
Do you have anything to say in your defence?
You have the right to remain silent

We believe this is not the first incident
We will search the premises for evidence
And you are guilty till proven innocent

Please Mr Buxton if you are resistant
Force will be necessary, at your expense
You have the right to remain silent

Right, Andy cuff him, no use getting violent
You're only going to make this more intense
And you are guilty till proven innocent

Or we can have your co-operation spent
Helping our inquiries to make some sense
You have the right to remain silent
And you are guilty if proven innocent

**Payphone**

Yes blud, wuss up?
**Sound bruv, iss al'rite**
**Jus 'oldin it down**
Safe, u got anyfing lef?
**Nah, in a bit, call me back**
**gotta geddit off dis head**

Oi I got no cred, bell me ahead
**Yo, I'll drop u a line when I pick up**
Safe I'll hold out till u call back
You is gonna bell back ... right?
**Standard blud, u won't get lef**
**out, jus keep it lock down**

Shall I come down?
**Nah, best not, u don't know dis head**
Oi jus make sure ders sum lef
**Blud jus chill, u know me, hold up**
**you got ma back right?**
Safe bro I got your back

So when u gonna be back?
**Look man I's gonna go down**
**like now, I'll bell u right**
**after, den come straight ahead**
*Excuse me could you hurry up*
*I haven't got all night left*

Can't u see I is on di phone, best if u lef
*But I need to call my wife back.*
I don't give a shit. U wanna get bruck up?
*Sorry? Look, all the other phoneboxes are down*
So fuckin what! u ain't ahead
of me, so u best step down, u ged me right?

**Oi!, who u chattin to? jus bell me alright**
Nah, u call me, I aint got no cre … eh eh e's lef!
Man, I is on de phone to this 'ead
and you is all over ma back
*Look I'm sorry I may not be down*
*with your lingo but he clearly hung up*

Right dats it, I told u back down
but nah, u posh cunts act like u always ahead
we de ones get lef out! Now u get bruck up.

**Marathon**

After Auden's *Airman's Alphabet* ( I still can't catch him)

Amateur –
        First to flag
        and flustered face
        and most of masses

Bang –
        Signal for start
        and sound of shot
        and got from gun

Cramp –
        Sudden spasm
        and searing strain
        and pang of pain

Distance –
        Miles to move
        and met with motion
        and always ahead

Endurance –
        Seriousness to sustain
        and savage suffering
        and length of lasting

Foot –        Pad of pressure
              and pusher of paves
              and burst blisters

Glycogen –    Granules in muscles
              and giver of glucose
              and emerges as energy

Heart –       Pace of passion
              and personal pitch
              and throb of thunder

Instep –      Aching arch
              and angle of agony
              and bridge over bumps

Jog –         Action of athletes
              and able advance
              and sensibly steady

Knee –        Solid support
              and set in synovial
              and hinge of haste

Ligament –    Elastic exertion
              and elongated by exercise
              and joiner of joints

Metamarathon –  Length of language
                and letters in lungs
                and alphabetical athletics

Numb –        Result of repetition
              and reaction to reason
              and varnish of vanquished

Oxygen –         Abundant in air
                 and absorbed by alveoli
                 and bronchial branches

Pheidippides –   Messenger from Marathon
                 and arrived at Athens
                 and dropped dead

Qualify –        Proof of passion
                 and position in pack
                 and given as guarantee

Road –           Clear of cars
                 and crowded by competitors
                 and repels runners

Stitch –         Side-splitting
                 and stabbing sensation
                 and breathe belatedly

Time –           Eternally temporary
                 and tense ticking
                 and personal position

Urge –           Individual division
                 and decisive decision
                 and power to prevail

Vowel –          Announcement of agony
                 and assertion of anger
                 and cry of completion

Water –          Splash on sweat
                 and saturate saliva
                 and quaffable quench

| | |
|---|---|
| X-ray – | Sight of skeleton |
| | and surgeon's slideshow |
| | and bare bones |
| Year – | Period of preparation |
| | and prolonged patience |
| | and annual anticipation |
| Zone – | Mental mode |
| | and marshalled by members |
| | and objective to overcome |

**Soulmates**

Brunette, 40s slim, attracted to dark-eyed
Romeo still seeking fun and romance
For countryside and animal love
Looks equally good in walking boots and lipstick.

Still seeking Romeo, fun and romance
Seaside Venus requires demi-God
Lipstick, walking boots and equal good looks
For conversation and meaningful r/ship.

Demi from Venus requires seaside God,
Or Martian for brief encounter and
Meaningful conversation in spaceship
With attentive M without children.

Brief encounter Martians or a
Long kiss goodnight with
Attentive M without children
With sexy smile and naughty twinkle.

Goodnight kiss with long
Time model WLTM solvent male
With naughty sexy smile and twinkle
For comfort and security.

Solvent Time™ Model WLTM male
Something wonderful will happen!

For comfort and security
It has been worth the wait.

*James E.C. Buxton*

Something wonderful will happen
Completely different, one in a million
It has been worth the wait
One call could change everything.

Completely different, one in a million
Tarnished knight seeks F to quest for
One call could change everything
Must have crass SOH & bumbling social graces.

Tarnished knight seeks maiden
To rescue for happy ever after
Must have bumbling SOH & crass social graces
Must enjoy paragliding, scale military figurines.

For Happy ever after rescue
Front row seats, fresh bed sheets
Must enjoy paragliding, scale military figurines
Yorks moor, dance floors, Indian food.

Front row seats, fresh bed sheets
Red wine, walks by the Tyne
Yorks moor, dance floors, Indian food
Seeks honest, F, 48, loves walking, poetry.

Red wine, walks by the Tyne
Countryside and love? For animal
Love, honest poetry, seeks walking F, 48,
Attracted to dark-eyed Brunette.

---

James E.C. Buxton, 22, London-born, Norwich-based, UEA English and Drama graduate, seeks poets, publishers and press for meaningful long-term relationships. His collection of poems, *22*, is available at www.theillegiblebachelor.com.

# Mark Harrell

*Six Men*
*(i) François Villon*
*(ii) Kamo no Chomei*
*(iii) Picasso at La Californie*
*(iv) Caligula*
*(v) Peter the Great*
*(vi) Hemingway in Madrid*

**Six Men**

O, what a piece of work is a man ...
(Hamlet)

**(i)**  François Villon

His gift sought him out, bent over his desk,
skulking mongrel, head on paws, uneasy
with the Angelus. Turnip-head, dagger-
carved harelip, a villain's eyes, he became
all Paris, the tentacled city; bore his
laurels well: poet, theologian, thief.
The Mule toasted him, funny, lovesick, ung
bon follastre, Mistress Overdone quipped...
From his crabbed pen leaked the real stuff, hard-edged,
not carved from butter: he played cuckold to
each vanity, loving filths like onion skins
overlaid; not wholly foolish, never quite sage.
Dead at thirty-two. He was his own Testament.
In the end his neck knew what his weighty arse meant.

**(ii)** Kamo no Chomei

Not one to make office, and O, how
Kyoto burned! He removed himself hill-
ward, in the dead empress's steps, far, yet
near enough; snow weighed heavy on the
old Ohara bus. – Summer, and a summer
and a summer ... He watched the crystal rain-
drops flop from the eaves of his shack – foolish-
ness to invest in a habitat! He boiled
himself some tea, examined a snail, stared
westward over mauve clouds of wisteria
praying, 'I am river foam'; tears at his sleeve ...
Gradually he vanquished the demon
wine, but the karma of longing remained,
so teaching him doubt that he could believe.

**(iii)** Picasso at La Californie

The telephone rings and it's Cocteau,
decorator of books. He greets him, like
Proteus from the bathtub, striped pants, false
nose, Pierrot with his joie de vivre.
Two dogs, one owl, a goat, he turns the
animal world to caricature, re-
finding childhood. His stare will up-seat Goya:
he magics his bull into a coathanger –
What if he stocks the world with creation;
can he outwit time ticking over like
a taximeter? How not to exist
as the Colossus, self-styled bull-man of
his perfected lust ... ? Lunch is called. Picasso
sits at table. His hands are bread rolls piqued with crust.

**(iv)**   Caligula
Many-necked Rome hailed him 'Little Chick.' He
liked that, sucking in his lower lip, bald save
for a kiss-me-quick curl, Brylcreemed like Hitler.
Capri schooled him, who defends the cult of
pleasure: he mastered buggery on magenta-
stained knees; feasted on his darling sister
cunted in blancmange, and turned his turds to ingots.
He took counsel from his warhorse, steeped the
Senate in red: bleating, impotent popes …
His acts blazed there like acetylene: for his
finale he would slaughter a flamingo,
hand the Empire to a drooling cretin,
and to his philosopher's hot-poker
agonies; 'Now that is true philosophy!'


**(v)**   Peter the Great

Six foot seven inches and off his rocker,
an air of greatness though, flounced in gold braid;
his 'mad, Medusa, pewter' eye, and the
quarts of brandy to see his vision through.
Petropolis: this frosted caprice,
premeditated, abstract, its nicknames
spawn a litany: Paris, Rome, Palmyra –
though foreigner in its own fatherland.
Along the Fontanka, palaces proffer
their brand of rococo cigarette;
statues bosom, uncovering their sex,
while sunshine tips the spires like hypodermics
gold; city more far-fetched than New York;
ice-new in a country Ice-Age old.

**(vi)**  Hemingway in Madrid

'Africa ends at the Pyrenees; the sky
is taller here: Italy is sentiment ...'
Hem. at the bar, drinking wine. And then the regret, face hardening, snout of blood: to know
all this, and to one day miss it; the essential city, with a fine road to Toledo;
the Goyas in the Prado, fists of bitch-
umen. – In the corrals, the bulls sway calm and
heavy, black as olives, waiting sacrifice.
'It is a subject, death, a man may write of,
being the simplest thing', he said ... 'But better
to live, to have a palate for an Haut
Brion than a liver shy in acquiring it.'

---

**Mark Harrell** is a London-based artist doing the part-time poetry course at UEA, having written verse for around 12 years. He has been published in several magazines and one poetry anthology.

# Aundi Howerton

*Cantilever*
*The Thing Studying Itself Secretly*
*Giacometti's Thumbed and Standing Woman*
*Love Note to Self*
*Ionic Compound*
*Natività*

**Cantilever**

Graph over map over barometer

I set you and find a trajectory
of pinched interstices: myself.
Reliability folds and faults with
excessive parameters. The study

is confused with ribbons of reality.

Notice the launch, the standard deviant,
how Paris and the peat bogs are each pulsed
by the same oscillation. Neither would
call you home. Notice your splintered limbs,
my sensational heart, apex,

and song, our similar curve: my river

clinging to my sphere, your corrugated
flow. Superimposed sine waves weave to your
harmonic and invisibly divide:
multiples to crucible. What beryl-
headed beast so exquisitely drags my

vectors? It twists. The pressure by torsion

filters from you to me along the faults,
the oblique folds. There is much talk of flood,
and the model predicts me jumping. These
sounds are artificial and loudest. My
purple sky dusts my sugared reeds and my

placid heart. Your winter tree rakes the sky

as it penetrates the loose between the
igneous prisms. Both, equally and
opposite. The cadence of your thoughts. My
racing heart. They call this a moment. Me
from you. I lend you my stress, shear, walking.


**The Thing Studying Itself Secretly**

argues and wrestles the black dirt
into the clay. Sometimes it simply
reaches down and plucks the strings, says
we have perfection wanting us like an old man
planting the word trinity into the mind
of a small girl. He whittles the words core and skin
and flesh as she cracks teeth-first into an apple.
The words work like an aristocracy, casting her
by way of page, by heredity of tree. The noble,
old, secret self: advocate, soldier, plowman, hacker.

It churns the violin solo into the hillside
and back through the floodlights, capturing it
with strange awareness into the unfilled blanks.

### Giacometti's Thumbed and Standing Woman

*'The Sainsbury Collection is primarily shown in a gallery known as the Living Area,*
*where modern European art is interspersed with works from across the globe,*
*grouped by geographical region. In 1978 the presentation of ancient world art*
*alongside modern masters was greeted as a revelation – today it continues to*
*provide juxtapositions across time and culture that can inspire and surprise.'*
*from the Sainsbury Centre for Visual Arts website*


We are the voyeurs full of her posture.
The other me sits in my breeze block:
Diego, atop my cot. He loves her

less, has known her longer. I am taken

by the way his brother thumbs her. He cannot
stand the way his brother handles her like
pie crust. The shadow of spiral stair is

as illustrious as the green copper

idol here discarded like me from me
by epidemic. This want is contagion.
She translates us to one another. He

watches her as though he saw her being

born. She is muddy and thumbed; a family
circles her, and I cannot see my other
self. This is solid rejection, her gorgeous

posture; she does not love us. The wooden

*Aundi Howerton*

grandmother watches the baby, several
centuries older. We let our simultaneous
selves loose. She is mine, the baby, ours: he

and I. We keen for the copper and dough.

She demands it of us. Picasso's plump
woman holds our lady's hair back. This, while

the other me cannot get off the bed.


**Love Note to Self**

You silenced the dogs with food so that I
would not hear you stealing my everything.

At least you could have cut through the door
with the grain. I can see you only in

retrospect now, a goldsmith crafting a
globe, unfaithful but beautiful. I am

fishing the torchlight. You are both lacquered
and tapestry, thing in my memory

of what happens next. Still full of the glowing
charcoal. I have untied my bundle of ribbons,

let them loose along the fishing lines; nothing
comes close. Fastened to variables,

I eddy like plum petals. I would wait
like the dog for you. Go back, take me

with you when the hour comes. I can change.

**Ionic Compound**

*for the translators*

They lift the form from glass, an ovule scrolled
in orbits frenzied by volute and voice.
They go. And scattered iron pulls to lode.
By Heracles and hydrogen the noise
is broken up into a hum and spells
the dead as hybridized of horn and ode.
Possessed are songs inside the valence shell
that pull the charges in to balanced node.
The proton seed unfolds to swag and hoard,
and Asclepius threads it through like twine.
The fusion like a compound word
shares meaning with the ghost around the spine.
The loss and gain converge into ionic
at atom's speed: an image made rhapsodic.

**Natività (Piero della Francesca c.1470)**

Cleaning the streets with fire, the woman
became boy. She laid him in the blue sky
or what she loved of it.
If I were Mary I would peel the baby
from the Jesus just to keep him from becoming
anything but iron dust.

My holy father used to peel the holy magpies
from the sky, leave them draped across the barbs;
I would cradle the savior.
There is my old home now, marine snow
below the cline, drifting manger and angels
in the eye's globe.

The baby blooms in a spread of luminescence,
a deep-sea blast of carbon, skeletons awaiting
a warm reassembly.
The violin has lost its strings. The wise measure the violent
din, and the shepherds, rubbed as faceless as the rocks, praise
the constant drift of flock.

*The world's oceans have historically absorbed and off-set a third of all human
carbon emissions. The oceans' ability to sequester carbon is rapidly declining, and
one suggested solution involves fertilizing deep seas with iron dust to induce
phytoplankton blooms. These have been observed to generate more sea life and
possibly remove carbon from the atmosphere.*

---

**Aundi Howerton** is an American poet and essay writer. Her poetry has appeared in the Seattle Literary Journal *Cranky*. She grew up in the Pacific Northwest and, as an adult, has called both Seattle and Los Angeles home.

# Meirion Jordan

*Monster*
*The Amazing Mandragora*
*Home, 1919*
*The ochre country*
*The year of the flood*

## Monster

**I.**

The monster said it could be done where our best architects had failed. We would not believe that something so grotesque, this pulsing mass that sprouted pseudopods to write and feed could help our city, but then we saw his plans. We were amazed. The structure he proposed, so slim, so elegant! Its arches seemed to flow like water down the page, each weight of stone and glass so delicately poised. We hardly could refuse: our councillors agreed. Of course we disapproved. But privately we dreamed of stone and glass reaching heaven, of columns and gold domes that flew.

**II.**

In his lair in the sewers there were many designs. I saw them later, zeppelins and ornithopters that spilled from the walls in frameworks of wood and canvas. And siege engines, and mining gear, a future that soared and whirred in my mind. By then it was too late. I can remember stealing what I could, models and rolls of drawings crumpled and stuffed into my shirt. And the stench of the monster as he rotted, the twitching pseudopodia dissolving into ooze.

**III.**

When construction began we celebrated in the city for nearly seven nights. The bright lanterns hanging from every portico and gable, the crowds of torches lighting the sky, the masked young men and women singing in the street. And on the podium the monster sat among the councillors and aldermen, hearing the speeches that were given in his honour. He made no reply, but sat there glistening. Slowly he dragged his bulk away from the firelight, trailing a single pseudopod behind him, until he disappeared from view.

IV.

My father was a watchmaker and built the town clock into its tower. When I was young the springs and balances amazed me, the thin gears that tucked into each case. I know the monster had designed a timepiece more accurate than any yet on earth, but I never found the papers in his lair. The legate burnt his models and his plans in secret afterwards. The few drawings I have, the models of the arbalest and mining gear, I study every day. I hear my father's clock count off the night hours, the drawing and redrawing of my plans.

V.

After some time construction stopped. The workers, listless, slept in the sun, grew sick of dysentery. The arches stopping mid-step to heaven. They hung in air, never completed. The monster stopped appearing above ground and there were no more speeches made. All summer ivy started to climb the unused stonework, the master-masons left for other cities. Travellers too ceased to come, and the merchants' quarter was subdued, full of old men who went at sunrise to the empty river-wharves.

VI.

On Lammas night we killed him. Drunken and angry, a group of us went down into the sewers and beat the monster to death. Yes, I was there. I heard the smack of clubs on protoplasm, I watched as he disintegrated into ooze. The flailing pseudopods went still. The streets are quiet now, hollow with the chiming of my father's clock. The structure dismantled, the stone re-used. Many of us moved away. But I still dream. At night I look over the plans again. The perfect timepiece I will make. The buildings that will soar as if the angels held their roofs.

**The Amazing Mandragora**

**I.**

Although the poster is pitted and splotched with rain, they will not take it down. At five o'clock, when the lights come on across the town, over its steep streets, its sooty brickwork, the people gather there. Beside it stands the last gas lamp, that they light and gather under as the dusk comes on, each staring up into that thin face, that wicked smile the rain and vaudeville colourings have made mysterious. Come, the poster says, and for tonight only The Amazing Mandragora. That thin moustache. That wicked face. And for tonight only. Come.

**II.**

The rain sweeps in again tonight, but still they wait. In the distance the chimneys lumber from abandoned wharves, toppling toward the river. The Amazing Mandragora watches from his poster, putting up his pristine glove to twirl his moustache while the girls in garish dresses gasp at fireworks of primary colours. Some of the girls are missing, where the paper has torn away to show the wood beneath. And still they wait, the circle of upturned faces in the lamplight, their eyes wide open, catching a brilliant rain.

**III.**

There was a house behind the hoarding, before the war. Now it is a pile of bricks and weeds, ragwort and dandelion exploding in the carnival lamplight. Some days the salvation army plays there, guide me oh thou great redeemer with the red-haired girl at the back flashing her trumpet silver in the rain. And the vaudeville girls gasp at them, or at the fireworks behind. Come, says the poster, and The Amazing Mandragora twirls his moustache, and the rain twinkles on his black, black eyes.

**IV.**

The dusk comes on, and they wait, watching the monkey that capers round the feet of the girls. In his top hat The Amazing Mandragora smiles among the fireworks, the rains of yellow and blue: some nights the monkey chases a spark caught in his tail, others he snatches blue fire from the eyes of the girls. And other nights there is a cabinet of mirrors in which the magician pulls a million rabbits from a million hats. Come, the poster says. And for tonight only. It is the greatest show on earth.

**V.**

That wicked smile, it never moves or sleeps, although the rain washes new colour into the red cheeks of the girls each night. That wicked face, it watches the musichall bawdies honky-tonk their way through worn-out acts. Any old iron, and still those wicked lips that catch and hold and keep. The Amazing Mandragora. Never look. The rain glimmers and brightens every night.

**VI.**

They wait, and night comes on. Across the town, gasometers lurch west under a steady rain. Old strips of poster flapping now might be a curtain coming up, a row of blushes on the vaudeville girls. And then they part, turning their collars only now to duck down steep streets headed for the clatter of the last trams. That wicked smile, for as the dusk returns they will all gather here again. That thin moustache. And for tonight only, among the stained brick, over the hiss of rain. The Amazing Mandragora. Come, the poster says. Come.

**Home, 1919**

He sees it now, flooding
in evening light over the copperworks,
up Balaclava street, up Sebastopol drive,
into the blushes of his wife's face
after sex. And spreading
to albums, to orchids pressed
between suppurating pages,
to photographs of summer, 1912,
the colour of it, dried.
He finds his books
uncomfortable, their spines
sticky to touch, the crimson plush
of theatres quivering, rippled.
Just whose he cannot say.
Jenkins's, is it? Or Davies's,
whose sons still clatter
hobnails up the cobbled hills
to a bundle of scrawled letters,
the worn blinds down.
It could be worse, he thinks,
he could still pace
his sector of the front at night,
or flatten, prone,
at every slamming door.
At least now he finds company
in his nicked skin, shaving,
in his rows of hyacinths urging
their hundreds of red faces sunwards,
the insects nuzzling
at their slick lips.

**The ochre country**

I. The shy foal

Dusk is come into the fields, the shy foal:
where it has gone the furrows dimple
by the stamped hoof, the poplars move
under their burdens of mist and frost.

Under the clouds the lakes furrow, the clods
are still, mirrored and dark with moss. Moorhens
break from the reeds, the grey light settles.
The felled trees flicker in the lakes like ghosts.

All England sleeps now. Gone is the hum
of M1 traffic headed home. The flickers
in the dark above us might be stars.
All England sleeps. The chalk horse dreams

into the dusk of torchlight, the furrows dream
a gust of manes and fetlocks running past.

II. The ochre country

Into the dark the trees rust. The rusted gates
and Bath Stone houses sink into the woods:
in lodge and parlour, rectory and manse
the televisions sit and must be watched.

From elm-row and birch-copse silver lawns
flicker the schedules of a broadcast moon.
The parks are shut. On littered avenues
the cars are piled up to their sleeves

in rowan-berries, rowan-twigs and dust.
The ochre country keeps its burning
through the night. The clouds rust through,
and moonlight trickles between curtains

into sitting-rooms. Under the streets
the loam is brandishing a spray of roots.


**The year of the flood**

After the Ark had sailed and silence
settled back, like an easy chair,
nobody fled but quietly we
said our goodbyes, paid off our debts
and battened down our doors.

We sat in old conversations
for days, watching the rain,
as our gardens buckled
and knelt into the soil.
The radio bubbled and went still.

And sill by sill our windows
gave a view of silt, swirling
and settling at last; the drains too

flourished treasures we had lost,
my red socks, father's barometer,

mother's tennis shoes. Then
there was nothing but old papers
flicking their pages and games
of solitaire. The rain stopped.
Those of us who mentioned air,

a covenant, dry land, we killed.
We would not come. Here
we tend polyp rows, the fields
of whalefall. The gramophone
wheezes, halts in its galliard.

The piano paces from wall to wall to wall.

---

**Meirion Jordan** is from Cwmllynfell, in South Wales. His work has been widely published in magazines, including *Poetry Wales*, the *TLS* and *The Rialto* and in 2007 he won the *Newdigate Prize*. His first full collection of poems, *Moonrise*, will be published in October 2008 by *Seren*.

# Kelly Kanayama

*from 'Lilith'*
*The man who was almost my grandfather*
*from 'Memento Mori'*
*In White*

## [from 'Lilith']

### I

Because she was molded from silt and muck,
the leavings of the dust that made him, I thought myself
safe. I was marrow of his bone,
flesh of his brawn, and nothing base
could haunt our steps. Only after

we stumbled from the gate, cringing
in borrowed skins, did I know what she was.
When we labored in our poor substitute
for a garden I coaxed nothing but weeds
from the stubborn loam; but for hours
he furrowed the rotting soil, watered each grain

with his palms' sweat. Now every year
I harvest thorns and wilted fruit husks,
smell her in the raked earth.

**III:** Building the first Eve

Since he'd watched divine hands string
optic nerves through sockets,
her blood-damp heart unclenching
and shrinking around its affections,
his touch made her flesh teem
with afterimages: flayed sinews
throbbing, nests of capillaries, bowels
wadded in her stomach. He thought then
of past hands busy with their brush
before the mirror; remembered staring
over those brittle shoulders, the gleam
of a reflection winking back.

### The man who was almost my grandfather

Richard had *good blood*, my grandmother said
several times a day in her accent-laden English,
reminding me that *he one hard worker,*
*was one good man, was healthy until*
*he get the kidney trouble* after two brief years
of marriage and leaving my future uncle
to grow in her belly. *Not like your grandfaddah,*
*who nevah do nothing,* who, if he timed it

correctly, would already be sanding
or nailing or sorting through bolts
by thread size in the garage, or peeling
sheaths from the orchids whose pots circled
the house until she junked them all
*so no waste water,* when she returned to Richard

who *went buy the apartment* she'd occupied
for sixty-plus years. *Not like your grandfaddah.*
*He no good, das why, with the bad heart —*
angioplasty, shunts, a triple bypass meant

his cardiac muscles were half alive, half constructs
he could have plotted with T-square
and plumb. *He get the bad blood,* sickness
that dripped through generations, coursing slow
and venomous in my mother's veins and mine

though only he endured the symptoms of it:
resetting shelves someone else's fortune
had erected; building, bare-handed,
the family shrine for a first husband's portrait
in flawless monochrome; too weary
to even straggle behind the dead.

*Kelly Kanayama*

*from* **'Memento Mori'**

**IV.**

Lotus

*Do you want nothing? No one to adore*
*Your hollow cheeks when you grow old? No grand*
*House, no husband's wealth? Nothing means more*
*To me than you.* Though she understands
Her mother's warning as: tender feet pressed
Beneath the crushing stone, the cracked toes curled
Like frightened larvae, the insteps humped like breasts,
The arches pushed into tight clefts, the girl
Is too young to hear that *Don't cry* means *I know*
*What that scream feels like. Smell the blackened rot*
*Of my flesh? My voice shattered like yours, years*
*Ago. Now I break only what I ought*
*To break; this is my gift to you* – and so
She wails, blind to her mother's waiting tears.

**In White**

*(for my father)*

It was 1967 when the army stationed him
In Korea's forgotten center, some village powered
By rural sweat and cricket music, where farm wives
Buried clay pots of slowly pickling cabbage
To ferment for months beneath the rich soil.
On leave one Sunday, he saw a rattling bus
Clunk bravely down the dirt roads to release
Its stream of white-clad passengers. Laughing, singing,
Chattering, they filed into a solitary house

Too small (it seemed) to hold the group. The driver
Rolled a cigarette, closed his eyes, inhaled.
The songs had stopped now. The soldier edged
Toward the walls, barely stirring the dust
In the heavy silence, but stopped at the first shriek
Of *Ai-go!*: female voices lamenting
In harmonic howls. The men joined in:
*Ai-go!* Through the parted curtains
He glimpsed black hair fluttering
Against homespun white. *Ai-go!* For twenty minutes
Bottomless keening burst from the house –
Then quiet. Then the festive clink of glasses,
Loudly proposed toasts, and a tide of white
Stumbling toward the bus, red-faced
Except for the oldest man, whose tearless lids
And parched cheeks had been picked clean
Of sorrow, wildness, or any scraps
Of spirit by too many years of wailing
For other men's losses. He shuffled past the soldier,
Who looked away. Inside the house, water
Splashed, cleansing used cups: the sound of order.

---

Originally from Honolulu, Hawaii, **Kelly Kanayama** studied English Literature and Creative Writing at Washington University in St Louis before coming to UEA. She plans to work and write in the UK after completing her degree.

*Kelly Kanayama*

# Nicole Lyn Lawrence

*Our Funeral*
*The Work-Out*
*The Anniversary*
*Prayer*
*The Machinist*
*Independence, New England*

## Our Funeral

As the summer begins
its slow retreat into fall, and the breeze quickens with intent to take over,
the ocean lining carves itself ever-increasingly into the pliable shoreline while I sit here,
toes drenched in froth, fretting once again
over the countless questions the ocean has posed for us – what is this life?
and when does one end and the next begin,
and why can't we ever catch the changeover, that fleeting
clutch of transition, or even this very instant in which I soak my toes in the ritual
of our talk about the way in which we wish for our last rites to be carried out,
a pair of twins without religion or the force of any understandable or tangible God
and what is that, this sense of God, unless it is found in the water
its salt washing over bronzed and cooking skin,
in the sand which claws its way around the indents of our feet
on the obese stretching floor of the earth ... yet we digress, as always
we do digress, thinking of the many times we have run as though half-insane
into the barely forty degree frigidity in last season's bathing suits which always seemed
to be too small and somehow uncomfortable although they served their purpose,
and raced each other to dunk, to dive all the way under and touch
the floor of our youth through the rough sand and floating legs of crabs already reclaimed
by the ocean's needy hands, and then, you become a brutal wave drawing back
and rearing its great head like a serpent to strike, redirecting my thoughts by telling me
that you want to be pitched into the ocean, and I say,

pitched
in questioning, to which you reply, of course, dear sister, pitched back into the sea
where we belong, rolling in the salty tears of the earth –
but what about rolling the enormous belly of a whale –
isn't that more significantly visual and to the point of being devoured by life
instead of being pitched desirously back from whence we came,
in the beginning, only to find ourselves lived again upon this shore, the same shoreline
we have walked almost daily, and look there, isn't that the frozen footprint
of our yesterday stroll into some grand question: is it right how we have lived this life?
wondering when does one end, and why can't we all go together, before I pitch her,
pitch her ever so tenderly as I am able, in my rage, in my own sickness,
back into the growling, gaping mouth of what we have named the Godless sea –
for what is this life, I demand to know, and when will it end, or rather how
so that I too can be pitched – only wait! hurled, I request, I insist on being hurled,
tossed caustically after so that I can catch her, floating amongst dolphins and even
such beings known as mermaids, to rejoin as her other half, the second voice of her
what, cruel non-existent God, I beg of you, is this wretched life, if not a twin's beauty
and the comforting terror of

**The Work-Out**

Three meters down
inside the muteness

of bubbles, everything
else is traded in for fog –

breath goggles and
artificial flippers.

Unfocused bodies
float plank tonic

in the deep end
as though they'd

always been there. We
make ourselves known

with waving limbs
and flutter-kicks:

our slight currents
quell the undertow

of anger, erode
the tension of slighted

ego. No walls to throw
glass at here. Just still

water to push up against.
In tandem, we maneuver

silence below the surface,
absorbing properties of

the cooler water, until we are
pale-white and spent of it all.

## Anniversary

*(for Gracen)*

November twenty-ninth falls on a Thursday this year. She won't sleep or eat for twenty-four hours before going back in. Only this time, she'll crawl under blankets. Stay all day in the dark womb of her bed. With what was lost. He wanted a kid … Someday. It had to be … Perfect. But he'd Do. What. He. Had. To. Do. What he was taught was Right. If he Had To. Without even placing a finger on her he punched her below the navel. Until she bled. Then she was eating an IV and it was ten … nine … eight … before she forgot the four sets of hands gripping and splitting her limbs. Doing things no regret can ever put right. Coming to, the anaesthesia had taken everything, even her own name, so she called his. Which brought him to her side for one of the last times. Shoved crackers between her lips, forced in a straw. Suck. I was. So. Worried. About. You. Holds her hands down on her lap to stop their shivering. Offers to take her home, make soup. For her. For their souls. I just want to sleep, she breathes. I just need to sleep. He dresses her. Like a child. Out of the hospital with her body inside a wheelchair. Countless sterile hallways. Where the lights judge in cold fluorescents. He forces his own way out clean. Leaves the blood between her legs, in her gut. On her hands.

*Nicole Lyn Lawrence*

**Prayer**

He sits on an uncushioned pew and remembers his wife,
how she could make him believe that trekking up
to touch the doorknob to God's room was salvation
if you made it forty days without whatever it was you loved more.

Today when the congregation is asked to give of themselves
he looks the priest in the eye and says: Take me to the desert.
Lay me in my wife's tomb. Forty nights and more.
Miserere mei, Deus. I have nothing left to give you.

Driving home he contemplates each guardrail, every ancient tree
squinting through dusk. Wondering how he will make another day.
Domine, exaudi vocem meam. There is nothing left for you to take.
At six o'clock, ash flakes in the washbowl. We are but dust.

**The Machinist**

He'd rise move about
the house in shadow
grab the lunch mother prepared
keys from the hook, his coat
and disappear the red Subaru
casting up a dusty farewell
At dinner he'd reappear
hungry, smelling of oil and
sharp metal the factory still
clinging to his cheeks, mouth
sagging open for mother to shovel in
plates of food, like charcoal feeding a gas stove
thumping down his fork 'finished!'
he'd move about the house
in growing shadows find
his brown armchair and stretch his legs
becoming still
occasionally he'd roar like the engines he built
for us to be silent four small daughters
afraid of their father so much like a machine.

*Nicole Lyn Lawrence*

## Independence, New England

### I.

We were strangers even then
Taking turns pulling from the flask
Spelling our names out in
The crowded air with lit sparklers
Fireworks spitting and shouting overhead;
At moments celebratory and anonymous,
Then claustrophobically agoraphobic
Faces lighting up and disappearing
In the spray of dying pyrotechnics.

### II.

The lot of us, once riotous, stormed
Beacon Hill, searching out the old homes
Of Plath and Sexton, before giving up and
Slinking into groomed doorways, down steps
Where we crouched, hitched up skirts
And jerked down trousers, the steam of urine
Incidental. How transitory we were, marking the slight
Passage of time, thinking we actually mattered.

### III.

How I loathed those summer nights
Staggering drunk on Memorial Bridge
The oppressive colony of heat, and its
Violent arpeggio of sound and human bodies.
How quietly I stood among
Considering the water of the Charles.
If it weren't for all those revellers
With clean sailboats and cameras
I would have jumped then and been free of you all.

---

**Nicole Lyn Lawrence** was born in 1981 and hails from Boston, Massachusetts. Upon completing the Creative Writing MA at the University of East Anglia, she plans to move to Chicago, Illinois where she will continue to write and study the craft of poetry.

# Ben Parker

*The Pure*
*City of Glass*
*from Autobiographies*
*Day's Last Wave*

## The Pure

Born with hydrophobia
he soon found that though
water was his fire, fire
was his water. His resistant skin
keeping him close to flames
curiosity drew him to.
He loved the hurried twitch
of their tongues on his body,
the fret of heat on his chest.
He learnt what was required
to achieve the perfect thrash
of fever from the fuel;
of the wood and coal
with the sweetest taste.
And the end of every day
was marked by a pyre:
immersed in a bath of fluid
in which everything burnt
but him. Emerging with skin
tight and clean as a foetus.
The thrum of the blaze
still just above his flesh.

**City of Glass**

One morning we woke to find the city
composed entirely of glass, prismatic
in the low sun glancing off sharp edges.
Not one object remained that had not bled
its colour into the ground in the night.
From the deep shock-proof shells of offices
to the etched headlines on delicate sheets
of stacked papers, everything was washed clear.
Only the pavements, foundations and roads
kept unaltered their original form
supporting the city's fragile sculpture.
And, exposed behind glass walls, carefully
closed glass doors, life continues. A woman
cautiously taps a piano's frail keys,
the silica strings resonate, each note
a high-pitched, drawn-out crystalline scream
that quavers, threatens to but does not break.

*from* **Autobiographies**

**(1689)**

I open my doors to the rhapsody
of summer air, to a land dressed in gilt
and verdigris, and to friends sat silent
in expectant waiting. Our church, not high

nor closed, is pure and as true as the hay.
The simple room's active hush, Inner Light,
thanksgiving for the work of the Valiant
founders. By these we fight apostasy.

Though the year sings towards amber, our
dress in its diurnal plainness avoids
the distractions of fashion, the fire

of jewellery and adornment. Our greys
and whites are symbols enough of belief:
Christ has come to teach His people Himself.

**(? – 1747)**

Stub candles. Tenebrous workshop. Spread leaves
of quarto and folio. The musk of skin
dried to vellum, the snag of a quill pen
on rough paper. And a needle that plies

its task, squinting thread through philosophies
as if guided through garter and stocking.
The flawed seam I unwittingly stitched in
is the warp and weft of the fastened muse.

*Ben Parker*

And although some of my work is published
I starve. Desperate in the loud streets I sell
a restorative jelly to be rubbed

on the ambiguous wounds of the ill;
by now there is nothing I will not try.
Having none I write an ode to money.

**(1836)**

A dry morning of sweat and talk. White flag
in a blue sky with four tribes beneath it.
And I ride out on a ribbon of dust
to meet them. Air as under a thick rug:

silence and heat. Then the bark of my dog
at my side. They tell me that all they want
is some food and a place to set their tent.
Knives and numbers mean they don't have to beg

or ask twice. Behind the defensive walls
and the spice of our cedar stockade, beef
is packaged. The rough flank of my horse swells

and subsides as I jolt it back and jump off.
Daubed faces, unreadable as broken
compasses ring me. The sprung snare bites down.

**Day's Last Wave**

Each afternoon he would make the drive
15 miles west from his house to see
the breaking of the last wave of the day.
One eye on the sun, or, if obscured
by a peremptory cloud, on the second hand
of his waterproof watch and an accurate
prediction of the time of the setting,
the other on the lick of the surf
as it ran along the parched lip
of this small, secluded gravel beach.
As the end of the sun teased the edge
of the horizon he would prepare
to record the details of the final wave
unfolding in daylight. Noting down
in his third, thick notebook the volume
as it sprawled against the stones, the height,
approximately, before it fell
and the hue and tone of its body.
When he arrived home he could still hear
the push and sigh of the sea working
at the shore in the thickening dark.

---

**Ben Parker** was born in Worcester in 1982. His work has been published in a number of magazines including *Iota* and *Agenda* and he has two pieces appearing in the forthcoming *Cinnamon Press* anthology *In The Telling*.

# Genevieve Schiffenhaus

*For Closeness*
*The Search*
*The Boy Whose Skin Fell Off*
*The Classified Ads*
*December 25th: San Francisco*
*For the Taking*

### For Closeness

The child cries out at birth, after its stay inside.
Proof of life but also its want to stay inside.

Fingers clenching around a car door's window frame;
a woman's voice saying: *We can talk pay inside.*

Why were we molded into this fragile tissue?
It would be kinder if we were still clay inside.

A man feels horses running through his mind all day.
His wife's ear to his temple; hears them neigh inside.

Strange how women have eggs like birds, featherlessly.
We roost, our body a nest, only lay inside.

When the time comes, I will ask you where you want me.
I will not wait long for your answer. Say inside.

**The Search**

Don't call it a blanket
of snow. Missing for
two months now and students still
look anxiously at certain
mounds, on their way to class.
Last seen leaving his friend's dorm,
his only winter coat later found
in his room. His mother speaks
of him in the past tense on the local
news, but still it goes on.  Men, up
to their thighs, crisscross patterns all
over the campus. Each has a stick,
inserted with every step. Like roadside
trash collectors, trying to pick up scraps
no one else can see. But they are not
trying to make contact with anything.
The holes are made to open up the scent
for the dogs, who smell nothing again.
After rain falls in the night, an icy film
forms over everything.  Let's be brave
enough to call it what it is: a crust, a
scab. How can April be so cold still?
When it all melts, it is always a surprise
to see the grass so green underneath,
so ready to begin where it left off.

*Genevieve Schiffenhaus*

**The Boy Whose Skin Fell Off**

is actually a man. He is having a party tonight.
He has invited family and friends and a pretty

girl who cries at the sight of him. He knows
her tears only come from understanding, or

lack of understanding, and that there is really
no difference between either of those kinds.

Both have the same amount of salt. Both would
sting the places where the soft of his cheeks used

to be. Both would dry too soon. The boy whose
skin fell off has gathered everyone together for

one last time. He is dying in one week. He has
hand-picked his own coffin; decorated it with pictures

of snakes, insects. He says that is the only way he will
ever come back to earth: if he can be something that

sheds its skin only when a new one has formed underneath.
Instead of his raw, seeping muscles. Instead of the blisters

that seem to hold an ocean of fluid in them. The boy whose
skin fell off does not want a pity party. Although he

doesn't mind if people feel moderately sorry for him. The
guests will murmur their apologies; their wonder at his

acceptance of the end. He will assure them that if their
skin fell away at the slightest rubbing, they might be

ready to embrace death at a moment's notice. *But surely,*
they will whisper among themselves, *he can still enjoy*

*the scenery, the simple pleasures in life.* The boy whose
skin fell off's hearing, however, is quite sharp, and he will

chastise them lightly, saying: *simple pleasures? Masturbation*
*is impossible.* And they will fall silent with realization and

feel a coldness spread throughout the deepest part of themselves.
Or at least the boy whose skin fell off hopes they will. He has

decided that life is a lesson that must be learned and his lesson
is about skin. That much wasn't hard to figure out. What

about skin though? The lack of it. Again, not a difficult
deduction. The pretty girl will look at the boy whose skin fell

off and say: *You are what I would be if someone dragged*
*me from the back of a car, down a long, paved road.* The boy

whose skin fell off will tell her to turn that into a metaphor, and
it is basically what happened to him. The girl will ask what

happened to the people who were driving the car and the boy
whose skin fell off will not reply, not because he has tired of

her and her trouble grasping figurative devices, but because
his lips will have cracked at the corners and it will be too

painful to speak at that moment. After a while the boy whose
skin fell off will clear his throat and address those at the party.

They won't perceive him as a prophet or a martyr only because
his suffering has no point. But still they will listen. I want to

*Genevieve Schiffenhaus*

*tell you two things. The first is that when I was younger my*
*father thought my sores could use some fresh air and so he*

*put me outside all day, naked, for the flies to land on me like*
*a piece of rotting meat. The second is that if I could bear*

*to hold each and every one of you. I would. I would wrap*
*my arms around you so gently. I would hold you until it hurts.*

*(In response to the documentary by Patrick Collerton: The Boy Whose Skin Fell Off)*

**The Classified Ads**

were like a wound on the page.
Before, they had purpose in mind;

thought themselves a space for things lost
and found, wanted and needed,

and priced to sell: The woman who lost
her grandmother's small opal ring.

The owner of a '98 F-150 truck in good
condition but needed it to sell fast.

The diversity suited the pages; kept
things interesting. There seemed to be

a strange continuity between some things:
A woman searching for her lost, elderly

dog – a lab mix, and a man selling a litter
of new Labrador puppies that very week.

These occurrences amused the Ads; allowed the
imagination to wander. But it all began

to change. More and more things were
described with too much meaning:

The woman who needed a plain dress,
long enough to cover the entire body,

in shame or sadness and sometimes
in loneliness. The man who had recently

lost his mother and was looking for a
baby's pacifier that accurately mimicked

the feel of a nipple because he missed his
childhood. The Ads began to feel edgy

and unsure. Some things were better left
unsaid after all. But, the Ads reasoned,

this is why we are here. A place for things.
Still, the changes caused unrest among them.

Some quietly missed the unspoken symbolism
that people's search for things gave rise to.

Others forcefully restricted their word limits
in hopes that they could get back to the way

things had been. Still others, a few, softly whispered
about the chance to understand the reason behind

all the needing and wanting; how it felt like it
was about to break upon them like some bitter wave.

The volume of the Ads kept increasing everyday.
They had to reduce their font size in order to fit

everything in. But the people still had holes
to fill and the Ads kept voicing their cries for

them. Then came the day when some of the Ads
contained pleas from people for other people:

An elderly woman looking for a man who remembers
the same things she does; to talk to.

A male seeking a young female who does
not mind dry skin and kisses that might start

to feel like bites from dull teeth. A girl who
says exactly what she does not mean but whose

hair smells like gardenia at the end of summer.
The Ads were restless. They demanded to know

what the people were using them for. Did they not
know what service they provided? For things only?

But none among them had an answer. One bravely asked:
*Are people things themselves?* But a shuddering was

the only response. It seemed that the change was fully
underway. Now when the Ads weren't all consumed

with expressing the desire of a man whose penis
had left him for some time but he still hoped to regain

its confidence in the company of a female of any age
that would allow him to do unspeakable things before they

ever spoke a word, they were immersed in mourning for the times
before they were stripped of subtlety: When an ad taken out

by a young girl looking for a shiny red bicycle with solid wheels
and wide handlebars really meant that she had realized she deserved to

be loved in a way that wouldn't eat her heart. And the
man selling a couch, used gently, to a couple, preferably,

meant his wife who he loved faithfully for 47 years had died of
breast cancer but he still felt her quiet presence in their home.

And turning to the Classifieds section began to feel
like heaving a sigh. And the font continued to grow

smaller until there was hardly any white left on the
pages; only dark ink which smeared when touched.

## December 25th: San Francisco

The tiger escaped its cage. Hours later people
learn that Siberian tigers, bred in captivity, lose

their natural fear of humans. Similarly,
17-year-old boys, bred in California, lose

their natural fear of Siberian tigers contained
at the zoo. A human footprint, on the wall

of the exhibit, seems to demonstrate this nicely.
Three mangled bodies, one dead, and a Siberian

tiger shot and killed by police, again, gets right
to the heart. The dead boy's mother says: *Our*

*Christmas is with him. No more Christmas.* But
a part of Christmas has always been ripped and

bloody and in the belly of a dead tiger. The careful
know this. The wise man who brought myrrh knew

that the end is already there at the start. That the tiger
who eats the arm of its feeder will have a taste for flesh.

That the boy who puts his neck out will have teeth sunk
into it. That to think there's more to this story is wrong.

**For The Taking**

As for the tree, it was dying. Sprawled along
the side of the path, roots in the air, its branches

brittle and pale. As for the season, it was autumn,
just, but already the air felt like a denser thing.

Sitting in the limbs of the tree, we bedded down
against the wind. As for our clothes, it never would

have mattered. As for your words, they came out
in muscular sentences, doing things your hands would

learn. As for your hands, I don't remember. As for
the sky, it was the same as on any other day when I have

wanted to tell you everything that could ever make
you change your mind about me. Which is no other day.

As for the ground, it held us. As for the ground, I dug
my heel into the grey soil until it turned a soft black

and then you covered it in a few, deliberate strokes. As for
the earth, it never said it was ours. It didn't have to.

---

**Genevieve Schiffenhaus** was born in New Jersey but grew up between Provincetown and Key West. She completed her undergraduate degree in English Literature at Middlebury College and attended the *Bread Loaf Writers' Conference* before coming to UEA. She plans to live and work in the UK for the time being.

# Sarah Wallis

*The Patience of Travellers*
*Breathe into Water*
*Sister*
*The Peach House*
*The Secret Life of Puppets*

### The Patience Of Travellers

I

So rain makes time travel slowly
and trains make elephants of us all.
We sigh to forget through mist-leavened windows
and break bread our mothers made with strangers.
Miles unravel in our minds behind the distant headlines
breathing rumours of the weather or politics;
soundbites occupy empty seats.
Music systems hum and blip and pencils tap
the brain for crossword solutions but the country
pulls me on out into the darkening world,
where it is possible to imagine hooting ghosts
and fields of sleeping sheep. We wait.
Shifting slightly in the bucking stops
as signals slowly change and lines reeking wet
squeak with rain; changing north to east.

## II

Thrumming past the blurry cows
it gets colder for us, we get bored.
But we need the travelling time to transition,
jet packs would not suit us; although we don't
believe it, instant arrival, shooting like stars along
the pylons we pass to crash and burn far from home.
Fields of snorting, braying donkeys
chase the train, mimic the clarion call.
Houses on hills glimmer a candle, a pinprick
in the dark about 14 miles distant.

## III

A spider spins a pentagram underneath the
luggage racks and we should hope protection outweighs
fear when he is discovered; illegal alien.
Platform scenes from movies crowd the humid lens
under sodium lights and we watch reunions in play;
English handshakes and a mother's kiss.
The travellers smile, faintly sad and thinking of home
until the train shrugs and blurs the view beginning to move out.
It might make us dizzy with sadness, the departure from home
and the imminent approach of the feared unknown. We wait.
Lulled by the constant rhythm of wheels and the chasing rain,
we wait with the necessary patience of travellers.

**Breathe into Water**

Borrowed scales,
breathe into water

hiprise on the curve, sensuous,
dolphin the element, belong.

Unscramble fear, feel your power
flipper your feet

enjoy the wave
return to your origin

re-live the haven,
a nine month water-sleep

remember it now
cycle it into your powerhouse muscles

build on the turn
tumble into a new routine

feel the beat of the engine
flipper-kick, tumble

curtain your heart, make it stronger
as the training days grow longer

breathe into the blue light
half aquarium glow

swimming pool karma
harness this calm for a gala

a swim-meet with like minded fish,
bring us a ball of gold, talented child
rise on the curve,
breathe into water
mermaid us to glory
breathe into water.

**Sister**

Breathe, baby, breathe
blue lights called
bedevilled, unknown to you

brought to the bed
a silent cough in the night,
why won't you breathe little sister?

We three next door, all unknowing
the automatic breathing clock,
had stopped going.

Breathe, baby sister
a deep lungful of air,
a gaspful, a light feather-handful.

Grasp tight, through this terrible night
keep your cot-full of colour
your clutch of hands

wave your rattle, call for the O2
you were supposed to grow with, learn about;
maths in your DNA, words in mine.

Unexpected. Like a wound down watch.
Or broken laces. Or a fridge burned out.
The breathing in our lives. Turned inside out.

Girl, interrupted. Abruptly cut off.
The once lively.
The domestic scene.

Our parents took a break not too long after,
to Jersey. They stopped short of a world tour,
perhaps, remembering at home

the daughter just turned four.
Breathe, baby sister
it should be so easy

to laugh together,
made for company
to go together like hand and blister

like salt and vinegar.
That day is coloured bricks to me,
Grandma's knees, closed doors.

Just a little longer,
keep your blindsiding twister
your scary news, little sister.

Breathe baby breathe
take a note of your mother's
gasping sobs to follow

the shout of disbelief, your father's
only song
Why has this happened? Where is she gone?

No belief grew up in this house
little sister, where panic took root
for breathing. Mine was the spare part in the drama

yet now they say, we couldn't have gone on
without you,
they don't know what they'd have done

*Sarah Wallis*

gone on, I suppose, just breathing
taking breaths, it's what you do when
you're not thinking of the breath not taken.

### The Peach House

Colours; pure theory of peach and nectarine tangle
slowly spidering over yellow stone work and the shining
timbers of the peach house in the late September sun.

Ceramic tiles hide under-floor heating like a Roman bathhouse,
such extravagance here, keeping warm the delicate trees of the peaches
an exuberance amongst the remains of Victorian austerity.

At the side entrance to the garden it reveals,
the great glass windows reflecting small bombs of sunshine
the peach house, an oasis, an Edwardian interlude.

### The Secret Life of Puppets

Set the cycle, oh to delicates
push the button on the anecdote robot;
hear the tumbling dreams pour out
catching a conger eel in cold Irish seas
travelling the globe
doing odd jobs in Oz.

Now the program's skipped a bit,
slip a few years down the timeline
to the daily wash and a conundrum
of grey crusty socks, off-white lingerie

to the colourfast work shirts and T-shirts,
that'll do for today.
The automaton doesn't question
where the odd socks wander
but now and then wishes them a good journey
and turns to counting pairs.

The secret life of puppets
alluded by a glazed middle distance gaze
filling the machine and setting the cycle
catching the sky reflecting in the drum
recalling a boat race, fast tacking
and the sails rising, switching port to starboard.
The bed-sheets flub out on the line,
the full wash basket is slung hip to hip.

Humming campfire songs at the ironing board
remembering flipping pancakes on a makeshift hob
turning now to consider the sparkling worktops,
the absent family pulls the strings,
maid marionettes out the motions
in place of purpose mere notions.

---

**Sarah Wallis** has been published by *Six Sentences*, *Aesthetica*, *Writing Magazine*, *Rubies in the Darkness* and *Trespass*. She lives in Leeds and is working towards a first collection of poetry, building on the work of the course and encouraged by the meeting of inspiring minds at UEA.

# Life Writing

*Introduction by* **Kathryn Hughes**

*M.C. Burns*
*Lorna Webb*

As biographers we live in interesting times. The old ways of doing things – the familiar subjects, the tried and tested narratives – will no longer do. But the new ways are not quite clear either. Where are the fresh subjects, the new forms, the previously unimagined ways of telling that oldest story of all, the story of human experience?

On the MA in Life Writing at UEA – still the only one in the country – we are uniquely placed to chew these matters over. First we immerse ourselves in the history of the genre, marvelling at Plutarch's modern touch, seeing Dr Johnson once more through Boswell's adoring eyes, wondering yet again at Lytton Strachey's brazen cheek. Then we keep a beady eye out for what is happening now, today, in the world of commercial publishing. What are the big hits? What are the best books (not the same thing at all)? Which titles do we itch to take apart and rewrite ourselves?

For everyone who comes on the MA in Life Writing is a biographer-in-training. Over the space of a year the 'Lifers' work on their own material, fashioning prose that serves their subject best. Statesmen, rogues, grandparents, poets and piss-artists have all come under our searching glance. And, while this isn't the only outcome we strive for, the fact is that a good proportion of this work ends up in print.

This year just two Life Writers have chosen to submit work for the anthology. Lorna Webb's finely-wrought piece reflects her family's heritage as weavers and her own fine ambition to write about Mary Somerville, that extraordinary Scotswoman for whom the term 'scientist' was first coined. M.C. Burns, meanwhile, has sent in a piece of short fiction. Her story is set amongst the Onondaga, native Americans who continue to pull off the trick of living between two cultures – their own, ancient and settled, and the new, jumpy world of New England. She is currently writing the biography of an Onondaga chief whose life has taken him from the reservation to a guest spot at any venue where world leaders gather. A Victorian woman scientist rubbing shoulders with an American Indian. It's what Life Writing at UEA is all about.

KH

# M.C. Burns

## *Antlers*

Andy Tarbell slept in a bed with two of his little brothers. The younger boys slid between sheets so cold they felt like panes of glass. Andy, the eldest at 14, would press their clothes into a pile on top of them and then lift a blanket corner and slither in. If they stirred, the loose-springed mattress would pitch and roll the clothes off. Four more brothers slept under their own pile in the other bed. The room wasn't too cold at bedtime – early, while traces of heat still rose from the stove downstairs. If a brother woke up in the freezing night he would struggle not to shiver, knowing if he disturbed the others he would be shoved out onto the floor.

It was still dark when Andy awoke and eased out from under the blanket. The oak floor, bleached by his mother's determined scrub brush, felt like an ice rink. When his feet touched down, the muscles in his soles shrank and hardened. Outside was all shades of silver. A bright crust sparkled on the snow and the trees, etched with frost, reached toward a gun-metal sky.

Onondaga village houses were mostly ramshackle – no electricity, water or heat. Banks don't give mortgages on Indian land, since they can't repossess. Everything was paid for in cash, built by Onondaga hands. It didn't matter that Andy's ice-lined windowpanes distorted his view, he knew every tree, path and berry patch. He came alive in the woods – on Indian territory among hunters' spirits – where he could forget that Onondaga is surrounded by New York state. White people stole most of the hills and since the Depression, they stole the animals too.

The windows shuddered and a dissonant whistle blew through the wallboards. Andy plucked jeans from the bed and drew eight socks from the tangle of underpants and t-shirts. His eyes landed on his dad's boots, pushed against the peeling baseboard and he remembered the last time he saw his dad, the day a chief was appointed at the Longhouse last summer. Edward Tarbell stood with the singers at one end of the crowded oak-log Longhouse, a small water drum tucked under his arm. The men wore leggings and ribbon-trimmed shirts. Some had gustowehs, a clutch of feathers sticking up from their heads. The women wore dresses over longer skirts, embroidered shawls hung over one arm.

A clan mother placed antlers on the new chief's head then everyone joined in a circle dance – rocking forward and back, massaging Mother Earth with their feet. Andy danced but didn't nod at the singers when he passed. He studied his beaded moccasins or straightened the ribbons hanging from his good shirt. His father's stare felt like a sunburn. Andy wanted to look, to exchange matching grins, but he feigned interest in the middle distance. When the dance ended, Andy went out past the feast-laden tables and headed for the forest, a knot of hunger and emptiness.

Andy stroked the soft leather of his dad's hiking boots. He'd kept them when Edward hurled himself out the front door in a drunken rage – and hid them when he came looking for them. Andy usually wore them hunting, but he wanted lighter feet today – sneakers. Since the dry, powdery snow had been on the ground a while, it wouldn't soak through. He yanked on four pairs of socks; the wool chafed the pads of his thumbs and tore at his cuticles. He struggled to tie the trainers. The ripped lacers were too short to knot around his bulked-up feet, and the frayed ends resisted eyelets. His frosted fingers got in the way.

He threw on a couple T-shirts, a red-checked flannel button-down and tip-toed downstairs. His mom Yvonne was passed out on the couch, her right arm flung toward the floor, a bottle of Mad Dog 20/20 rested on her left. Moonlight picked out new threads of grey in her long black hair and turned the print of her calico dress to shadow. Life was quieter since his dad left. The brawls ended, but Andy missed Yvonne's throaty laugh and forgot the shape of her wide smile. She knew Andy belonged to his dad – as a baby, even when she nursed him, his alert brown eyes searched for Edward.

Andy put the bottle to his lips. The last shot seared his tongue and down his throat. He put the bottle in the garbage so his brothers wouldn't find her like that. Andy sliced off two pieces of bread, thin as he could manage. He pulled a couple of last night's potatoes from the metal bowl on the windowsill – hard and heavy as stones. He squashed them in the bread and slid the sandwich into his front pocket.

The rifle, a 44-calibre Winchester 1873, was under the front porch. Old Man Bucktooth lent it to Andy in exchange for the promise of some deer meat. That wasn't likely. The only time he saw a live deer Andy was 9, hunting with his dad. 'You be the dog,' his dad said. 'You go into the bushes and chase out every living thing.'

Andy fell into step beside Edward, a sinewy Mohawk who worked high steel. When he was happy, Edward played ragtime on their upright piano – his powerful hands spanning the chipped ivory octaves, his laughter a descant to Joplin's melodies. Drunk, he was a snake coiled on the best living room chair.

Branches whipped Andy's face as he flung himself into the undergrowth, but Edward never had a reason to lift his gun. In the steep slanting shadows, Andy spotted movement – a doe stretched its neck between two trees and looked straight at him. 'There's a deer,' he hissed. At once, Andy was on the ground, spitting crushed leaves. Edward's powerful roundhouse punch to the back of Andy's head knocked him face down. The deer was long gone, alerted by Andy's voice. They went home empty-handed.

Edward taught Andy that when Onondaga hunters take a deer, they waste nothing. They eat the meat and carve the bones. They use its brain to tan the hide, and the leather makes moccasins and gloves. When Andy killed a sparrow with his slingshot, Edward made him pluck it and eat it for dinner. Then his dad disappeared, went to live with another woman and her kids.

On that silver morning it had been weeks since Andy's family had meat. They ate potatoes and carrots from the dwindling root-cellar supply. The day before, Andy had walked six miles into Syracuse to see Red at the pawn shop. Red's dad sold jewelry, guns, pool cues – anything valuable. If broken boxes of ammo came in, Red would slip Andy some cartridges. That day Red had just one for the Winchester, pressed it into Andy's hand behind the dust-furred shelves so his dad wouldn't see.

Andy slipped the shell into the barrel. He laid the gun on the porch and poked around in his shirt pocket for a crumpled paper packet and matches. The old tin can was under the porch, right where his dad left it. Andy set it in snow, dropped the parcel in and lit it. The tobacco inside flared, then curled. The smoke rose, bearing his prayers up to the Creator. In Onondaga, he spoke his thanks for being a human being and for the trees, birds and animals of the forest. He finished, "Nya wenha. Ho." It shall be. When the fire fizzled, he scooped snow into the tin and put it back.

Andy took light, silent steps and the powdery snow fell easily off the tops of his sneakers. He headed for the highest Onondaga mountaintop, his muscled calves springing upward. From the ridge, he surveyed the territory. A swamp lay at the base of the mountain, a valley stretched out from the other side. A sliver of sun threw shadows on the distant city buildings and lamplight flickered in some Onondaga houses – Andy's was still dark.

The only animal tracks were hardened little snow-holes, so Andy set off along the ridge. He entered a still, white clearing and heard a twig crack. He snapped toward the sound and saw an enormous buck standing in profile. Trees blocked each spot where Andy could kill with one shot. He could hit the deer's haunch, but he knew it took days for a shot in the leg to kill. The buck would limp off and die in agony.

Andy eased the gun off his shoulder, shut one eye and put the deer in his sight. They stayed still until the buck snorted, then leapt into a canter bobbing between trees. Andy, startled and panicked, knew he would lose the trail if the deer went into the swamp. He shortcut across its path and skidded to the water's edge, where the buck stood among tall spiky grasses. It leapt forward, its front feet crashed through and caught in the ice, but the buck leaned back on its powerful hind legs and drew them out. It jumped further into the swamp. Andy slid his feet over the black gossamer surface. It collapsed and he plunged into water up to his knees. He took huge ungainly steps, breaking the ice with each one. The deer turned and led Andy up the mountain, his calf muscles throbbing under frozen jeans. The buck stopped at the top and Andy came up behind, steam poured from its flared nostrils, scarlet oozed from a gash on its front leg.

Then it was off again, over the top of the mountain and down. Half-running, half-sliding, Andy strained to stay upright. The deer sprinted into the valley. Andy was relieved to be on flat land but the deer was out of sight. Andy followed the tracks, but ended up going round in a circle of several sets of prints, with none leading off its circumference. He was nearly all the way around when he noticed a deeper pair of tracks and a similar set blending into the pockmarked snow under a nearby bush. He leaned into another shrub and found more prints. Andy followed the hidden tracks and groaned when he realised the deer had gone up the mountain again. He pulled out his sandwich and bit into it. Warmed in his pocket the potatoes and bread congealed, he chewed every bite so long, there was little left to swallow. Then he headed into the mountain's lengthening shadows.

Breath burned in his chest and his leg muscles cramped as Andy sprinted toward the peak. He thought of the hunters who ran these woods for thousands of years. The old chiefs said his ancestors brought down mastodons with slings, and could kill anything with arrows. Head down, Andy asked those hunters to lighten his freezing, throbbing feet, to get him up their mountain.

And when he lifted his head, the buck was right in front of him. Standing in blood-pink snow, the curve of its neck darkened with sweat, it looked directly at Andy. 'Ska nonh', he blurted, 'peace' in Onondaga. 'Grandfather', he called the deer and it all tumbled out; his six starving brothers and his mother at home, the hunger and emptiness since his father left. He thanked the buck for its sacrifice – its body would nourish his family, but the spirit of the deer would continue. Andy thought the buck dropped its head slightly, accepting, but couldn't be sure. He lifted the rifle and squeezed off one clean shot.

The buck fell and died instantly. Andy was elated and crushed, he longed for the deer already.

At noon the next day, his mom woke Andy with a steaming bowl of stew. He shoveled the meat and potatoes into his mouth. He scraped the last bits of gravy from the bowl and didn't look up when she came back into the room. She tousled his hair and gently eased the bowl out of his hands. She held them tight for a moment and then wrapped his fingers around buck's antlers.

---

**M.C. Burns** was a journalist in the US and moved to Norwich in 2003. She won a *Robert F Kennedy Journalism Award* in 1994 for *Somalia's Sorrow*, a report on the famine. She also won several *Associated Press Writing Awards*. She is a freelance magazine editor and is writing the biography of an American Indian Chief.

# Lorna Webb

## *Bricolage*

*A*riadne stood on the threshold. In the palm of her hand she held a ball of finely spun thread and Theseus' life. Weave the thread into the heart of the earth and it will lead you to your desire. Free the soul of the minotaur and you will find your way back to me. Theseus gazed into the labyrinth and heard a mighty roar ...

'I am Theseus', came the challenge as the small figure beside me leapt off the sofa sweeping his wooden sword through the air.

'Who are you, Mummy?'

'I am the minotaur', and my roar echoed with laughter from my youngest. I catch hold of his feet as they are momentarily thrust towards me in combat, joining his brother in imitation. Suddenly I am suffused with the memory of his spring dawn birth when reaching down I touched his small damp foot. Startled we both withdrew as though we were strangers and had not been so intimately connected; an undiagnosed breech birth, which turned my life upside down and forced me to mine sources I didn't know I had, to rethink the feminist theory I had gobbled up in my twenties and live and love, more fully than ever before, the meaning of difference.

Later, in search of my brain, I watch a documentary my brother has made with our cousin about a project to raise the wreck of the Blessing from the silted depths of the Firth of Forth. The boat, the Blessing of Burntisland, had been built by Andrew Watson in the early 17th century. He did not know that the boat he built would survive for 400 years and be the object of desire of a 21st century cartographer.

There is treasure on board the Blessing of Burntisland which surveys reveal to be about a mile from the Fife coast. On 19th June 1633, King Charles I rode north from London to Edinburgh to be crowned at Holyrood, in part to appease the

Scots who were angry with the absent King and in part to collect his treasure and take it to the Palace at Whitehall, his English home. Charles travelled in complete self-sufficiency, which included a 200-piece silver dinner service and as many from his court to eat from it. After the ceremony, Charles toured the lowlands and returned to the bustling, prosperous port of Burntisland with his treasure. On July 10th, gold, silver and jewellery were loaded aboard the Blessing in anticipation of the crossing to Leith and the journey south. The Firth of Forth is an unpredictable and treacherous stretch of water. A storm blew up from nowhere and a short distance from the harbour, the Blessing capsized and sank. Neither man nor treasure was saved, so quick was the tragedy. In search of an explanation which did not include God's judgement on the young King, the following year a group of Lancashire women were tried as witches and found guilty of sinking the King's boat that summer's day. Their powers may yet be at work, hovering around in the gift of a map dowser, also from Lancashire, who pinpointed the location of the wreck on an Admiralty Chart months before the survey confirmed his finding.

But there was treasure of a different kind hidden in the story. Andrew Watson the ship owner had built his own house in Burntisland, which had become the home of Mary Somerville's family. When the house was restored in 1957, painted ceilings were discovered, hidden by subsequent alterations. Planetary deities, astral scenes depicting the signs of the zodiac and amorini encircling the sun against a background of sky, stars and cloud were revealed. On one ceiling was the figure luna by the name of Lovna, with the crescent moon on her forehead. For a split second I thought the word was Lorna and my skin tingled. That simple mistake started me on a journey in search of Mary Somerville.

The sasines of Burntisland record that on 20th December 1754, Samuel Charters and Christian Murray, Mary Somerville's grandparents, took possession of the house and decided to alter and extend it. Mary was born in 1780 in Jedburgh and soon after the family moved to Burntisland where Mary spent her childhood. She was a free spirit on the seashore and in the wild countryside, a curious child whose fascination with the natural world would shape the woman she was to become.

From her bedroom window Mary gazed out at the night sky studying the stars with the aid of the celestial globe, oblivious to the concealed representations of the sky so close above her head. She was hungry for knowledge until one day she was intrigued by algebraic equations in a magazine and found a puzzle to satisfy her hunger. Mary followed a path which was to make her one of the most admired mathematicians and scientists of the 19th century, the woman whose work inspired Whewell to coin the term 'scientist', whose calculations predicted the existence of as yet invisible planets and who perceived the sciences as integrally connected disciplines.

Perhaps this sense of integrity, which characterised Mary's life, was the cord which drew me to her as it had drawn her contemporaries. Making marmalade, teaching her children, studying calculus were of a piece in the same way as the constellations, the body and the word both essential if sometimes adversarial.

There were questions which I wanted to ask, from what was Lady Byron like and how easy was it to mentor Ada, to how did she feel being in the centre of an internationally renowned scientific community? Would she have studied had she stayed in Scotland? How fortunate was she that her first husband, who thought a woman's life was measured by the walls of her home, died? The questions opened on to the lives of other women. My curiosity led me to the intoxicating delight of archives. There was much marmalade to be made before the first trip was possible and a tenacious grip to be kept on the researcher who bobbed about on the familial sea.

I decided to take the train to Scotland, returning to that stretch of the Fife coast, where I had spent my early years. I wanted to walk along the beach where Alexander III had plummeted to his death in 1286 and where my father, also Alexander, had crumpled with a heart attack at the age of thirty-eight. I longed to look again into the rockpools and smell the briny air, to visit Mary Somerville's house knowing what I now knew.

As the train left Norwich station, I ran through the checklist of domestic notes and reminders and let them flutter out of my head. I unwound the shawl I was knitting and let it cascade down over my knees, warm colours inspiring its own poetry. For centuries my family had been weavers, now I was weaving words.

---

**Lorna Webb** lives in Norwich with her family. She knits shawls and poems and she is writing a book about the constellation of women scientists in the 19th century. She is also editing a collection of writings about the lives of families who have children with special needs.

# Scriptwriting

*Introduction by* **Val Taylor**

*Jenny Brogan*

*Alison Falconer*

*Colette Gunn-Graffy*

*Alexandra Leaney*

*Stephen Robert Morse*

*Molly Naylor*

*Luke Oakes*

*Janice Okoh*

*Hannah Puddefoot*

In the Scriptwriting MA, we focus our attention upon each individual writer's development. The script drafts, scenes, synopses, outlines and treatments written during the course are accompanied by analytical and self-reflective essays demonstrating the writer's understanding of the practices of established writers and of the drama production industries, as a means to locate and improve his/her own creative work. There is always a tension to be negotiated between the writer's own instinct for story and character and the painstaking expression of themes and ideas within the highly formalised structures of screenplay, theatre and radio script formats.

The MA maps the writer's progression through a series of explorations that engage, in different ways, with this essential tension. The journey begins with learning to read scripts well, unpacking the subtleties layered into the codes and conventions of script formats. It's a truffle hunt: rooting through the plainness and simplicity of linguistic expression required by stage/screen directions and lean, economical dialogue, to uncover the rich motivations, feelings and behaviours of characters embarked upon their own voyages through their story worlds. The yield, for a skilled script reader, is akin to the pleasures experienced by a reader of poetry. For scriptwriters, it's crucial to understand these pleasures and how they are created on the page. Although scripts are rarely read by the majority of the audiences who come to see and hear them in performance, they must nonetheless be able to enchant the people who do read them: literary managers, producers, directors, actors, designers, and other key production personnel. These are the gatekeepers; the script is the key. A script must be a good read, but should leave the reader hungry for the performance still to come. It must not, itself, satisfy that hunger; its job is to whet the appetite.

VT

# Jenny Brogan

## *Fury*

***FADE IN:***

***EXT. CITYSCAPE – NIGHT – FLASHBACK***

Dark tower blocks lit by flashing neon signs.

Rain-spattered windows, cars, asphalt.

PEOPLE jostle along busy sidewalks.

> ***LUELLA (VO)***
> There was a time I called the
> city home.

A COUPLE shelter in the glow of a late night drugstore. They are arguing about nothing.

Moonlight reflected in the flow of the City's grey river.

A WOMAN (LUELLA, 29) idles down an empty side street. She's bathed in shades of green; calf-length trench coat, headscarf, nails. She's soaked through with rain.

> LUELLA (VO)
> Then I got a calling.

She's carrying a small satin bag. It has a large gold catch. Her metal heeled-shoes are black. The sound of her footsteps punctures the night.

### INT. MAIN LOBBY OF A SHABBY APARTMENT BLOCK – NIGHT

One light bulb burns brightly; the rest are dead.

A staircase at the end of the lobby leads to the first floor apartments. It is shrouded in darkness.

> LUELLA (VO)
> I needed to go west. Get out of the rain,
> find some sun.

Luella puts her satin bag on the hallway table and sifts through the tenants' mail that is scattered over the table.

Rain from her wet fringe splatters envelopes. There's nothing for her. She walks towards the dingy staircase and walks to the first floor.

> LUELLA (VO)
> Mostly, I wanted to forget that night.

### INT. LUELLA'S LOUNGE/DINER – NIGHT

Light from flashing neon boards plays through the Venetian blinds, casting shadows across the wooden floor. The lounge is littered with papers, plates and glasses. A pile of newly washed laundry sits on an armchair. Luella enters and surveys the mess. She takes off her trench coat and pulls a clean towel from the pile.

### INT. LUELLA'S BATHROOM – NIGHT

With a loud click Luella is illuminated in a large mirror above the bathroom sink.

She's wearing a towel like a turban. Her mascara has smudged her cheeks.

> **LUELLA**
> Well, hello, doll face.

She steps back, gazing appreciatively.

She edges further back, almost to the bathroom door, studying her chest in the mirror.

> **LUELLA**
> Great rack.

She's almost out in the hallway. She turns her back to the mirror and twists round to see her reflection.

> **LUELLA**
> Nice ass. Poor man's Betty Grable.

DOOR BUZZER rings off. Luella ignores it. It rings again.

**INT. LUELLA'S HALLWAY – NIGHT**

Luella is staring at the front door. It begins to rattle.

> **DODIE (OS)**
> You in there, Lu?

> **LUELLA**
> You gotta love y'neighbours.

Luella opens the door an inch. Her tiny neighbour DODIE (78) stands smiling up at her. She's wearing a new lacy dressing gown. She places her frail hand on the door frame.

Luella holds the door firm. Dodie places her foot in the gap. Luella holds her gaze.

She notices Dodie's new night-time finery.

**LUELLA**
Dodie, he ain't here yet.

Dodie tries to push further into the gap. She's smiling all the while. She's not so frail.

**DODIE**
Where is he? He's here. I heard him.
You're playing games. Where's he
hidin'?

**LUELLA**
He's gonna be real late tonight,
past your bedtime. Go along now.

Luella eases Dodie out onto the landing and closes the door.

**INT. FIRST FLOOR LANDING – NIGHT**

Dodie makes her way to her front door. She uses the landing walls to steady herself. She mumbles:

**DODIE**
Jack ain't never this late.

**EXT. GAS STATION – EARLIER THAT EVENING**

JACK (31) pumps fuel into his car. He's laughing with the FORECOURT ATTENDANT who has come out to chat with him.

**EXT. *the opposite side of the street* – NIGHT**

Luella stands in a shop doorway across from the gas station. She is half hidden in the shadows. A nearby street light casts an orange glow; her nylons shimmer, her shoes shine in the light. She smokes.

> LUELLA (VO)
> Jack. Everyone loved him. Had that special
> something; y'know, children, small
> animals, old ladies. Not so old ladies. We
> all wanted a piece of the action.

**EXT. GAS STATION – NIGHT**

Jack hands over notes to the attendant.

A car pulls up at the opposite pump. The door opens. A SHARPLY DRESSED MAN
gets out and heads for the cigarette machine.

The passenger door opens and a YOUNG BLONDE alights. Jack locks his eyes on
her. They start to flirt. The woman's throaty laugh rings out across the street.

> LUELLA (VO)
> He really knew how to work it.

The sharply dressed man returns with a packet of cigarettes. He kisses the blonde
on the cheek and opens the car door for her. The woman gazes at Jack.

> LUELLA (VO)
> Take her right from under her man's nose
> if he wanted to.

Jack watches the car drive off before getting into his own.

> LUELLA (VO)
> Thing about Jack was, he didn't
> concentrate so well. He flitted here and
> there. Butterfly man.

**EXT. THE OPPOSITE SIDE OF THE STREET – NIGHT**

Luella walks along the sidewalk. She flicks her cigarette into the gutter. It starts to rain. She hails a cab.

### EXT. ED'S DINER – PARKING LOT – NIGHT

Jack pulls into the parking lot. He eases himself out of his car. He takes off his hat and places it on the passenger seat. He runs a comb through his hair.

> LUELLA (VO)
> He was sweet on Sally though.

### EXT. STREET ADJACENT THE PARKING LOT AT ED'S DINER – NIGHT

A cab pulls up.

### EXT. ED'S DINER – PARKING LOT – NIGHT

Jack watches SALLY (19) through the large diner windows. She's waiting on a handful of customers. Jack watches the men watching her walk away from the table.

He's pleased with himself.

### INT. ED'S DINER – NIGHT

Jack finishes the remains of his burger. The diner has emptied of customers.

### EXT. ED'S DINER – PARKING LOT – NIGHT

The light of the diner shines bright in the parking lot. A lone MAN stands at the cash register. Sally counts out his change. The man is generous with his tip. He's too generous. Sally blushes with embarrassment.

> LUELLA (VO)
> She was real pretty. A honeypot
> for sure.

**INT. ED'S DINER – NIGHT**

Sally glances over the man's shoulder and catches Jack's gaze. Jack winks and smiles at her.

The man picks up his hat from the counter. He shoots Jack a look as he yanks open the door.

Sally walks slowly over to Jack. He watches her every step.

> **LUELLA (VO)**
> Just couldn't help himself.

He stands up, towering over her. He takes her hand and leads her to the counter. He hoists her onto it.

> **SALLY**
> I ain't putting on a show.

**EXT. ED'S DINER – PARKING LOT – NIGHT**

Jack switches off the lights. The glass-fronted drinks cooler is the only source of illumination. The parking lot is dark.

Jack and Sally are silhouettes. He leans into her. He places a hand on each of her calves. He trails his fingers slowly up her legs. He kisses her neck.

**INT. ED'S DINER – NIGHT**

The driving rain smashes against the windows. A strong gust of wind blows the door open. It stays open.

The lovers startle.

> **SALLY**
> Forgot to lock it.

Sally looks at him, waiting.

> **JACK**
> You gonna invite me in?

Sally lifts up the hem of her uniform and opens her legs wider. She takes one of Jack's hands and guides it under her skirt.

She's holding his head, pulling him towards her. They move in time with each other. Sally clings to Jack.

> **LUELLA (VO)**
> When I first met Jack, it was, it
> was like some kinda door had opened,
> y'know. And I was invited
> in. And when he kissed me, I held on.
> I held on.

Luella stands in the doorway. She's silhouetted in the light of the drinks cooler. She watches.

> **JACK**
> Sal, honey, you're hurting me.

> **LUELLA**
> Jack.

Jack and Sally pull apart. Jack sees Luella in the light of the cooler. The moment lasts.

The door swings back shut with the force of the gale.

Gun shots in the dark.

### EXT. STREET NEAR ED'S DINER – NIGHT

Luella jogs to the main road. She is soaked through to the skin. She stands out in the road to hail a cab.

### INT. LUELLA'S LOUNGE/DINER – NIGHT

Luella sits at her dining table. Her towel-dried hair hangs in rats' tails. She pulls out a revolver from her satin bag and places it on the table.

*She cleans the gun with a cloth. Her cleaning is slow and precise.*

> **LUELLA (VO)**
> Picture in my head. Me and my daddy
> sitting on the back porch. And I'm
> watching him real close. He's cleaning
> his favourite gun. It's a rifle. Blow your
> face clean from your skull. Noboby'd
> recognise ya.

She holds the revolver like a museum exhibit.

> **LUELLA (VO)**
> Now a revolver. It's a prettier kill. That's
> what he said. He said it was a woman's
> gun.

### INT. FIRST FLOOR LANDING – NIGHT

Dodie stands in front of Luella's door. She wears a shabby nightie. She's agitated.

She hesitates to ring the door.

### INT. LUELLA'S LOUNGE/DINER – NIGHT

Door buzzer, off. Luella stops cleaning. The door buzzer rings again.

***INT. LUELLA'S HALLWAY – NIGHT***

Luella stares at the door.

> ***DODIE (OS)***
> It's only me.

Luella opens the door wide. She glares at Dodie.

Dodie makes no attempt to move. She's afraid. She's looking at something in Luella's eyes but she can't read it.

> ***LUELLA***
> Now I told you before. Jack is gonna be
> late. Way past your bedtime.

> ***DODIE***
> Just wanted to see him. Say goodnight.

Luella stares at Dodie.

> ***DODIE***
> I'll … I'll speak to him in the mornin'.

> ***LUELLA.***
> You do that now.

Dodie shuffles to her own front door.

> ***LUELLA (CALLING)***
> Sweet dreams, Dodie.

***INT.  ED'S DINER – DAWN***

> ***LUELLA (VO)***
> I shoulda put her out of her misery.

Jack is motionless, spreadeagled on the diner floor.

His eyes stare at the ceiling. He's lying in a halo of blood.

Up near the cash register lies the body of Sally. She's unrecognisable.

### INT. STAIRCASE TO THE MAIN LOBBY OF THE APARTMENT BLOCK – DAY

Luella descends the stairs. She struggles with the weight of her suitcase.

She's dressed in a cream trench coat.

### INT. FIRST FLOOR LANDING STAIRWELL – DAY

Dodie follows her down the stairs. She has to clutch the rail to steady herself.

> DODIE (CALLING)
> Lu. Luella.

Her voice doesn't carry too well.

> DODIE (CALLING)
> Lu.

### INT. MAIN LOBBY OF THE APARTMENT BLOCK – DAY

Luella stops in her tracks. She watches Dodie reach the bottom stair.

> LUELLA
> He didn't come home last night Dodie.

Dodie is visibly distressed. The stairs have taken her breath.

> DODIE
> Where ... where'ya goin'?

Luella pulls the front door open. The light of the day shines in. She blinks.

Dodie stumbles up the lobby. She stops short of the front door.

>                          **DODIE**
>                   Where'ya goin' to?

Luella stares at Dodie. She shrugs her shoulders.

>                          **LUELLA**
>                You be sure to say goodbye to Jack for
>                me now.

She turns and closes the door behind her.

**EXT. FISHERMAN'S WHARF IN SAN FRANCISCO – DAY – PRESENT**

CROWDS fill the boardwalk on a summer's day. People eat lunch at the waterside cafés, STALL TRADERS do a brisk trade, CHILDREN play among the adults.

Luella mingles with the crowd. She's stunning in red and white. Her hair is different. She stops and scans the crowd. She notices her type, a TALL DARK MAN, standing at an arts and crafts stall.

>                          **LUELLA (VO)**
>                   The air's different here.

A summer shower drenches the crowds. Luella's laughing.

>                          **LUELLA (VO)**
>                Hell, even the rain's different.

**EXT. CAFÉ PORCH – DAY**

Luella takes cover under the café's canopy. Her eyes are drawn to the TALL DARK MAN who is now standing near her. He sees her. She smiles then looks away.

He crosses to her.

**MAN**
Robert Leigh. How do y'do?

***LUELLA***
Dorothy Roles. Dottie, if you like.

Robert grins at Luella. Luella produces her killer smile.

***LUELLA***
I'm doing good.

He's hooked.

**THE END**

---

**Jenny Brogan** is a drama teacher. Her first play made the shortlist for Channel 4's *The Play's The Thing*. More recently, her proposal for a six-part television comedy made the shortlist for the *Brocken Spectre Production Company*, as part of Channel 4's *PILOT* competition to find new writing talent.

# Alison Falconer

## *Mother's Day*

### INT. HOSPITAL WAITING AREA

Patients are variously bandaged or showing signs of damage. JULIA, 39, is clothed from head to foot, including a balaclava. NURSES emerge and take other patients to booths. Only Julia remains. Finally a DOCTOR, male, 56, crosses the area about to go off shift. He notices her.

> *DOCTOR*
> Mrs Wilson?

> *JULIA*
> Yes.

> *DOCTOR*
> You were due two hours ago.

> *JULIA*
> I was here but no one ...

> *DOCTOR*
> Follow me.

He strides off. She follows him.

### INT. HOSPITAL BOOTH, CONTINUOUS

He picks up a clipboard.

> So, what's brought you here?

> #### JULIA
> Well, bits of me had been disappearing
> for years.

> #### DOCTOR
> Common complaint among women of a
> certain age.

> #### JULIA
> I just learnt to work my way round it.

### INT. SITTING ROOM, FLASHBACK

BEN,14, and LUCY,12, sit on the sofa watching television.

> #### JULIA (VO)
> You, know ... wearing gloves.

Julia serves them plates of fish fingers, chips and broccoli. She wears large rubber gloves with rings and fluffy cuffs. *Die Another Day* is on. She sings along to the theme tune.

> #### LUCY
> Mu-um ...

She freezes. Perhaps they've noticed the gloves.

> #### LUCY (CONT'D)
> Stop singing, you're ruining it.

She stops singing and continues to serve.

> **BEN**
> Can't we ever have something different
> for tea?

### INT. BEDROOM, DAYLIGHT

Julia walks past a long mirror in a skirt and sandals. Her legs are invisible. She steps back to look again, then hunches down so that her skirt covers her legs. She moves awkwardly to a dressing table from which she pulls a tub of fake tan. Her legs reappear as she rubs it on.

> **JULIA (VO)**
> … Using fake tan.

### INT. BEDROOM, NIGHT

SEAN,41, bespectacled, is in bed, reading papers from a folder. Two bedside lights are on. Julia, dressed in high-necked pyjamas, a headscarf, socks and gloves, sits at the dressing table inspecting her face in the mirror.

> **JULIA (VO) (CONT'D)**
> And, mainly, wearing a lot of cloths.

Her left ear has become invisible. She tucks it under the scarf. She looks at Sean with concern. He puts down the papers.

> **JULIA**
> Sean …

He grunts and turns off his light without looking at her. She gets into bed and he turns away from her. Julia undoes the buttons of her pyjama top to reveal empty space where her neck and chest should be.

> Sean, please look at me.

He looks over his shoulder briefly.

**SEAN**

What?

He turns away from her again.

It's late. I'm too tired for this.

**JULIA**

Soon there's going to be nothing left.

**SEAN**

Bill missed the ten o'clock today, which
meant I didn't have the figures for the
afternoon meeting. I told Angela but she
didn't listen. It's my job to know and I
didn't know.

Julia lies back and looks at the ceiling.

**JULIA (VO)**

And then I started having this dream, the
same one, over and over again ...

### INT. OPERATING THEATRE, DREAM

All implements in the room are domestic equivalents of operating instruments,
whisk, bread knife etc. The POV hovers above. Leaning over the operating table in
gowns and domestic rubber gloves are Sean, Lucy and Ben.

They stand upright to reveal Julia's clothes flat on the table as if the body inside
has dissolved. Sean takes off his gloves.

>               SEAN
> There'll always be some you can't save,
> no matter how many hours a day you
> slave away.

>               LUCY
> Can we go now?

>               SEAN
> Might as well.

Ben and Lucy leave.

>               SEAN
> If they'd given us the upgrades but it's
> always budget, budget, budget.

He turns off the light. Julia screams.

### INT. HOSPITAL BOOTH

The doctor's head on one side, his eyes closed.

>               JULIA
> I had entirely ... dissolved ... So I went
> to the GP and he said something could
> be done before it's too late. (PAUSE)

The doctor wakes and rubs his eyes.

>               DOCTOR
> Sorry. Long shift. He told you to bring a
> recent picture for us to work from?

>               JULIA
> Oh ... yes.

She takes two pictures from an envelope in her bag and looks at them, making her mind up. One is of Julia as she appears in flashbacks and another digitally altered with red hair, freckles and green eyes. The doctor looks up.

> **DOCTOR**
> Keep it with you for now.

Julia puts them away.

> Don't want your picture mixed up with
> someone else's. You'd both have a big
> surprise when you woke up. Ha?

Julia rubs her chin and looks guiltily away.

> If you could just sign here.

### INT. HOSPITAL SIDE ROOM, LATER

Julia, in balaclava, scarf and hospital gown, sits in bed and sorts through her handbag. She pulls out a used tissue, which she bins, then a fluffy pen she strokes and puts on the bed. Next is a toy Jedi light sabre, too large to fit in the bag. She swishes it with appropriate noises, remembering a younger Ben, and adds it to the pen. Then she pulls out a baby sock, which she sniffs deeply, rubs against her face and adds to the pile. Finally she pulls out a large beachstone with a hole in it.

### EXT. BEACH, 1983, FLASHBACK

It's summer. Julia, 21, long floating skirt, interesting jewellery, and Sean, 23, shorts, both barefooted, race along the beach to the breakwater. Sean reaches it moments ahead of Julia.

> **SEAN**
> I win.

Sean, arms open, waits for Julia to catch up. She walks past him, speeding up.

Then runs on slowly.

**JULIA**

Best of three.

He catches her and spins her round.

**SEAN**

You cheated.

Julia gestures 'and?', laughing. They kiss, then walk, arms round each other. They stop and face the sea. Julia picks up a stone and inspects it. It's the one from her handbag. Sean picks a stone too but skims his. He picks up more and continues skimming.

**SEAN**

Soon be able to go freelance. Work on
my own ideas.

**JULIA**

Good. They've got potential. Linking up
computers ... that might be useful.

Sean squeezes her shoulder and they
walk on.

**SEAN**

Maybe. And you can make more
jewellery and sell it.

**JULIA**

And we can live on a boat ...

**SEAN**

And chase our six children round the
deck ...

*Alison Falconer*

> **JULIA**
> I'm going to keep this stone so we
> never forget.

> **SEAN**
> Look, a starfish.

They both look.

> It's still alive.

Sean picks it up and rushes into the sea, swimming out until Julia is worried about him. He swims back without it and comes out of the water shivering. Julia dries him with her skirt.

> **JULIA**
> You're freezing.

> **SEAN**
> You have to go rer-right out.

She hugs him to warm him up and rubs his arms.

> You have to go far enough so they won't
> get washed up again. Otherwise they dry
> out and die.

She kisses him.

> Can't let that happen.

## INT. HOSPITAL ROOM, PRESENT

Julia looks at the stone for a moment then puts it back in her handbag. She jumps out of bed, pulls off the balaclava and removes the rest of her clothes. She picks up her handbag and pauses in front of the mirror. She is completely invisible, although the bag is not. She stuffs it in the bedside locker, opens the door, looks around, then steps out.

### EXT. FRONT STEP, JULIA'S HOUSE

The front garden is sterile grey brickweave with one spiky plant in a gravel bed. She checks, no one's looking, then gets a key from beneath an insulated milk holder and opens the door.

### INT. HALL

Julia enters and shuts the door behind her.

> SEAN
> (OFF) Lucy, is that you?

> LUCY
> (OFF) What?

> SEAN
> (OFF) Is someone at the door?

### INT. HALL/STAIRS

Julia follows Lucy's voice upstairs. She freezes as Sean peeps from the dining room to check the front door, moves on.

### INT. BEN'S BEDROOM

She goes into Ben's bedroom where tomorrow's school shirt hangs from his electric guitar. A chest of drawers by the door features a mess of CDs, plectrums and hair products. Ben strums his acoustic guitar. Lucy sits on the bed, reading a magazine.

> BEN
> … the one that starts, (SINGING)

Walking all night in the city ...

> **LUCY**
> Still don't remember it.

> **BEN**
> That's what I'm doing for the
> song contest.

> **LUCY**
> What if mum's not back in time?

> **BEN**
> No problem. Mr Burton's helping me
> write it out.

> **LUCY**
> Oh. Dad says we're having take-out
> again.

> **BEN**
> Cool.

Lucy heads towards the door and Julia pulls back.

### INT. LANDING

She watches for a moment as Ben retunes one of his strings. Lucy picks up some heat-proof serum. Julia turns away.

> **LUCY**
> (OFF) This is mine.

> **BEN**
> Is not.

*INT. STAIRS*

She walks downstairs and the argument fades out.

*INT. HALL*

She can see Sean in the dining room.

*INT. DINING ROOM*

She enters and looks at him. He sits back in one antique reproduction dining chair, his feet on another, beside a table covered in papers. He's on the phone.

> **SEAN**
> You know what he's leaving to do? ...
> Nothing as sensible as that. He's 'going
> travelling' and he's 40 for God's sake ...

Julia walks around the room. There are school photographs and one of their wedding. Julia picks it up. They are holding hands. Sean looks proud, Julia happy. She's wearing a white wedding dress but large, unusual earrings. She puts it down and heads towards the door. Sean is unaware of her. She watches him.

> **SEAN**
> No. I'm here till I get my pension, with a
> bit of luck ... Suits us perfectly. Julia's
> got the children, I've got the Rotary.

> **JULIA**
> (PAUSE) Goodbye Sean.

Sean drops the phone and falls off his chair looking for the source of the voice. Julia leaves the room.

### INT. HOSPITAL ROOM – LATER

Julia is in bed holding a photograph as the door opens. There is another, face down, beside the cupboard. The doctor comes in. He picks up a chart.

> **DOCTOR**
> Mrs Wilson. Good to see you.

He shakes her hand.

> Sorry. Ha ha. Soon will be.
> I mean, soon will be good to see you that
> is. Er, picture?

Julia pauses, then hands the other picture to the doctor.

> Ah, family'll be glad to have the
> old Julia back I expect. Er, not old
> as in …

### INT. HOSPITAL, RECEPTION AREA (AS SCENE 1)

Julia, 39, now a fair-skinned redhead with freckles, green eyes and light summer dress – unrecognisable but for her bag – waits on a chair by a window. She sees something and goes out.

### EXT. HOSPITAL STEPS

Her family approaches. She holds the door for them.

> **BEN**
> Thanks.

She watches them go through the door and into the foyer. Then sadly walks away.

### EXT. STREET

She walks along the street, her step becoming lighter, freer. She sees a bus stop. And looks at the timetable. There is a bus to the station. A LARGE, OLDER WOMAN with a shopping bag joins her.

> **WOMAN**
> Been waiting long?

> **JULIA**
> Years and years.

> **WOMAN**
> Should be one along soon then.

A young ASIAN WOMAN joins them. She carries several bags of food.

> **ASIAN WOMAN**
> Are you waiting for the fifty three?

> **WOMAN**
> It'll be here soon.

The bus draws up just as an elderly lady approaches with a stick, which she waves as she gets near.

> **OLD LADY**
> Wait for me.

Julia gets on the bus.

> **JULIA**
> The station please.

She sits down. The bus is peopled by WOMEN of all kinds. The large woman sits next to her with her bag on her lap. The bus moves off. The Asian woman has left her bags at the stop. Julia watches out of the window as the streets go by. She notices a flat with a bright windowbox in a dull block. A bag lady pushing a trolley has a fresh flower in her hat.

**WOMAN**
Where are you going?

**JULIA**
The station.

The bus stops alongside a house where a teenage boy feeds an iguana pieces of banana.

**WOMAN**
Then?

**JULIA**
I don't know where I'm going.

She thinks for a moment.

**JULIA**
I don't need to know.

She looks out of the window again.

**JULIA**
(TO SELF) As long as it's far enough.

---

**Alison Falconer**'s performed work consists of four theatre pieces, including one full-length professional commission. Two radio submissions have led to requests for further work. She's currently working on a full-length play around a hostage situation on an oil rig and hopes to expand her range to television following the MA.

*Mother's Day*

# Colette Gunn-Graffy

*Amara*

FADE IN:

*EXT. BEACH – DAY*

Rough sea, overcast sky. On the horizon is a fishing boat. Dark cliffs rise above the deserted beach – at their top, something orange billows. The tide smoothes over the strange tracks – like twin snakes – that cross the sand.

*EXT. CLIFFS – DAY*

An orange pavilion tent whips in the wind at the top of the cliff. Beyond is a circle of caravans, each painted a different garish colour.

*EXT. ROAD – DAY*

A sledge pulled by an ALSATIAN speeds across the dusty road towards the encampment. The DRIVER's legs are wrapped in a heavy grey skirt, her face is not seen.

*INT. ESTELLA'S TENT – DAY*

The wall of the tent glows red-orange from the light of a fire. Outside, some way off, the sledge skids to a stop. A SMALL BROWN HAND lifts the flap of the tent.

### EXT. CIRCLE OF CARAVANS – DAY

The sledge rests in the middle of the circle of caravans. Just beyond is the orange tent – the flap is still lifted, but the occupant cannot be seen. The Alsatian is lying down, panting.

The driver of the sledge, AMARA, a slight girl of 15, unhooks a pair of forked staffs from the underside of the sledge.

Caravan doors bang as their occupants hurry outside to view the visitor: a HUNCHBACK with a toothbrush jutting out of his mouth; a WOMAN covered head-to-toe with fine golden fur, in the process of taking out her curlers; SIAMESE TWINS, each with a single eye made up, each holding an eye pencil.

A MAN WITH TUMOURS COVERING HIS FACE (ESTEBAN) reaches out to help Amara. She knocks his hand aside and pulls herself upright on the staffs. As she does so, her skirt lifts slightly, revealing swollen, veiny flesh. Amara glares at the man.

**AMARA**
I'm here to see Estella.

In the background, the tent flap drops.

### INT. ESTELLA'S TENT – DAY

Esteban lifts the tent flap for Amara as she enters with the aid of her staffs. The flap drops behind her.

The tent is luxurious – much larger on the inside than it looks on the outside – decorated with animal furs and dark wooden furniture. In the centre of the tent, surrounded by a circle of high-backed armchairs, a log fire burns but does not give off smoke. Show posters spanning several decades hang on the wall.

Amara examines a poster of an enormously fat woman wearing a baby-doll outfit and holding a parasol. The poster reads: 'The Lovely Lolateena, she's larger than life at Starlight Novelties Show'.

Amara snorts. She turns to go, but her eye is caught by the distorting mirror in the corner. In the wavy glass, Amara's grey-shrouded lower body appears as though it were spliced in two – as though she were wearing trousers. Amara stares at her reflection.

### EXT. BEACH – DAY – FLASHBACK

Amara stares into the ocean. She sits on a large rock several metres from shore. A small brown hand offers her a white card. Amara does not take it.

> **AMARA**
> I'm not one of your circus freaks. There's
> nothing you can offer me that I want.

Amara lurches into the ocean with a splash. Her clothes float to the surface.

**END FLASHBACK**

### INT. ESTELLA'S TENT – DAY

Amara reaches out to touch her reflection.

> **ESTELLA (OS)**
> I had a feeling we'd meet again.

Amara turns. ESTELLA, a tan-faced midget of indeterminate age, pokes her head around the side of one of the armchairs. She is wearing a gold-sequined tailcoat and a mask of make-up.

Estella gestures to a side table crowded with liquor bottles.

> **ESTELLA (CONT'D)**
> Something to wet your whistle?

Amara does not respond. Estella picks up a spritzer bottle.

> ***ESTELLA (CONT'D)***
> A glass of water then!

Estella winks at Amara and fills a glass with water. She fills a second glass with gin.

> ***ESTELLA (CONT'D)***
> They say water keeps you young, but
> I have to say, it's the gin that keeps
> me going.

Estella leads Amara to one of the armchairs. She starts to hand her a drink, then sniffs it.

> ***ESTELLA (CONT'D)***
> Whoops!

Estella hands Amara the other glass, and with the aid of a small step stool, settles herself into another armchair. Estella sits like a child with her short legs splayed open.

> ***ESTELLA (CONT'D)***
> I think you'll find it's nice to
> be appreciated.

> ***AMARA***
> I'm not looking for appreciation –

> ***ESTELLA***
> No? Value, acceptance, love – call it what
> you will –

> ***AMARA***
> I want to be left alone!

Estella chuckles.

> **ESTELLA**
> Oh my dear, that is the one thing they'll
> never allow you.

### EXT. BEACH – DAY – FLASHBACK

Amara sits on a rock several metres from shore. Estella, wrapped in a tawny fur coat, stands over her, holding out a small white card.

Amara rejects the card and dives into the ocean.

### EXT. UNDERWATER – DAY – FLASHBACK

Amara swims naked underwater among kelp and coral. Her lower body is a veiny, flesh-coloured mass with webbed appendages where the feet should be – but underwater it moves as gracefully as a fish tail. Amara's long hair streams around her. She is smiling, strong and free.

> **ESTELLA (VO)**
> If you were to live among them in the
> village, they could turn you into a
> charity case. They could view your
> deformity up close, witness your
> anguish. Set up funds in your name.

### EXT. OCEAN – DAY – FLASHBACK

Amara surfaces for air. Nearby is a fishing boat.

### EXT. FISHING BOAT – DAY – FLASHBACK

MEN with red, raw faces and hands pull on ropes, bringing a net of fish up from the ocean. Fish cascade over the deck.

**EXT. UNDERWATER – DAY – FLASHBACK**

A net falls on Amara. She struggles.

**EXT. FISHING BOAT – DAY – FLASHBACK**

Amara slides onto the deck with the fish. The fishermen are shocked at first, then begin to leer and grin at one another and at Amara. They approach her, try to touch her breasts, grab at her tail. Amara bites, scratches and spits.

> ESTELLA (VO)
> But you keep yourself apart, like a wild
> savage. How can they tell what you are?
> If you feel pain? They need to know.

**EXT. UNDERWATER – DAY – FLASHBACK**

The hull of the fishing boat is visible. Amara lands underwater with a great splash. She screams but makes no sound. The boat starts up. Amara tries to chase it.

ESTELLA (V.O.)

Turn your back, it doesn't matter. The stories will spread ...

**EXT. OCEAN – DAY – FLASHBACK**

Amara comes up for air. The boat is just a dot on the horizon.

> ESTELLA (VO)
> ... Getting wilder and more fantastic ...

**EXT. BEACH – DAY – FLASHBACK**

Amara lies sobbing with her face in the sand as the tide rolls in across her body. The Alsatian sniffs at her, licks at her face and hands.

> **ESTELLA (VO)**
> And one after the other, they'll come
> after you. Some just for a look, others
> for more …

**END FLASHBACK**

## INT. ESTELLA'S TENT – DAY

Amara's glass of water shatters on the floor.

> **AMARA**
> No! You said –

> **ESTELLA**
> I offered you escape – not in body,
> in mind.

Estella stares into Amara's tear-filled eyes, takes her hand.

> **ESTELLA**
> They've caused you to suffer –
> make them buy the right to enjoy
> your pain.

The firelight catches on Estella's sequined tailcoat.

## INT. FREAKSHOW – DAY – FLASHFORWARD

Amara wears a golden crown that catches the light. On her face is a haughty expression. Her breasts are hidden by clam shells and her lower body has been painted a shimmering greenish-gold – a realistic tailfin has been attached. She sits on a pedestal encrusted with coral and starfish in the middle of a white pavilion tent. The MEN, WOMEN and CHILDREN who crowd around the pedestal, gaping, are kept at a distance by a red velvet rope.

> ### ESTELLA (VO)
> Knowing what they want gives you
> power over them.

The rest of the company are exhibited around the room in similar approximations of their own 'natural habitats': the hunchback, in blood-stained rags, stands above a woodpile, holding an axe; the furry woman, chained to a post, bays forlornly; the Siamese twins, wearing a leotard, cavort with balls and hoops.

> ### ESTELLA (VO – CONT'D)
> You play into their hands. You act the
> expected part.

Amara catches the eye of Estella, who is across the room, collecting money at the door.

A YOUNG BOY reaches for Amara's tail. She whacks it against the pedestal, barely missing his hand. The boy looks up to meet Amara's stare of menace. His frightened MOTHER pulls him roughly away.

Amara and Estella smile at each other from opposite sides of the room.

### INT. AMARA'S CARAVAN – NIGHT – FLASHFORWARD

The caravan is cosy, decorated with show posters and dried flowers. A lantern casts an orange glow. Amara sits on a chair next to a table with a make-up mirror. She uses a sponge and small bucket to rinse the make-up off her body.

> ### ESTELLA (VO)
> They see what you want them
> to see.

Amara catches sight of herself in the mirror. A tear rolls down her face.

> ### END FLASHFORWARD

### INT. ESTELLA'S TENT – DAY

Estella stares into Amara's eyes.

> **AMARA**
> And what if one day I want to leave, to
> return to the ocean?

> **ESTELLA**
> You won't. We'll get you pools. Private
> ones, whatever you need.

Esteban appears behind Estella's armchair and hands her a sheet of parchment and a quill pen.

> **ESTELLA (CONT'D)**
> Thank you, Esteban.

Estaban leaves. Estella places the parchment and quill on the small table between their chairs.

> **AMARA**
> What if I decide, one day, I no longer
> wish to play the role?

> **ESTELLA**
> Then they'll slaughter you. For
> betraying their most innocent beliefs.

Estella smiles.

> **ESTELLA (CONT'D)**
> But you won't have to worry about that,
> because I think you are going to be very
> happy here. Now you'll have to learn to
> sing ...

Estella hands the quill to Amara, who takes it.

>                         **ESTELLA (CONT'D)**
>               Hope you don't mind.

Estella points to the parchment.

>                         **ESTELLA (CONT'D)**
>               Just here ...

## EXT. CIRCLE OF CARAVANS – NIGHT

Firelight flickers over the caravans. Music and laughter indicate that the caravans' occupants are nearby. Amara's Alsatian lies with his head in his paws. Esteban approaches the dog and looks down at it.

>                         **ESTEBAN**
>          Go.

The dog stands and looks at him.

>                         **ESTEBAN (CONT'D)**
>               Go on. Go home. Leave.

Esteban aims a kick at the dog. The dog runs off.

## EXT. CLIFFS – NIGHT

Firelight flickers over the orange tent at the edge of the cliff. A dog howls.

## EXT. BEACH – NIGHT

The tide is high, waves crash against the cliffs. A dot of light on the top of the cliff indicates the encampment. A dog howls.

**Colette Gunn-Graffy** grew up in San Francisco, California. She studied theatre and acting at Yale University. Her first play *By Any Other Name* premiered at the *Yale Playwriting Festival*. Colette has written several plays, most recently with London Soho Theatre's Core Group. She is currently writing a full-length stage drama.

# Alexandra Leaney

## *Eau de Fox Merde*

*INT. KITCHEN – MORNING*

Oak cabinets and tiled counter tops line the front of the large country kitchen.

Under an oak table at the back of the room is an empty dog's bed, which is filled with splinters from chewed wood, the remains of an old leather slipper and a large bone in the latter stages of decomposition. The S and the E from the embroidered name Dickens on the side have been torn off.

CYRUS, a sleek reddish brown Saluki dog, dozes on a large neatly folded purple blanket in front of an open fire.

FLOSSY, a small white fluffy Havanese showdog sits in her pink padded basket on the window ledge gazing out into the countryside beyond.

> ### *FLOSSY*
> Cyrus, Cy ...

Cyrus stirs. He opens his eyes and stretches.

> ### *CYRUS*
> Mmmmmm?

**FLOSSY**

Why can't I go out and play?

Flossy glares at the empty bed under the table.

**CYRUS**

You are a young lady. A young lady
with the world at her feet.

**FLOSSY**

No I'm not. It's out there and I'm
in here.

**CYRUS**

I meant it metaphorically speaking.
You can't win Crufts if you tear around
in the brambles and mud.

**FLOSSY**

Dickens does.

**CYRUS**

Dickens is a mutt.

**FLOSSY**

I thought he was a Terrier?

**CYRUS**

Same thing.

DICK, a medium-sized terrier covered in muck, pokes his head through the cat-flap. He squeezes his left shoulder through and then in one large grunt bursts into the kitchen.

**DICK**

So, what d'ya think?

Dick turns a few times, inhaling deeply. Cyrus turns his head away in disgust. Flossy sniffs tentatively.

> **CYRUS**
> Wonderful Dickens, never a thought for
> your fellow dog.

> **DICK**
> How many times do I have to tell you it's
> DICK. Not Dickens or Charles. Dick. What
> is it with you and all the big words and
> stuff? I only need one name, just keep
> it simple.

> **CYRUS**
> Yes, yes. I suppose one should attempt to
> address others on their level.

Dick stares at Cyrus, eyebrow raised in confusion.

> **FLOSSY**
> I like having a long name. I think it
> flows. Flossy Finola Finton. Flo-o-ssy,
> Fino-o-la, Finton.

> **DICK**
> Well babe, it suits you.

Dick sidles up to Flossy, leaning on the windowsill to gaze into her eyes.

> **DICK (CONT'D)**
> So do you like my new scent?
> I call it 'Eau de Fox Merde'.

**FLOSSY**
Oh. Well, it's … certainly different.
I haven't smelt that one before.

**DICK**
I know, there's no point just following the
pack. See that's what I am, a born leader.

Cyrus rolls his eyes and sits up to keep an eye on Flossy. Dick goes to the cat-flap,
sticks his head through and returns with a black rubber object.

**FLOSSY**
What's that?

**DICK**
I don't know, but it chews good.

Dickens places the piece of rubber under the table on his grimy bed. Flossy jumps
down from the windowsill to take a closer look.

**DICK (CONT'D)**
I found it by the heap after I'd killed,
like, fifteen rats.

**FLOSSY**
Did you eat them all?

**DICK**
No. You don't eat rats.

**FLOSSY**
Then why do you catch them?

**CYRUS**
Good point Flossy. A dog of pedigree
hunts for food fit for consumption.

> **DICK**
> Yeah, whatever Cyrus. Rats need killing
> and I kill 'em good.

Dick turns his back on Cyrus. He hunts around his bed pulling out a small raggedy teddy bear, which he places in the middle of the kitchen floor and then turns to Flossy.

> **DICK (CONT'D)**
> Rats are sneaky and vicious, so to be a
> good ratter you've got to be bold, brave
> and brutal.

Dick snaps his head round and bares his teeth.

> **FLOSSY**
> Goodness.

> **DICK**
> Watch. You pick up their scent.

Dick turns, nose to ground and begins sniffing about.

> **DICK (CONT'D)**
> Stalk them.

Dick crouches low to the ground and creeps towards the helpless teddy bear.

> **DICK (CONT'D)**
> Then –

Dick flies through the air snatching up the teddy bear. His head is a blur as he shakes the limp teddy.

> **DICK (CONT'D)**
> *(muffled)*
> You shake 'em.

He throws the teddy in the air and it lands at Flossy's feet.

> **FLOSSY**
> Wow.

> **DICK**
> Go on, why don't you give it a try. It's a
> real buzz.

> **FLOSSY**
> Well, I don't –

Cyrus shakes his head in disdain.

> **CYRUS**
> Flossy ignore him.

> **DICK**
> Afraid I might be able to teach her something you can't?

Cyrus gets up and stands between Flossy and Dickens.

> **CYRUS**
> Flossy was not bred to catch rats.
> She does not have the propensity.
> She is not –

Cyrus sees Flossy's head drop and pauses.

> **CYRUS (CONT'D)**
> But we all have to learn the hard
> way sometimes.

> **FLOSSY**
>
> You mean ...

Cyrus nods. Flossy giggles with excitement, as Cyrus lays back down on his blanket. Dick gives Cyrus a look.

> **DICK**
>
> OK, now that the old goat has finally
> shut up.

Dick positions the teddy in the middle of the floor.

> **DICK (CONT'D)**
>
> Smell him out. That's it.

Flossy sniffs around the kitchen floor.

> **DICK (CONT'D)**
>
> Now stalk, pounce and shake.

Flossy skips up, gently picks up the teddy and jiggles it meekly from side to side.

> **DICK (CONT'D)**
>
> No. No. No. You've got to really get your
> teeth into it. Watch.

Dick pounces on the teddy and violently shakes it. He throws it into the air and poses for Flossy. As the teddy falls, it knocks a vase which crashes to the floor. Dick shoots under the table. Flossy, motionless, looks at the broken vase and then at Dick, who quivers under the table.

> **FLOSSY**
>
> Dick?

> **DICK**
>
> Oh, what, yeah.

Dick emerges from under the table.

***DICK (CONT'D)***

I didn't –

***GERALDINE (OS)***

Dickens!

There is an almighty thumping above. The door bangs open, revealing GERALDINE, a frumpy older woman. Dick backs under the table, Cyrus smirks as he licks his paw to straighten his eyebrow. Flossy is still, except for a faint wag of her tail.

***GERALDINE (CONT'D)***

What have you – Aaarrghh Dickens!

Geraldine holds her nose.

***GERALDINE (CONT'D)***

You foul little beast. Come here.

Geraldine lunges forward to grab Dick, who darts through her legs and out the cat-flap.

---

**Alexandra Leaney** is a British scriptwriter, who works predominantly in the field of film. She is currently working on a feature-length thriller aimed at the mainstream international market.

# Stephen Robert Morse

## *Moses and Rachel*

JOANNA, 23, and SCOTT, 23, sit on one side of a four-person table, with an additional seat added at the head of the table. Three seats are empty. UDI, 26, a waiter, approaches.

> **UDI**
> Can I interest you in some drinks before
> your companions arrive?

> **SCOTT**
> They're taking forever.

> **JOANNA**
> It's not Dani's fault.

> **SCOTT**
> Mind if I go for an aperitif?

> **JOANNA**
> Can you hold off? I don't want to
> be rude.

Scott turns to UDI and shrugs as he smiles.

> **SCOTT**
> I don't call the shots around here.

Scott winks at the UDI who walks away.

> **SCOTT (CONT'D)**
> So her sister's a nut?

> **JOANNA**
> Absolutely insane.

> **SCOTT**
> Good crazy or bad crazy? I'm crazy, but
> I'm good crazy, and I can admit that I'm
> crazy, which is the first step on the road
> to being good crazy.

> **JOANNA**
> I think she's good crazy, but until you
> know her well, you'll disagree.

Joanna's cellular phone rings. She answers.

> **JOANNA (CONT'D)**
> Hi Dani! We're in the back room.

DANI, 23 and petite, walks in to the dining room followed by a tall, handsome Israeli man, RAFFI, 26, and her blonde bombshell sister RACHEL, 19, who teeters on extra high heels and sports an inappropriately short skirt. Dani and Joanna embrace one another.

> **DANI**
> Hope you guys haven't been waiting
> too long.

**JOANNA**
Not at all. This is Scott.

Scott stands up and shakes hands with Dani and Raffi while Rachel scans the room, oblivious of the ongoing greetings. Raffi sits down at the head of the table next to Scott. DANI sits beside Raffi.

**RACHEL**
I want to sit at the head of the table.

Dani rolls her eyes disapprovingly, but Raffi takes the cue and switches seats with Rachel. Rachel turns to Scott in an almost hostile tone.

**RACHEL (CONT'D)**
So what are you doing in Tel Aviv?

**SCOTT**
Vacation. See some sights, hit the beach.
Nothing extraordinary.

**RACHEL**
Are you trying to force your way into
Joanna's pants?

Dani is taken aback. Joanna chuckles. Scott doesn't react.

**SCOTT**
That's exactly what I'm trying to do, get really deep inside.

Scott growls. Everyone laughs, except for Rachel. She has been outwitted.

**DANI**
*(To Rachel)*
I can't take you anywhere.
Will you ever act your age?

A beat.

> **JOANNA**
> So where did you go today?

> **DANI**
> We were supposed to go on a hike,
> but clearly the word hiking is not in
> someone's vocabulary, so we went to
> the mall instead.

Dani turns to Rachel, scornfully.

> **RACHEL**
> Shut up Dani, you didn't want to
> go either.

> **DANI**
> Because I knew if we went hiking, one
> of us would wind up dead.

Scott tries to ease the tension.

> **SCOTT**
> Why don't we order some wine?

> **RACHEL**
> I only drink dry whites.

> **SCOTT**
> Shucks. I'm a red man.

> **RACHEL**
> I think red wine is pitiful, the way it stains
> your teeth and forces everyone around you
> to have to look at such oral hideousness.

                              **SCOTT**
                    Raffi, up for a bottle of red?

                               **RAFFI**
                    Sounds good.

                              **RACHEL**
                    Dani, will you share with me?

                               **DANI**
                    I can't, I'm driving.

                              **RACHEL**
                    Joanna?

                              **JOANNA**
                    I'm on Zithromax from a sinus infection.
                    I can't mix booze with meds.

Rachel becomes loud and obnoxious.

                              **RACHEL**
                    Nobody will go splits with me?
                    You all suck. Dani, take me home.

Other restaurant PATRONS turn and stare at Rachel.

                               **DANI**
                    Just order the bottle, I'll have a glass.

                              **JOANNA**
                    I'll have one too.

                              **SCOTT**
                    Crisis averted.

> **RACHEL**
> No crisis. They're just losers.

> **DANI**
> Tone it down Rachel.

Udi returns to the table and sets up plates and silverware in front of the diners, each set atop a different neon-colored placemat. He places a neon green mat in front of Rachel.

> **RACHEL**
> I want a pink one.

> **DANI**
> How old are you? Six?

> **RACHEL**
> Sir, please bring me a pink one.

Udi runs off to fetch a new placemat.

> **SCOTT**
> I would've given you mine.

> **RACHEL**
> I don't want yours. I want the waiter to
> bring one especially for me. He's much
> more attractive than you'll ever be.

Udi returns with a neon pink mat for Rachel.

> **UDI**
> Can I interest you in some drinks?

**RACHEL**

One bottle of Chablis. Don't you
just love that word? Chab-leeeee …

**SCOTT**

And a bottle of the Merlot, please.

Everyone begins to peruse the dinner menu.

**JOANNA**

What are you thinking?

**SCOTT**

The Porterhouse Moses Steak medium
rare. It's what they're famous for.

**DANI**

I'm up for some red meat.

**JOANNA**

Me too.

**RAFFI**

Same.

**RACHEL**

You people disgust me. Innocent cows,
even if they're kosher, dying so you can
get fat. Is that right?

**DANI**

This isn't the appropriate venue to
espouse your ever-so-elegant political
views.

> **RACHEL**
> Is it my fault that you're a bunch of
> cannibalistic beasts?

Udi returns to the table with the two bottles of wine.

> **UDI**
> Do you care to hear the specials?

> **RACHEL**
> Nope. We're A-OK. They'll all be eating
> whatever causes the most damage to
> the food chain.

> **SCOTT**
> Four Moses Steaks – medium rare, and
> four sides of fries. Et tu, Brute?

> **RACHEL**
> Veggie burger – extra rare. Try not to
> screw it up. And a salad, but no
> cucumbers. I don't get the Israeli
> obsession with cucumbers. I'll probably
> wake up tomorrow looking like a
> cucumber.

Udi writes down the orders and pours a bit of red wine into one glass and a bit of white into another. Scott sniffs the glass of red, takes a sip, and nods to Udi that it is fine. Rachel chugs the white.

> **RACHEL (CONT'D)**
> Fill 'er up.

Udi leans over and pours more wine, Rachel pinches his ass, startling him. She's the only one laughing.

> **RACHEL (CONT'D)**
> Just having some fun, jeez.

Udi can't help but to blush. He walks away. Rachel turns to Scott as he passes the wine to Raffi.

> **RACHEL (CONT'D)**
> So what do you do with your life,
> big shot?

> **SCOTT**
> I write movies.

> **RACHEL**
> Oh yeah? Well, now we've got something
> to talk about. Maybe you won't continue
> to bore me. What type
> of movies?

> **SCOTT**
> Documentaries, but I'm getting
> into features.

> **RACHEL**
> *(Dramatically)*
> Can you picture me starring in any of
> your work?

> **SCOTT**
> Not really.

> **RACHEL**
> Well, fuck you then! I'm sure your movies
> are no good anyway. Documentaries aren't
> worth shit these days. Every idiot with a
> camcorder is a 'documentarian' on YouTube!

**SCOTT**

So you're an actress?

**RACHEL**

Oui Monsieur. A damn good one.

**SCOTT**

And your medium of choice?

**RACHEL**

I'm the epitome of versatility. I'll
probably start out on Broadway for
my first few years, then move on to
the soaps, and take on a sitcom,
before living out my later years on
the big screen.

**SCOTT**

Lack of ambition doesn't seem to be
an issue.

Joanna nudges Scott, indicating that he should end the conversation, immediately!

**JOANNA**

The decor in here reminds me of El
Coyote back in LA.

**SCOTT**

Ugh. Such bad memories.

**JOANNA**

What's so bad about El Coyote?

**SCOTT**

Not the decor, or the food. Remember the
last time we were there? It was that
horrible public relations girl, that friend
of a friend who I got stuck sitting next to,
the one who wouldn't shut up about how
important she is over at Dreamworks.

**RACHEL**

Our mother's a PR executive, and she's of
the utmost importance.

**DANI**

Not anymore.

**RACHEL**

Yes she is.

**DANI**

No, Rachel, she's not.

**RACHEL**

What are you talking about? Of course
she is.

**DANI**

No, Rach, she's not.

**RACHEL**

What? Since when?

**DANI**

Since earlier this week.

**RACHEL**

Since what earlier this week?

**DANI**

Let's talk about this later.

**RACHEL**

No, tell me now.

**DANI**

I'm not airing out the dirty laundry at the dinner table.

**RACHEL**

Was mom ... fired?

**DANI**

No ... Yes ... it's complicated.

**RACHEL**

I don't believe you. Mom couldn't have been fired. She's been there forever.

**DANI**

Nothing lasts forever.

**RACHEL**

But ... my career! I need Mom to make me a star.

**DANI**

You're a 19-year-old college sophomore. You have no career.

**RACHEL**

How will I ever be able to get auditions without Mom?

***SCOTT***

You make it sound like she's dead.

***RACHEL***

If she's not in the business, she might as
well be. Answer me Dani. How will I ever
be able to work without Mom?

***DANI***

I don't know Rachel. Call her. Talk to her.
Maybe if you asked her about her life
some time ...

Rachel bursts into tears, picks up her purse and runs outside the restaurant.

***SCOTT***

Is she always like this?

***DANI***

Born a drama queen, and she'll die a
drama queen. I retract my earlier
statement. Some things are forever.

Joanna giggles.

***SCOTT***

That was her Little Miss
Sunshine moment.

***RAFFI***

Huh?

***JOANNA***

What do you mean?

***SCOTT***

There's that scene in Little Miss
Sunshine when the kid realizes that he's
color blind and can never become an Air
Force pilot. We just witnessed the real
life version of the same phenomenon.

> DANI
>
> My sister is one crazy bitch.

> SCOTT
>
> I got the warning talk earlier.

> DANI
>
> I hate to break it to her, but she'll never
> be on Broadway, or on TV, or in the
> movies – with or without my mother –
> not only because she's a god-awful
> actress, but because she's a headcase.

> SCOTT
>
> Thanks for the punishment.

> JOANNA
>
> Huh?

> SCOTT
>
> Making me sit next to her.

> JOANNA
>
> Come on Scott, she's not that bad.

> DANI
>
> I've been stuck next to her for
> a lifetime.

The unmistakable click-clack of Rachel's heels draws nearer. She emerges into the dining room.

**SCOTT**

At least she's got her looks.

**DANI**

They'll only get her so far. The second
she opens her mouth she drops from a
ten to a two.

**SCOTT**

How'd the chat go?

**RACHEL**

I can't believe it!

**DANI**

Told you so. But who cares? Mom only
worked for foreign films anyway. It's not
like Roberto Benigni and Danny Boyle
would ever need California fake-blonde
Rachel Schwartzman as their female lead.

**RACHEL**

Shut up and thank me Dani.

**DANI**

Thank you for what?

**RACHEL**

For telling Mom what she wants
to hear.

**JOANNA**

What does she want to hear?

**RACHEL**

That Dani looks thin, and that she's lost
weight, and that the highlights in her
hair are absolutely stunning.

**SCOTT**

Pretty deep stuff.

**RACHEL**

All Mom ever wanted for us was to be
skinny, pretty, and successful – and
fortunately, we're all three.

**DANI**

Thanks to the nose jobs inflicted upon
us at age twelve to glamorize us prior to
the well – photographed year on the
pubescent Bar and Bat Mitzvah circuit.

**SCOTT**

Are noses even fully developed
at twelve?

**DANI**

Who knows?

Udi carries two plates to a nearby table.

**RACHEL**

Look at that steak. I can't eat in here.
Give me the keys. I'll be out in the car.

Dani willingly hands over the keys. Rachel rises from the table, walks over to the nearby table with the hot steaks and spits in the food before laughingly running out of the restaurant.

### SCOTT
After two thousand long years, there's
peace in the Holy Land.

---

A Long Island, New York native, **Stephen Morse** graduated from the University of Pennsylvania in 2007. He has written six feature film scripts and developed three television series. He wrote/directed the award-winning films *Ain't Easy Being Green*, *DUET*, and *The Morning After*.

*Moses and Rachel*

# Molly Naylor

## Columbia Road
*An extract*

### EXT. STREET. EAST LONDON – DAY

Two TEENAGE GIRLS lean against the glass window of a pie and mash shop. A TEENAGE BOY balances on top of a street sign to the left of the shop. It reads: Columbia Road.

Two JAPANESE WOMEN speed past on a push-bike.

A YOUNG MAN walks by, pushing a pram.

An OLD MAN shuffles along slowly, smoking a roll-up.

The teenage boy falls off the street sign. The teenage girls shriek with laughter.

A woman appears from a front door next to the pie shop. This is EMILY OSBORNE (27). She is tall with long, auburn hair. Laden with bags, she smiles at the laughing teenagers and goes on her way.

### INT. PAUL'S HOUSE. BATHROOM – DAY

A tall man with dark hair and slight stubble leans over the sink and stares at himself in the mirror. This is PAUL HEATH (39).

He moves closer to the mirror and scrutinises his reflection, checking the corners of his eyes for wrinkles.

Paul heaves a sigh.

### INT. PAUL'S HOUSE. KITCHEN – DAY

Moments later. Paul stands at his kitchen window, smoking a cigarette and looking out over East London.

He stubs out the cigarette and picks up the packet.

Impulsively, he stands up, tears the remaining cigarettes in half and throws them into the bin.

> **PAUL**
> God, I'll miss you.

### INT. PROJECT CLEAN SLATE BEHAVIOURAL UNIT – DAY

ED (40), a well-built Afro-Caribbean man stands in front of a class of TEENAGERS. It's the end of the day and they're a little rowdy. Ed is losing them.

COREY (14, good-looking, Nigerian) has lost interest and generally when that happens, the rest of the class follow suit – lead by Corey's friends MIKEY (14, skinny, Pakistani) and BARESH (13, plump, Turkish).

> **ED**
> … so you're going to pick a painting,
> or sculpture, or like, whatever, then do
> a talk on it. It's really not hard –

> **COREY**
> No-one said it was hard, did they
> though?

**ED**

I'm just wondering why everyone has
such a problem with this. I thought
you'd prefer it to Maths or –

**COREY**

Yeah, you're making out like we're thick
now.

**BARESH**

Blatantly.

**ED**

That's not –

**MIKEY**

I'm thick.

**COREY**

It's shit man. I don't like art, so how am I
meant to stand up and talk about some
painting man, like it's not boring though?

**BARESH**

This gallery is gonna be well gay.

**ED**

We've discussed using homosexuality as
a derogatory term –

**COREY**

'low that man!

Ed flounders. Paul saunters over from the back of the class. He has a friendly,
enthusiastic tone and a soft Glaswegian accent.

**PAUL**

Okay, so here's the challenge. You think
the art's all gonna be crap, right? Right?

The class omit noises of agreement.

**PAUL (CONT'D)**

The challenge then, is to find the
one thing in there that you think
is absolute rubbish, the worst one,
and explain why you think so.

**COREY**

I reckon I can get behind that.

**PAUL**

Corey, I'm looking for something really
pretentious. Worst one gets a prize.

**BARESH**

What's pretentious?

**PAUL**

Can anyone tell him?

A pretty BLACK GIRL (14) sticks her hand up.

**PAUL**

Priscilla?

**PRISCILLA**

It's like, la-di-da innit?

> **PAUL**
> Yes, kind of. Another word would be
> showy, or ostentatious, conceited. Having
> unfounded airs and graces. So once
> you've found the worst one –

> **ED**
> Or –

Paul glances at him – I've got this one.

> **PAUL**
> And then after you've talked about the
> worst one, you have to talk for a little
> bit about the piece you found the most
> interesting. You don't have to like it, it
> just has to be engaging. Okay?

> **COREY**
> Yeah, alright.

> **PAUL**
> The best presentations get to pick teams
> for the football next week –

> **BARESH**
> Paul, you're not playing are you?
> No offence mate but you were wack.

> **PAUL**
> What was that Baresh? You'd like to put
> in a special request to have me as your
> striker? Sure.

The class all laugh. Paul turns to Ed who smiles and gives him a grateful thumbs up.

### INT. SCHOOL. CLASSROOM – DAY

KATE JONES(14) stands confidently in front of a class of her peers. She is quite short and slight with straight, dark, chin-length hair. MR. RODGERS, the teacher, observes her presentation, smiling warily. Kate has a strong North London accent.

> **KATE**
> So basically it all went tits up.

The class all laugh.

> **KATE (CONT'D)**
> No, seriously. They had to close the
> factory down 'cause people were getting
> like, their hands cut off and stuff.

### INT. HOUSE – DAY

Emily – dressed as a fairy – stands in front of a group of LITTLE GIRLS, all dressed as fairies. She is well-spoken with a clear, articulate manner and just an occasional hint of a London accent.

Well-dressed MOTHERS stand on the peripherals as Emily gets the girls to run around the room, flapping their arms like wings. Saccharine, Disney-style music plays quietly.

One girl, ROSIE, draws back from the group, annoyed.

> **ROSIE**
> I don't want to be a fairy, I want to be
> a dragon.

> **EMILY**
> Okay, so you be the dragon and you have
> to chase all the fairies.

The girl complies enthusiastically and starts chasing the others. They are all in fits of giggles, including Emily, who runs away from the 'dragon'; squealing dramatically.

> **EMILY**
> Right, who wants to play pass the parcel?

All the girls cheer loudly in a resounding cry of agreement. Emily throws her head back and laughs.

### INT. CLEAN SLATE – DAY

Paul and Ed place the last of the plastic chairs onto the desks in the classroom.

> **ED**
> You coming for a drink?

> **PAUL**
> No, no. I've got to go and meet someone.

> **ED**
> Someone female?

> **PAUL**
> Kind of. But not like you think.

> **ED**
> Well, have a good one.

> **PAUL**
> Cheers.

### INT. HOUSE – DAY

Emily stands in the doorway of a bedroom, talking to an elegantly dressed WOMAN.

> **WOMAN**
> Thank-you so much Emily. Olivia
> absolutely loved it! You were great.

> **EMILY**
> Oh, thanks! I had a really good time. I
> always have a good time, I'm a big kid
> really –

> **WOMAN**
> Darling, I've just got to say bye to
> someone. Look, here's …

She hands Emily a wad of notes.

> **WOMAN (cont'd)**
> I'll let you get changed. Thanks again.

### INT. HOUSE. BEDROOM – CONTINUOUS

Emily glances around the sumptuous bedroom, complete with four-poster bed. She strokes the linen longingly then shakes her head and laughs at herself before turning away.

She opens her handbag and glances at her mobile phone.

There's a voice-mail. As she listens to it, the bottom falls out of her world and she sinks to the floor.

### EXT. HOUSE – DAY

Emily rushes from the house, still in costume, carrying her bags and clothes. She dives into an ancient Ford Fiesta and speeds away.

**EXT. SCHOOL CAR-PARK – DAY**

Emily clambers out of her badly parked car. She looks down and notices she is still dressed as a fairy.

> **EMILY**
> Fuck.

She leans into the back seat and tries to grab her coat. It's caught on something. It won't budge.

> **EMILY**
> Fuck it.

She sprints towards the school.

**INT. SCHOOL. CLASSROOM – DAY**

Kate stands in front of the class, who all applaud. She takes a dramatic bow.

> **KATE**
> Thank-you Archway!

She walks back to her seat and grins at the BOY sitting beside her.

> **KATE (CONT'D)**
> Was that completely shit or what?

There's a knock at the door and an INDIAN WOMAN pokes her head around it. Mr. Rodgers walks over to her and they have a quick discussion. The class take this opportunity to have a discussion themselves.

> **MR. RODGERS**
> Quiet. Shut-up. Kate Jones, please go
> with Miss Chanza.

Kate is caught off guard. She stands up, all bravado, rolling her eyes at her friends, STACEY and SHANIQUA.

> **STACEY**
> Naughty girl Kate.

> **SHANIQUA**
> She's got special needs.

The class grow rowdy as Kate strolls out.

> **MR. RODGERS**
> Okay, calm down. Stacey, you're very
> vocal, perhaps you'd like to do your
> presentation next, yes?

> **SHANIQUA**
> (laughing)
> Gutted.

### INT. SCHOOL. CORRIDOR – DAY

> **KATE**
> What's this about?

She trails off as she looks down the corridor and notices Emily at the end of it, dressed as a fairy and looking terrified.

> **KATE (CONT'D)**
> Emily … what the hell are you doing
> here?

### INT. HOSPITAL. WAITING ROOM – DAY

Emily and Kate sit on white plastic chairs. Emily has managed to locate her long, navy coat that just about covers the sparkles.

DOCTOR MACKINTOSH, a woman in her forties, enters and sits down opposite them.

> ### DOCTOR MACKINTOSH
> As you know, your mother suffered
> a serious brain haemorrhage.

She pauses and her face becomes solemn and tense. Emily looks at her and suddenly she knows.

> ### DOCTOR MACKINTOSH
> I'm so sorry. There just wasn't enough
> time. We lost her.

> ### KATE
> What?

> ### DOCTOR MACKINTOSH
> I'm afraid we couldn't save her.

> ### KATE
> I don't know what you mean.

> ### DOCTOR MACKINTOSH
> I –

She glances at Emily, who turns to Kate and addresses her softly.

> ### EMILY
> She's gone, Kate. She died.

> ### KATE
> No, that's wrong. She was alive this
> morning. We talked about the Industrial
> Revolution at breakfast.

> **EMILY**
> Oh Kate, darling …

She tries to hug Kate who is as stiff as a board.

> **KATE**
> Is she telling the truth?

> **EMILY**
> It's true Kate.

She watches Kate carefully, her face creased with pain.

> **DOCTOR MACKINTOSH**
> Would you like to see her?

Emily and Kate both stare at the doctor.

**INT. HOSPITAL. ROOM – DAY**

Emily stands at the door of a white room, looking over at the bed. Kate weeps openly, clutching their mother's body.

**INT. HOSPITAL. CORRIDOR – DAY**

Emily and Doctor Mackintosh stand in the corridor.

> **DOCTOR MACKINTOSH**
> Is there someone else we should call?

> **EMILY**
> Anyone else?

> **DOCTOR MACKINTOSH**
> Other family? Your father?

**EMILY**

No. Kate doesn't have a father. Mine's in
Cornwall. I'll tell him.

(Stricken)

Oh god, I have to tell him. I have to tell
everyone ...

**DOCTOR MACKINTOSH**

Are you going to take Kate with you?

Kate appears by Emily's side. Emily is confused.

**EMILY**

Take Kate with me?

**DOCTOR MACKINTOSH**

Yes, you're... sisters?

**EMILY**

Yes, yes of course. Of course I'll take
her with me.

Kate looks at her, dazed.

**KATE**

I live with you?

**DOCTOR MACKINTOSH**

Would you like to speak to our
bereavement councillor?

**EMILY/KATE**

No.

They glance at each other.

> **EMILY**
> Thanks. Thanks, we'll go now. She's
> coming with me. I'll look after her.

### EXT. HOUSE – DAY

Paul stands outside a small terraced house. He looks up at it, then goes to knock.

He stops, mid-knock, lets his hand fall and leans his head on the wall before taking a deep breath and gathering his courage.

He knocks.

A few seconds later, TAMARA BONETTA (30) opens the door. She's an attractive West-Indian woman, with rather stern features. She is wearing no make-up and is dressed casually. She looks at Paul – unimpressed.

> **PAUL**
> Tamara.

Tamara smirks.

> **TAMARA**
> You look exactly the same.

> **PAUL**
> You look … different.

> **TAMARA**
> Thanks a lot. I had a kid, so …

> **PAUL**
> You look great.

> **TAMARA**
> Come in then.

She turns around and starts walking into the house. Paul follows her in and closes the door behind him.

### INT. TAMARA'S HOUSE. KITCHEN – CONTINUOUS

> **TAMARA**
> D'you want tea or something?

> **PAUL**
> Yeah, thanks.

Tamara starts making tea. The sound of children's TV can be heard from a room down the hall and Paul glances anxiously towards it.

> **TAMARA**
> So how's the job?

> **PAUL**
> Oh, it's great –

> **TAMARA**
> What is it again?

> **PAUL**
> I work at a Unit for kids who have been
> suspended from mainstream edu –

> **TAMARA**
> (interrupting)
> Right, yeah.

> **PAUL**
> What do you do?

> **TAMARA**
> I'm a mother.

Paul is not sure how to respond.

> **PAUL**
> Is she … ?

> **TAMARA**
> Look Paul, just wait. I want to talk to you before you meet her. Like I said on the phone, I don't want her to be completely freaked out.

> **PAUL**
> Cool, of course.

He glances around.

> **PAUL (CONT'D)**
> Nice place.

> **TAMARA**
> Oh, yeah.

She plonks a mug of tea down on the counter beside him.

> **TAMARA**
> We haven't got any sugar.

**INT. CAR – DAY**

Emily and Kate sit in Emily's car. Tears stream down Kate's face. She is shaking as she lights a cigarette. Emily stares at her and opens the window.

> **EMILY**
> You shouldn't smoke.

Kate glances at her before taking a pointed drag.

> **EMILY (cont'd)**
> Where shall we go?

> **KATE**
> Home. I want to go home.

### INT. TAMARA'S HOUSE. LIVING ROOM – DAY.

Tamara and Paul stand in the doorway of the living room. Tamara looks at Paul and gestures into the room with her head. He tentatively walks into the room.

Knelt in the middle of the room, surrounded by Lego, is TAYO (5). Her skin is a few shades lighter than Tamara's and her hair falls in loose, dark brown curls. She looks up at Paul.

Paul kneels down, staring at her in awe.

> **PAUL**
> Hello Tayo.

She peers at him curiously for a long time. He holds her gaze, awestruck.

> **TAYO**
> Hi.

> **PAUL**
> My name's Paul. What are you making?

> **TAYO**
> Dinosaur house.

> **PAUL**
>
> Can I help?

> **TAYO**
>
> Are you good at making Dinosaur houses?

> **PAUL**
>
> I think so. You can tell me if I'm doing it wrong.

> **TAYO**
>
> Okay.

They get to work. Tamara stands and watches, a tight frown on her face.

> **PAUL**
>
> Do you know what the biggest dinosaur was?

> **TAYO**
>
> Yes.

> **PAUL**
>
> Have you ever seen a dinosaur skeleton?

> **TAYO**
>
> No.

> **TAMARA**
>
> Yes you have Tayo. At the museum, remember?

Tayo thinks about it.

**TAYO**

With uncle Isaac?

**TAMARA**

That's right.

Tayo glances at Paul and nods furtively.

**PAUL**

Cool aren't they?

She shrugs.

**PAUL (CONT'D)**

What's your favourite animal?

Tayo ignores him. Paul looks to Tamara for help and she shoots him a look – you're on your own.

**PAUL (CONT'D)**

Mine's a puma. They can run really,
really fast.

**INT. KATE'S HOUSE. HALL – DAY**

Emily and Kate open the front door and walk into the house. Kate slowly leads the way into the kitchen.

**INT. KATE'S HOUSE. KITCHEN – DAY**

Kate clocks the breakfast things still on the table and doubles over with pain, letting out a gasp. Emily helps her into a chair and they look around the room.

### INT. KATE'S HOUSE. LIVING ROOM – DAY

Kate and Emily sit on the sofa, comatose, watching a cartoon. On the coffee table is a bottle of port. Emily pours some into a mug.

Kate smokes, tapping the ash into an eggcup.

### EXT. VICTORIA PARK – DAY

Paul and Tamara watch Tayo playing on the slide.

> PAUL
> She's beautiful.

> TAMARA
> I know.

> PAUL
> She looks like you.

> TAMARA
> Don't.

> PAUL
> No, I'm just ... god, I'm not being ...
> you're making me feel like some –

> TAMARA
> Like what? How am I making you feel?

> PAUL
> Like an idiot.

She looks at him and raises her eyebrows.

> PAUL (CONT'D)
> Okay, okay.

Pause.

> PAUL (CONT'D)
> I really want to be her dad Tamara.

> TAMARA
> I don't know what you're trying to do.

> PAUL
> I've moved three-hundred miles away
> from my home. I left my job, got a new
> one, moved into a tiny flat that costs
> twice as much as my house in Edinburgh.
> I know you don't think much of me but
> you've got to admit – it's a start, right?

He smiles and tries to gain eye contact with her.

> PAUL (CONT'D)
> Right?

She nods, without looking at him.

> TAMARA
> I'm not promising anything.

Paul walks over to his daughter.

### INT. KATE'S HOUSE. BEDROOM – NIGHT

Emily and Kate lie in a double bed in their mother's room. Emily rolls onto her side and tentatively strokes Kate's hair. Kate twitches in her sleep and Emily backs off.

### INT. KATE'S HOUSE. KITCHEN – DAY.

Kate wanders into the kitchen, disorientated and confused. She spots Emily, sat at the kitchen table drinking coffee with a note pad, pen and the phone on the table in front of her.

> **KATE**
> What are you doing?

> **EMILY**
> Just sorting things out. Telling people.

> **KATE**
> Now?

> **EMILY**
> People have to know.

> **KATE**
> I'm not going to school.

> **EMILY**
> You don't have to.

> **KATE**
> I'm going back to bed.

> **EMILY**
> I'll bring you breakfast?

> **KATE**
> I'm not hungry.

### INT. CREMATORIUM – DAY.

Emily and Kate sit at the front of a small crematorium. HARRY (60, balding, rotund), Emily's father, sits in the row behind. A few other MOURNERS are spread over the rest of the seats. A PRIEST speaks in a rather perfunctory fashion.

> **PRIEST**
> ... and to be grateful for the life she
> had, the daughters who will miss her
> hugely, and the work she did that
> helped so many people, every day.

Music begins to play and Emily notices that everyone has stood up. She helps Kate to her feet and they watch as the coffin slides back through the curtains. Kate begins to howl and cry, collapsing back onto her seat. Emily holds her, poker-faced.

**INT. KATE'S HOUSE. KITCHEN – DAY.**

A selection of unappetising snacks are spread over the kitchen table, along with a pile of non-matching plates and some Christmas napkins. SUE and VIV, two middle-aged women, chat in hushed tones whilst helping themselves to food.

> **VIV**
> Yes, I worked with her at the Royal for
> years. Wonderful woman.

> **SUE**
> And is there no father on the ... ?

> **VIV**
> No. Well, that's Emily's dad in there.
> Harry. he's a doctor too – him and
> Hilary met at the Free actually.

> **SUE**
> Perhaps Emily could move in here, I'm
> not sure how it works ... she was only
> renting this place you know.

> **VIV**
> And rent these days.

> **SUE**
> I know.

> **VIV**
> Well, they're saying it's a buyer's market.

Sue reaches over Viv to take a napkin.

> **SUE**
> Poor girl. It's terrible. Fifteen is she?

> **VIV**
> Fourteen.

Sue shakes her head. Kate stands in the corner of the room watching them, swigging from a large glass of red wine.


**INT. KATE'S HOUSE. HALL – DAY**

Harry hugs Emily tightly.

> **HARRY**
> I'm sorry to rush off.

> **EMILY**
> It's okay dad, I'm fine.

> **HARRY**
> Last train's at six, would you believe it.

> **EMILY**
> I wish I could get on it with you.

                    **HARRY**
         Listen, just call me if you need anything.
         Anything at all, alright. That goes for
         Kate too. I wish I could have met her in
         better circumstances.

He opens the front door and adjusts his case.

                    **EMILY**
         You'd better go. Bye Dad.

                    **HARRY**
         Come and stay any time you like.
         Both of you.

They hug again and she stands in the doorway, watching him leave.

### INT. KATE'S HOUSE. BATHROOM – DAY

Emily sits on the toilet and pees. She notices a shadow behind the shower curtain and reaches forward to pull it back.

Sat in the empty bath is Kate, fully clothed and holding a half empty bottle of wine.

                    **EMILY**
         Jesus.

She finishes up on the toilet, washes her hands and looks at herself in the mirror before glancing back at Kate.

She walks over and climbs in to the bath with her. she carefully prises the wine out of her hands and is about to place it on the floor when she decides against it and has a swig.

                    **KATE**
         Make them go away.

> **EMILY**
> Okay.

Viv opens the door and walks in. She's almost at the toilet before she notices Kate and Emily. She starts.

> **EMILY**
> Hi.

Viv makes an apologetic face and leaves. Emily starts giggling, unable to help herself. Still crying, Kate joins in.

### INT. KATE'S HOUSE. KITCHEN – DAY

Emily sits at the kitchen table with a pile of papers, holding the phone to her ear with her shoulder whilst looking through them.

> **EMILY**
> I just need to take some time off. It's
> very difficult to say exactly how long …
> yes, I will let you know you. Veronica, as
> soon as I have an idea, I'll let you know.

She hangs up the phone and shakes her head in disbelief. Kate enters, wearing an oversized dressing gown and rabbit slippers.

### END OF EXTRACT

---

Before attending UEA, **Molly Naylor** worked as a writer, director and pupeteer with a number of companies and performance collectives. Writing credits include *Press Escape to Continue* (with Small Fires theatre company) which sold out The Pleasance Theatre studio and *Goodbye Friday*, first performed at The Diorama in Euston.

# Luke Oakes

## *The Wyvern's Tongue*
*The opening of a TV pilot script*

Adapted from *Cesarino and the Dragon* by Giovanni Francesco Straparola

*FADE IN:*

*WHITENESS.*

A texture to it, almost porous. A tide of watery red washes across it, bleeding into the surface. Paint on paper, moved by a paintbrush. It swirls the red watercolour, filling in an area marked by long wavering inked lines, describing:

A tongue, lolling out of the mouth of a monstrous set of jaws, teeth slick with saliva. Set above is a pair of angular eyes. They glow emerald in a dark-hued smog, staring down at a young peasant. He stands noble and defiant, bow and arrow held in attack.

*INT. GRANDFATHER'S STUDIO – NIGHT*

The paintbrush withdraws, held by the GRANDFATHER, a worn man in his seventies. He sits at his desk, hunched over, studying the painting. Absentmindedly he applies more paint to his brush. The desk is strewn with sketches and half-finished paintings that spill onto the floor in great, haphazard drifts.

A small lamp illuminates the Grandfather's desk. Next to it is an uneaten dinner on a plate.

Over the Grandfather's shoulder an ornate fireplace can be seen. Crouched, stoking the fire is the GRANDSON, ten years old with unruly hair. He throws a few logs onto the fire, rises and walks over to the Grandfather. He looks at the uneaten dinner.

> **GRANDSON**
> Mum'll be cross. She spent ages making
> that.

The Grandson reaches for the plate. The Grandfather WHACKS him lightly on the knuckles with the paintbrush.

> **GRANDFATHER**
> I'll warm it up later.

The Grandson peers around the Grandfather to look at the painting.

> **GRANDSON**
> Who's that?

> **GRANDFATHER**
> Cesarino.

> **GRANDSON**
> Never heard of him.

The Grandfather swivels in his chair and glares disdainfully at the Grandson.

> **GRANDFATHER**
> You've never heard of Cesarino and the
> Wyvern's Tongue? What do they teach
> you at that school of yours?

The Grandson shrugs.

> GRANDSON
Algebra.

The Grandfather grabs a thick sheath of paintings and flicks through them. He pulls one out and lays it on the desk.

**INSERT: PAINTING**

The young peasant, CESARINO, as a boy, running through a forest holding a bow. A quiver of arrows at his side.

> GRANDFATHER (OS)
Cesarino lived a long time ago, in
a land far beyond the borders of
our own –

Cesarino begins to move, slowly at first, the painting around him coming to life. The grass and trees begin to sway in the breeze.

> GRANDFATHER (OS) (CONT'D)
– on the edge of a great forest.

**EXT. FOREST – DAY**

Cesarino runs past a tree, leaps a low shrub and comes to a sudden halt. In the distance a plump pheasant pecks the ground. Cesarino crouches low, pulls out an arrow and places it within the bow.

> GRANDSON (VO)
He's not going to shoot the bird,
is he?

**INT. GRANDFATHER'S STUDIO – NIGHT**

The Grandfather looks at the worried expression on his Grandson's face.

> **GRANDFATHER**
> Of course, it's dinner.

**EXT. FOREST – DAY**

Cesarino draws back the arrow and takes aim. The pheasant pecks on, unsuspecting.

> **GRANDSON (VO)**
> Well this is a great start to a story.

Suddenly a black blur hurtles from the undergrowth and into the boy, knocking him to the ground.

Cesarino lays on his back, a small, fluffy BEAR CUB sprawled across his chest.

> **BEAR**
> Help.

> **CESARINO**
> Sorry?

> **BEAR**
> He got my mum. Now he's after me.

> **CESARINO**
> Who is?

A CRASHING of undergrowth, getting closer. The Bear Cub's fur quivers.

> **BEAR**
> The Woodsman!

The CRASHING turns into distinctive strides. Someone running towards them, breathing heavyily. The WOODSMAN, a burly, feral looking man, smashes through a group of ferns, axe at the ready.

But Cesarino is gone. And so is the Bear Cub.

The Woodsman scans the horizon. Nothing. Scowling he moves on, passing an oak tree. Hidden on the other side is Cesarino, back pressed against the trunk. He holds the Bear Cub close. Silently, Cesarino slips off in the opposite direction.

### INT. CESARINO'S HOUSE – KITCHEN – DAY

A small farmhouse kitchen with furniture blackened by years of soot and smoke.

Cesarino enters, wary. He clutches a bulge in his shirt, the Bear Cub hidden beneath.

**MOTHER-TROLL (OS)**
Where's supper?

Cesarino freezes. Sat in the shadows is a huge, beastly shape. It rises to reveal MOTHER-TROLL, a hideous creature, all fat, muscle and warts.

**CESARINO**
Sorry, Mother.

**GRANDSON (VO)**
That's his mother?

She towers over Cesarino, a meat-cleaver held in one tight, pig-like fist. She breathes with great, wet SNORTS.

**GRANDFATHER (VO)**
As far as he knew. He'd been stolen as a
baby, taken from his parents' bedroom
in the still of night.

**GRANDSON (VO)**
But what is she?

> **GRANDFATHER (VO)**
> A troll.

Cesarino looks up at Mother-troll as he edges towards the hallway.

> **CESARINO**
> I had no luck today in the forest.
> None at all.

Mother-troll slams the cleaver down, embedding the blade in the kitchen table.

> **MOTHER-TROLL**
> Liar. I can smells it.

Mother-troll grabs Cesarino by the arm and shakes him.

> **MOTHER-TROLL (CONT'D)**
> Where's you hiding it?

The Bear Cub WHIMPERS, poking his nose through the neck of Cesarino's shirt. Mother-troll reaches in, grabs the Bear Cub by the scruff of the neck and lifts him up.

> **MOTHER-TROLL (CONT'D)**
> Keeping it all for yous, were you?
> Worthless thing!

She slaps Cesarino across the back of the head, sending him crashing to the floor.

Mother-troll roughly lays the Bear Cub on the table and yanks the meat-cleaver free from the wood. She raises the cleaver over the Bear Cub's neck.

> **CESARINO**
> Wait! Don't! Let me. You should rest, you
> work so hard all day. Let me cook it, in a,
> ah, in a pie.

Mother-troll stops.

> **MOTHER-TROLL**
>
> Pie?

Cesarino rises, nodding. Mother-troll slams the cleaver down, narrowly missing the Bear Cub's ears.

> **MOTHER-TROLL (CONT'D)**
>
> So you should. But the pie's just for
> Mother! You getting nothing!

And Mother-troll stomps away.

The Bear Cub sits up, shaking. He looks at the cleaver and SNIFFS.

> **BEAR**
>
> I don't want to be a pie.

Cesarino crosses to the kitchen table in an alternating hop, removing his worn leather shoes. He slams them onto the table and grabs the cleaver.

> **CESARINO**
>
> Don't worry. I know the perfect
> alternative.

He brings the cleaver down, slicing one of his shoes in half.

### INT. CESARINO'S HOUSE – DINING ROOM – DAY

Mother-troll sits on a chair, rolls of flab spilling over onto the dining table. A napkin is tucked under her multitude of chins. She BANGS the table with both fists.

> **MOTHER-TROLL**
>
> Worthless thing! Where's din-dins!
> Me wants it! Me wants it now!

Cesarino enters, barefooted, holding a steaming pie.

Mother-troll snatches the pie from Cesarino's hands and rams it into her mouth, cramming the entire pie down her throat. She chews wildly, making happy GRUNTING noises as crust and gravy spill down her chins.

Then Mother-troll stops with a gagging COUGH.

BLURGH! She sprays the pie all over the dining table.

> **MOTHER-TROLL (CONT'D)**
> Ruined! Burnt it you did! Tough!
> Leathery! Tastes like feet!

She goes to smack Cesarino, but he swiftly ducks backward. She starts to gag again, choking.

> **MOTHER-TROLL (CONT'D)**
> Get out! Get out, worthless thing!
> Before I busts your skull!

### EXT. FOREST – DAY

Cesarino, bow and arrows slung over his shoulder, runs through the forest, weaving between the trees. From the undergrowth bounds the Bear Cub. They run alongside one another laughing.

They pass behind a tree and come out the other side altered. Cesarino taller, lanky. The Bear Cub larger, bulkier.

> **GRANDFATHER (VO)**
> As the years passed Cesarino and the
> Bear hunted together in secret.

They sprint, passing behind another tree and emerge full grown. Cesarino a young man, slender and handsome. The Bear, huge and powerful, eating up the ground with long strides.

> **GRANDFATHER (VO) (CONT'D)**
> They became so adept, that Cesarino's
> Mother –

### INT. CESARINO'S HOUSE – KITCHEN – DAY

Gold pieces tumble down from a velvet purse into Mother-troll's hand.

> **GRANDFATHER (VO)**
> – who sold the surplus at market,
> never had need to work and toil again.

Mother-troll, older, fatter and wearing expensive clothes, sits with her cloven hooves up on the table. Jowls shake as she CHUCKLES. Above her row upon row of game – pheasant, partridge, chickens – hang from the ceiling.

> **GRANDFATHER (VO) (CONT'D)**
> So busy was she adoring her
> new-found wealth she clean
> forgot to administer Cesarino
> his daily beatings –

### EXT. FOREST – WATERFALL – DAY

A small, peaceful waterfall, slipping down into a rockpool below.

> **GRANDFATHER (VO)**
> – allowing the young man to spend
> his days following other pursuits.

Cesarino jumps into the rock pool with a whoop and an almighty SPLASH!

The Bear lays beside the pool, resting in the shade, one paw trailing in the water.

> **GRANDFATHER (VO) (CONT'D)**
> But it was not to last.

At the apex of the waterfall a figure stands silent, watching Cesarino below. Only the broad back can be seen, covered by the mighty hide of a bear. A sharp axe rests casually over one shoulder.

> **GRANDSON (VO)**
> The Woodsman!

The Woodsman watches, a smirk spreading across his scarred face.

> **GRANDFATHER (VO)**
> Oh yes. And when he saw Cesarino, the
> renowned hunter, when he saw his
> secret ... What do you think he did next?

The Woodsman hefts his axe and knocks on –

A DOOR:

### *EXT. CESARINO'S HOUSE – FRONT DOOR – DAY*

The door whips open, the doorway filled by Mother-troll. She glowers at the Woodsman.

> **MOTHER-TROLL**
> What is it?

> **WOODSMAN**
> I come bearing news of your son,
> dear lady.

> **MOTHER-TROLL**
> What kind of news?

> **WOODSMAN**
> The kind that requires gold.

Mother-troll gives a curious leer. The Woodsman puts the axe across his shoulder and smiles.

> **GRANDSON (VO)**
> The sneak!

Mother-troll moves aside. The Woodsman enters.

> **GRANDFATHER (VO)**
> There's more money to be made in
> treachery than there ever was in
> bear hides.

The door SLAMS shut.

### EXT. CESARINO'S HOUSE – DAY

Cesarino leaves the forest and approaches the farmhouse, a sack full of game slung over one shoulder.

### INT. CESARINO'S HOUSE – KITCHEN – DAY

Cesarino puts the sack down on the kitchen table. He turns and comes face to face with Mother-troll.

> **MOTHER-TROLL**
> Wretched deceitful thing!

She strikes him across the face with a backhanded slap. He reels, staggering.

> **MOTHER-TROLL (CONT'D)**
> Betrayal! Subterfuge! The bear, where
> is it?

*Luke Oakes*

**CESARINO**

What bear?

Mother-troll kicks out with a hoof, knocking Cesarino to the floor.

**MOTHER-TROLL**

Lies! Mother knows! Mother
knows all!

**CESARINO**

I cooked the bear. In a pie. Remember?

**MOTHER-TROLL**

More lies! All these years! Laughing at
me! Laughing at your poor Mother!

Mother-troll takes the meat-cleaver from the kitchen table and brandishes it, her face scarlet.

Cesarino scrambles backwards along the floor on his elbows.

**MOTHER-TROLL (CONT'D)**

Slash and slice I will! Cut you up and put
you into a pie! Then I'll eats you! Eats
you all up!

She holds the cleaver high, ready to bring it down on Cesarino's skull, when –

**BEAR (OS)**

Hold!

In the kitchen doorway stands the Bear, huge, fur bristling.

Mother-troll turns.

>           **MOTHER-TROLL**
> You! Just you waits your turn! You'll
> makes a lovely stew!

With a wicked scowl she brings the cleaver down on Cesarino.

But the Bear is already moving, bolting towards Mother-troll, his jaws snapping open around her descending hand –

### EXT. FOREST EDGE – DAY

Cesarino, clutching his hunting sack, and the Bear run into the forest as Mother-troll's shrill SCREAMS resound in the distance.

>           **MOTHER-TROLL (OS)**
> Me hand! Me precious hand!
> I'll kills you! I'll kills you both!

>           **CESARINO**
> I can't believe you did that!

>           **BEAR**
> Neither can I. She tastes dreadful!

Cesarino and the Bear disappear amongst the trees.

---

**Luke Oakes** is a graduate of both the Royal Court's *Young Writers Programme* and their select *Invitation Group*. He wrote and performed for the BBC Radio sketch show, *Play & Record*. He is Currently developing a new comedy drama with a BBC producer.

# Janice Okoh

## Bella's Bathtime

### INT. RESIDENTIAL CARE HOME – STAFF ROOM – DAY

A dining table with wooden stools is in the centre of the room, mismatched comfy chairs line its edges. A tea area and a set of lockers are in the far corner.

LIZZIE, a care worker, 40s, in a blue and white overall, barefoot, massages her ankles and reads a trashy novel. The radio is on.

OLA, Nigerian, late 30s but looks younger, hair in braids, enters. She wears the same style overall as Lizzie's.

*OLA*

Hi.

Lizzie grunts.

Ola heads for the lockers. She opens hers and leans on the door for support, squeezing her eyes closed.

### INT. RESIDENTIAL CARE HOME – BATHROOM – DAY – FLASHBACK

The bathroom is small, functional. The door is slightly ajar. Ola bathes BELLA, 60s, overweight, mentally impaired. Eyes closed, hair all foamy, Bella enjoys the firm, impersonal pressure of Ola's hands as Ola scrubs her hair and soaps between the folds of her sagging flesh.

TONY, late 50s, shirt buttons straining over his belly, comes in and Bella raises her arms like a child who knows the routine.

> **OLA**
> What are you doing?

> **TONY**
> Ain't you finished yet?

> **OLA**
> I told you, five minutes.

Tony shrugs and leaves.

Ola finishes soaping Bella down. Bella giggles when Ola rinses off the soap.

> **OLA (CONT'D)**
> You like that?

Ola pulls the plug and bangs twice against the wall.

> **OLA (CONT'D)**
> Tony!

Tony enters and Bella raises her arms. Ola and Tony heave her out of the tub.

Ola wraps her up in her bathrobe and cleans out the bath tub. The bottle of Jif is empty.

> **TONY**
> I'll watch her.

Ola leaves. The bathroom door is wide open.

### INT. STOCK CUPBOARD – DAY

Ola rummages around and finds a new bottle of bathroom cleaner.

### INT. CORRIDOR – DAY

Ola notices the bathroom door is slightly ajar. She approaches from such an angle that she sees the whole of Bella's profile through the crack. Ola freezes. A HAND, definitely male, is between the edges of Bella's bathrobe, below the waist.

Ola races towards the bathroom, her approach triggering the hand's withdrawal.

She pushes the bathroom door further open. Tony leans against the wall, arms folded, casual. Bella sings to herself.

> **TONY**
> You got it then?

Ola avoids eye contact.

> **OLA**
> You can go.

> **TONY**
> She needs help up the stairs.

> **OLA**
> I can manage.

Tony loiters.

> **TONY**
> Suit yourself.

Alone, Ola studies Bella's face and adjusts Bella's bathrobe more securely around her. Bella giggles.

***END FLASHBACK***

### *INT. RESIDENTAL CARE HOME – STAFFROOM – DAY*

Ola retrieves her bag and coat from the locker and dumps them on the table. She rummages around the stacks of papers on top of the lockers.

> **LIZZIE**
> What you after?

> **OLA**
> The pink forms.

> **LIZZIE**
> They're by the radio.

> **OLA**
> Thanks.

> **LIZZIE**
> What's happened?

> **OLA**
> Nothing.

Now Lizzie's interested.

> **OLA (CONT'D)**
> I burned my hand. In the kitchen.

> **LIZZIE**
> *(Deflated)*
> That's the yellow one.

Ola takes a yellow form and sits at the table. Her bag and coat obscure Lizzie's view.

> ### LIZZIE
> You heard Connie's gone?

> ### OLA
> Yes.

> ### LIZZIE
> Went between *Doctors* and *Dial M*
> *for Murder*.

Ola studies the pink form. It reads 'Complaints Procedure' and has a number of personal questions on it. The first question asks for her name. She hesitates, writes 'Ola'and then stops.

### INT. HOUSE – SITTING ROOM – DAY – FLASHBACK

The wallpaper is peeling and the sound of cooking filters through from the kitchen.

A WOMAN, black, youngish, hair in braids, slides a BANK CARD, with the name 'MISS OLA TOBUN' across the coffee table towards Ola. Ola, head bowed, hair in a low afro sits beside ALEX, 50s, Nigerian, well-fed, on the worn out bucket-shaped sofa. They both have their coats on.

Alex picks up the bank card.

> ### ALEX
> She will need to use the passport for this
> small care job she has found.

The Woman gives Alex her BRITISH PASSPORT. Alex gives her an envelope containing money. The Woman starts counting it.

> ### ALEX (CONT'D)
> Two thousand as agreed.

**WOMAN**

When do I get it back?

**ALEX**

Wednesday. I will return it here.

Alex and Ola wait for the Woman to finish counting. When she is satisfied, the Woman leads them out of the room.

### EXT. HOUSE – DAY

Ola and Alex get into an old white Ford Fiesta.

### INT. FORD FIESTA – DAY

Alex sits behind the wheel. He hands the British passport and bank card to Ola, who gives him a wad of tens and twenties. He counts them.

Ola looks at the passport photograph of the Woman. In the photograph, the Woman has her hair in braids but bears a slight resemblance to Ola.

**OLA**

She won't let me use this more
than once.

**ALEX**

She will. But you must not be jumping
here and there from one job to the next.
Inchem, you are not like these English
people. You cannot be attracting
attention to yourself.

**END FLASHBACK**

### INT. RESIDENTIAL CARE HOME – STAFFROOM – DAY

Ola stares down at the name she has written on the pink form. She scrunches it up and puts it in her bag.

Tony enters.

> **TONY**
> All right?

> **LIZZIE**
> Hiya.

Ola makes a sound of acknowledgement but is unable to look at him. She prepares to leave. Tony adjusts the radio station, finds the news, and puts the kettle on.

> **LIZZIE (CONT'D)**
> I'll have a cup if you're making one. Know
> how to give a good foot massage?

> **TONY**
> Course.

He wriggles his fingers at her.

> **TONY (CONT'D)**
> These work wonders.

> **LIZZIE**
> Come on then.

> **TONY**
> What's your old man gonna say?

> **LIZZIE**
> Who's gonna tell him?

Tony and Lizzie laugh.

Tony sobers, looks at his watch.

> **LIZZIE (CONT'D)**
> So when you off then?

> **TONY**
> About an hour.

> **LIZZIE**
> You got time to move Bella now
> Connie's gone?

> **TONY**
> Not moving her.

> **LIZZIE**
> Bella's not gonna be too happy being up
> in that room on her own.

> **TONY**
> She's all right. There'll be a newbie in a
> couple of days.

Ola stares at the water boiling in the plastic KETTLE.

### INT. RESIDENTIAL CARE HOME – DAYROOM – NIGHT – FLASH FORWARD

An array of RESIDENTS, 70s upwards, sit in chairs either watching the final credits of EastEnders scroll up or just staring into space.

Ola pushes a medicine trolley from resident to resident, handing out pills, puffing up pillows. She looks around, searching for someone.

### INT. HALL – NIGHT

Ola ascends the staircase just as Tony comes down it.

> **TONY**
> All right?

Ola nods and lowers her eyes. He brushes past her.

### INT. LANDING – NIGHT

Ola crosses the landing. A faint SOUND emanates from one of the bedrooms. She follows it. Someone's crying.

### INT. BEDROOM – DAY

The room has four beds with a dresser and wardrobe beside each one. They are all bare except for one bed and its set of accompanying furniture, which are Bella's.

Bella whimpers in her bed, her back to the doorway, the sheet up to her neck.

> **OLA**
> Bella? Bella? What is wrong?

No response. Ola touches Bella's hair. Bella flinches.

> **OLA (CONT'D)**
> Bella? It is me. It is Ola.

Ola strokes her hair and makes soothing noises but nothing seems to work. She rubs Bella's arm. The sheet drops a little to reveal red marks, like scratches, on her shoulder.

Ola pulls back the sheet. The only item Bella has on is her bra. There are more scratch marks on Bella's arm and back.

Ola pulls the sheet back even further. Bella's completely naked from the waist down.

Bella turns towards her. Ola inhales sharply, triggering a fresh outburst of tears from Bella. The flesh at the tops of Bella's thighs is red raw and there are human bite marks around her stomach and groin area.

**END FLASH FORWARD**

### INT. RESIDENTIAL CARE HOME – STAFF ROOM – DAY

The Kettle boils forcing the button to POP UP.

> **OLA**
> I will have a cup.

> **LIZZIE**
> Thought you finished for the day?

Ola joins Tony over at the kitchen area.

> **TONY**
> Sugar?

> **OLA**
> Please, do not do it again.

> **TONY**
> You what?

> **OLA**
> Do not do it again.

Tony starts filling the mugs with boiling water.

> **TONY**
> Dunno what you're talking about, love.

> **OLA**
> I saw you.

Distracted, one of the mugs spills over. Boiling water splashes him.

> **TONY**
> Fuck!

> **LIZZIE (OS)**
> It's tea, Tony, not rocket science.

Tony attempts to wipe up the mess with serviettes.

> **OLA**
> If you touch her again I will report you.

> **TONY**
> *(BEAT)*

> Go on, then.

> **OLA**
> *(BEAT)*

> I said I will report you.

> **TONY**
> Go on.

He stares her out. Ola drops her eyes. She puts on her coat and grabs her bag. Triumphant, Tony finishes making the tea.

### LIZZIE
You changed your mind then?

### OLA
I will see you tomorrow.

### LIZZIE
All right.

Ola leaves.

Tony brings a mug of tea over to Lizzie.

### LIZZIE (CONT'D)
What was all that whispering for?

### TONY
Nothing.

### LIZZIE
You interested in her?

### TONY
Fuck off. I ain't interested in that lot.
Who does she think she is?

*(Off her look)*

What?

### LIZZIE
That lot? You're lucky it's just me, Tony.
If someone heard you talk like that, well,
it's a disciplinary offence, isn't it?

---

**Janice Okoh** is writing a full-length theatre play. She has written a 10-minute play for Theatre 503's *Urban Scrawl Project* and two plays for BBC Radio 4's *The Afternoon Play* slot. Her 10-minute short *Baby Jay's Bedroom* was selected for the 2007 *International Play Writing Festival*.

# Hannah Puddefoot

## *Disregarded*

**EXT. A COUNTRY ROAD. MORNING – FLASHBACK**

A group of three NURSES and four SOLDIERS, dressed in WW2 uniforms walk up the road. They are carefree, colourful, alive. Two remain behind the others, arm in arm, watching the world go by.

**EXT. BEACH. MORNING – FLASHBACK**

The group stand posing for a photograph, genuine smiles. The girls separate and the soldiers assemble. They see something off screen and burst out laughing. The photograph is captured. The vibrant colours fade to black and white.

**FLASHBACK ENDS – CUT TO:**

**INT. SUNDANCE NURSING HOME. MAIN LOUNGE. MORNING**

The same photograph, black and white – weathered and torn. A wrinkled hand passes across it.

The hand belongs to MAY HAMILTON [75] who sits in a beige armchair with a small table in front of her. She places more photographs around the first, some colour, some black and white.

The Main Lounge of the Nursing Home is bleak, few lively colours around the room. Sparse Christmas decorations have been arranged haphazardly on a Christmas tree in the corner.

May sits by the window, which looks out onto a beautiful snow-covered garden. She continues to place the photographs onto the table in front of her, one by one.

After a moment or two she looks at the assembled images and frowns, concerned. She moves the ones at the top aside so that there is a gap where another photograph could fit.

Leaning back in her chair she looks out of the window. A robin hops over the frozen ground and she watches it. Suddenly a tinny, metallic voice says 'I love you' and May seems puzzled.

She looks down in the direction of the sound.

Her slippers are white, a teddy bear lying across each one. Their noses are touching. May moves her feet apart and puts them back together again. The noses of the bears brush each other and the 'I love you' sounds again. She smiles in surprise. She looks around the room gleefully; no one else appears to be interested. She looks out of the window.

### INT. SUNDANCE NURSING HOME. MAIN LOUNGE. LUNCHTIME

May sits in the same chair with a foldaway table in front of her, on it is a tray with some fish, chips and peas. She eats hungrily. By her side is another patient, AGATHA, who sits with the same plate of food but eats nothing. She is in a wheelchair.

May finishes her meal and notices that Agatha has eaten nothing. She picks up the roll on the side of her tray and puts it on Agatha's plate.

Agatha starts to eat the bread.

### INT. SUNDANCE NURSING HOME. MAIN LOUNGE. AFTERNOON

May and Agatha sit in the same chairs, facing the window, their plates have been taken away but the tables remain, restricting their leg room.

May watches NURSE #2 out of the window.

May's POV: The nurse tips some bread onto a wooden feeder that is covered with snow. Wrapping her cardigan around herself she runs back inside. As she enters she closes the door but, in her haste, does not lock it.

CU – The keys swing from side to side.

NURSE #1 brings May her tea and puts it on the table. She places one on Agatha's table as well. The nurse bends down, looking closely at Agatha, who appears to be asleep. The nurse feels Agatha's pulse.

#### NURSE
Marguerite!

The nurse walks swiftly across the room to the Senior Care Assistant [MARGUERITE]. They approach Agatha. Marguerite feels Agatha's pulse at her wrist, counting against the watch attached to her cardigan. She motions to the other nurse to leave the room. Marguerite wheels Agatha out.

Through the door, May can see Nurse #1 using the telephone.

### INT. SUNDANCE NURSING HOME. MAIN LOUNGE. AFTERNOON

NURSES #2 & #3 approach May and remove the table from in front of her. They take her by the arms and lift her out of her seat. They walk her over to another armchair, close to the door that leads outside. The nurses leave her sitting there and go across the room to another patient [PHILIP] asleep in his chair.

May's POV: They wake him up and in the same manner move him over to May's seat.

Through the door opposite, where the corridor stretches towards the reception area, May can see the St John's Ambulance STAFF wheeling Agatha away, a mask covering her face. May is expressionless.

A piece of paper flutters past her face. A light breeze lifts it up and out of the window. May watches it, and as she sees it blow into the garden, it looks like a photograph.

*EXT. THE BEACH. MORNING. FLASHBACK*

A soldier [ROBBIE] smiles, posing on his own. He grins broadly. There is a flash.

*INT. SUNDANCE NURSING HOME. AFTERNOON*

The image, for a split second can be seen on the piece of paper flying out of the window.

May is breathless, excited. She pushes herself out of her chair with difficulty, but manages to stand. She walks stiffly over to the door and opens it.

Philip watches her. He raises one hand, indicating that she is leaving. The nurses are busy with another PATIENT and do not notice.

*EXT. SUNDANCE NURSING HOME. GARDEN. AFTERNOON*

May steps out of the door, her slippers still on her feet, into the frosty garden. The snow is only a few inches deep but it is bitterly cold. Oblivious, she watches the paper flutter higher in the breeze.

Staring upward she follows it, her feet stepping awkwardly over stones and flowerbeds, frozen beneath the snow.

From the fence, the robin watches her.

She stumbles slightly and has to look down to find her feet. She walks back slowly to the path that leads around the gardens and when she looks up she cannot see the paper any more. Desperate, she looks into the trees and along the grass verges of the garden.

### INT. SUNDANCE NURSING HOME. MAIN LOUNGE. AFTERNOON

Philip watches her from his seat by the window. The staff are helping one of the patients into a wheelchair. NURSE #2 looks up as if she has seen May, but instead reaches for a blanket and covers the patient's knees with it.

### EXT. SUNDANCE NURSING HOME. GARDEN. AFTERNOON

May is walking more slowly, miserable. She reaches the fountain and stares upwards at the sky. As she does this, something catches her eye.

She looks down again at the fountain. The water has frozen on the surface, a thin and translucent layer of ice. But she can see, beneath it, the smiling face of the soldier. The photograph lying at the bottom of the fountain.

May stares at it, elated. She removes her slippers. Places both her feet into the snow. She lifts up her skirt and sits on the stone base of the fountain, turning herself round with difficulty until her feet are resting on the ice.

### INT. SUNDANCE NURSING HOME. MAIN LOUNGE. AFTERNOON

The Nurses wheel the patient past the window, chatting to each other. One of them glances up and looks startled. She walks past the other member of staff and approaches Philip.

In his hands he holds a thread that leads from the stitching on the chair where he sits, he is unravelling it absently. The nurse angrily takes the thread away and snaps it free, preventing him from pulling on it.

She returns to the other nurse and they both leave the room.

Philip watches May out of the window.

### EXT. SUNDANCE NURSING HOME. GARDEN. AFTERNOON

May puts one foot against the ice, seemingly unaware of how cold it is. She breaks the ice without much effort; and puts her foot onto the bottom of the fountain.

She places the other one beside it and stands up, shin deep in the water. She keeps her skirt raised above her knees and moves very slowly, painstakingly, through the ice, breaking it as she goes, towards the photograph.

### INT. SUNDANCE NURSING HOME. MAIN LOUNGE. AFTERNOON

The nurses enter the room again and approach the tea trolley. Nurse #1 hands Nurse #2 the kettle, which Nurse #2 takes into the kitchen to fill. Nurse #1 starts to unstack the tea cups and put them on the bottom shelf of the trolley.

In doing so she must move round it until she is facing the window. Blurred in the background as she continues, we can see May through the window, bending down, one hand outstretched into the water.

The nurse puts a cup and saucer on the shelf and suddenly notices something straight ahead of her. The cup falls out of her hand and clatters against the others as she runs past the trolley, to the garden door. She opens it and runs through.

Nurse #2 comes back in to see what has happened.

### EXT. SUNDANCE NURSING HOME. GARDEN. AFTERNOON

*May's fingers are about to close over the photograph, when arms reach forward and pull her hand out of the water.*

*The two nurses, frantic, both have to climb into the fountain, hissing through their teeth at the cold and manage to get May out without a lot of effort, she is very light.*

*As she is led away, blankets being wrapped around her shoulders, she looks back in vein at the fountain. The photograph lost forever.*

***INT. SUNDANCE NURSING HOME. BATHROOM. EVENING***

May lies naked in the bath as two nurses bath her with warm water. She hardly moves, staring straight ahead. The nurses speak in hushed voices.

**NURSE #1**

Must be minus five today.

**NURSE #2**

About that.

**NURSE #1**

What was she doing?

**NURSE #2**

You know what they're like. I think she's
getting worse you know.

They both look at each other.

May stares straight ahead. A tear rolls down her cheek.

***INT. SUNDANCE NURSING HOME. MAY'S BEDROOM. EVENING***

May is being tucked in by a male nurse. He tucks the quilts up around her and turns off the light.

**NURSE**

Keep you snug and warm tonight. Don't
want you catching cold now do we?

He gives her a friendly grin and brings her slippers out from behind his back.

**NURSE**

I found these outside. I thought you
might need them tomorrow. Cute.

He puts the two noses of the bears together and the metallic 'I love you' sounds. May perks up a little, surprised by the sound and smiles up at him.

He gives her another grin and puts them on her bedside table.

***NURSE***
There you go May my darling.
Sleep well.

He leans over her and moves the pillows so her head is more elevated. Frowning, he pulls his hand from beneath the pillow and puts something on the bedside table next to the lamp. He looks down at May, who is sleeping with shallow breathing. He leaves the room.

It is very dark in her room, but some light comes in through the slits in the blind, there is a full moon.

May sleeps. On the bedside table beside her can be seen a small square object.

We move slowly forward until it comes into focus. It is the photograph.

ECU: The soldiers face. The photograph changes to colour.

### EXT. THE BEACH. MORNING – FLASHBACK

The soldier stands posing for the camera but stops just before it is taken and holds out his hand laughing. He walks out of shot and comes back with one of the nurses. She is laughing hysterically. He puts his arm round her and kisses her forehead.

They both look at the camera, his grin just the same as we have already seen it. A flash. She is caught, looking up at him, smiling happily.

***END FLASHBACK***

### *INT. SUNDANCE NURSING HOME. MAY'S BEDROOM. EVENING*

The photograph is illuminated by the window. The solider and the nurse frozen in time.

May lies in her bed, her eyes closed. The clock ticks.

**FADE TO BLACK.**

---

**Hannah Puddefoot** began writing at an early age and had a fascination for short stories. When she began her Creative Writing degree at Leeds University it was scriptwriting that most captured her imagination. It is this medium that she is continuing to explore through the MA, presently focusing on writing a serial for television.